STACKED

STACKED

Your **Super-Serious** Guide to Modern
Money Management

Joe Saul-Sehy and Emily Guy Birken

AVERY
an imprint of Penguin Random House
New York

AVERY

an imprint of Penguin Random House LLC
penguinrandomhouse.com

Most Avery books are available at special quantity discounts for bulk purchase for sales promotions, premiums, fund-raising, and educational needs. Special books or book excerpts also can be created to fit specific needs. For details, write SpecialMarkets@penguinrandomhouse.com.

ISBN (hardcover) 9780593330678
ISBN (ebook) 9780593330685

Printed in the United States of America
1st Printing

Book design by Silverglass

Timeline illustrations on pages 7–8, "the cube" illustration on page 54, and the champagne table on page 269 were created by Tina Ichenberg.

The asset "periodic table" on pages 5 and 287 was created by Paul Girard.

Einstein splitting atoms on page 119 and the policeman drawing on page 253 were created by Brad Lark for Stacking Benjamins LLC.

Fox and unicorn illustrations throughout the book were created by Emily Guy Birken.

A brief portion of Bonus Sub-Chapter 2A originally appeared in different form on the website Wise Bread under the title "4 Ways to Make Debt Repayment Fun," January 19, 2018.

Interviews included at the end of each chapter were originally published on the *Stacking Benjamins* podcast and are used with permission. These interviews have been edited for length and clarity. Longer versions of interviews are included in the audio version of this book.

Joe:
For Cheryl.
Remember all of those times I messed up with money
and told you it'd someday pay off?
#micdrop

Emily:
Dammit! I was going to dedicate this to Cheryl, too.
All right, I guess this is for Jayme. Thanks for always
laughing at my jokes. (Except the puns, of course.)

Contents

PART 2

Building a Stack of Benjamins 113

6

What to Expect When You're Investing 115

7

Taking Action, or "Let's Actually Do Something Here!" 147

PART 3

Holding On to Benjamins (Without Burying Them in the Backyard) 161

8

The Condom Broke and Other Risk-Management Horror Stories 163

8A

Insurance Bingo 193

9

Estate Planning: The Final Frontier 201

PART 4

Stacking Benjamins on Top of Your Other Benjamins: Buying Some Security and Comfort 221

10

Fighting Fear and Creating a
Benjamin-Stacking Mindset 223

11

What to Expect Now That You're
Invested (Investing 201) 239

Introduction

Wherein Joe Explains Why Us and Why This Book

In this time of health and financial uncertainty, there are two things I wish I'd known earlier:

1. Start with the basics.
Back when I struggled with money, I was always searching for short-cuts, easy fixes, and ways to cover up mistakes I'd made along the way—and I've made more than my fair share. A better path (and the only one I know now that works, after too much stumbling around) is to focus on building your house one brick at a time, just like the pig in that timeless tale.

2. Laughter is more important than ever.
If I hadn't had the ability to laugh through my mistakes, I wouldn't be here to roll out the red carpet for you now. If you're going to grow, mistakes are going to happen. Your goal should be to make those mistakes quickly and work past them. The ability to shake your head, stand back up, laugh a little, and keep moving will allow you to stay positive and focused on the prize.

With these two universal truths in mind, it's become clear to me that there's a *big* need for a financial book that can make you laugh as you read. Sure, countless financial books already hit store shelves year after year. (My co-writer, Emily, the brains of this operation and a former bookseller, wants me to clarify that I understand that financial books, like all other books, are placed lovingly on store shelves by professional English majors who understand the importance of the printed word and they do not go about throwing them willy-nilly at shelves like they're flying salmon at Pike Place Fish Market. She also points out that the number of financial books released each year is, in fact, countable, and that my description of them as "countless" shows laziness in my math.)

My point, already nearly derailed, is that there are lots of financial books out there. But in good times or bad, something important is missing from the genre. I know about this gap because nearly every author of the "top" titles each year asks to come talk about it on my podcast. In the course of creating and cohosting the *Stacking Benjamins* podcast, I construct three shows per week, forty-seven weeks of the year. With that many shows to record, I ask a number of experts to sidle on up to the microphone.

The majority of the world's top personal finance guests have ducked their head and climbed down the stairs to my mom's basement to discuss their latest project (you'll hear from Mom later because she owns our podcasting "headquarters" and has plenty of wisdom to share). In our corner of the world, finance and investing are serious sports. The prevailing attitude among many in my cohort seems to be "Money only works if you take it seriously. There are important retirement accounts to fill, and overly serious bank managers with somber mustaches and knowing gazes awaiting your next savings deposit. There's no room for giddiness in wealth building!"

Unfortunately, treating money as only slightly less fun than a colonoscopy limits the reach of our collective voices. We are pigeonholed with people promising wealth without work and riches beyond measure—and often for a much stiffer (and hidden) price than a free podcast. Enter *Stacked*.

The truth is, the sport of Benjamin stacking isn't played the way you may think. As it turns out, being a big shot and being wealthy are two totally different games. We're going to teach you the real game we had to stumble into—and happily for all of us, the real game is more unicorns and rainbows and less spreadsheets and deprivation.

Overpromising?
Just a bit?

- Emily

So if you've ever wondered, "Could *I* stack some Benjamins?" then you've come to the right book. Whether you're intimidated by money terms or can quote every line from *The Big Short*, you're sure to find something helpful in this handbook.

But don't just take my word for it. Emily Guy Birken has helped countless readers build their own stacks into intimidating towers, and she's agreed to help. If you've listened to the podcast, you'll know that we promise to teach you nothing. But I don't want to tarnish Emily's reputation, so it's high time to do something useful for once and make this book a fresh start: something you can actually learn from.

We have no clue how far along the journey you've come, so we're going to begin, as any good journey should, at the beginning. Our goal here is to stack that first Benjamin—which, frankly, any supervillain will tell you is the hardest part of world domination. The first section of this book is titled, well, Stacking Your First Benjamin, and these chapters focus on the strategies my friends and I used to build our financial foundation. We'll help you set up a budget and figure out how to save for the things you care about most. You'll learn how to increase your income and nix any money drains that keep your dreams from coming true. We'll also demystify the weirdness that is debt and credit so it's easier to reach your goal of a college education, early retirement, or maybe that volcano lair you've had your eye on.

The second section is called Building a Stack of Benjamins, and now that we've filled the backpack with the basics, we'll embark on the great journey of investing. Why invest? Because if you don't, you're going to need to save nearly dollar-for-dollar the same amount you'll want to spend in later years. If you're living a $50,000 life-style and planning for a twenty-year-long retirement, you're looking at saving a million bucks. Sure, you might be able to do that, but what if we taught you how to let interest do the work for you? Let's all jump on the lazy train. Less work for you and more work for your money. That's a big key to success.

From there, we'll teach you how to protect your money and potential income in the Holding On to Benjamins section. That means we're going to focus on something we money nerds call "risk management," which you might know by its more dreaded name of "insurance." You may need insurance, but starting off with such a loaded word is like walking up to the high school bully and asking for a wedgie. Talking about insurance may be a necessary mental wedgie, but the interesting part comes from discussing how it can skew the odds in our favor. In short, we use insurance to mitigate the risks of life, kind of like real-world cheat codes. That way, a broken dishwasher can't derail our plan to conquer the world. (Muahaha!)

Finally, we'll wrap up this whole package with the sexy stuff everybody wants to talk about, in a section we call Stacking Benjamins on

Top of Your Other Benjamins. We'll wind through tall-but-true tales about advanced-level investing, mitigating the effects of those shuffling hordes known as inflation and taxes, and hiring a financial advisor. We'll share examples from some of the best investors we know. We're confident you'll be such a money nerd by then that closing the book will leave you with a tear in your eye. You're welcome.

Now, go join us in Chapter 1 already. A richer, funnier, and infinitely Benjaminier life awaits you.

—Joe (and Emily!)

STACKED

PART 1

PART 1

STACKING YOUR FIRST BENJAMIN

The world is full of obvious things which nobody by any chance ever observes.
—SHERLOCK HOLMES

PART 1

PART 1

PART 1

PART 1

1

One Magical Idea to Rule Them All

TOOLS YOU'LL NEED:
- Paper
- Pen
- Some degree of imagination (Don't worry. It's not so much "Walt Disney" as "that cloud looks like Uncle Tony.")

Virtually every financial book starts with the same tired move: asking you to write out your goals. While there's nothing wrong with this strategy for financial planning, seeing it over and over starts to feel like hearing the same old pickup lines:

"Hey, baby, are those some well-thought-out financial goals in your pocket, or are you just happy to see me?"

"Is it hot in here, or is it just your thirty-year financial plan?"

"I like your money goals. They'd look great in a pile on my bedroom floor."

Here's the problem with goal setting: Many people mess up their plans from the beginning. They ask the wrong questions, and that makes the whole process far more difficult than it needs to be.

Back when Joe was a financial planner, it felt like everyone wanted to know the answers to the following completely irrelevant questions, long before they got into the important stuff:

1. *How am I doing compared to everyone I work with/live near/compete with in my fantasy baseball league/watch on television/etc.?*

If you're not doing better than a random sampling of people who don't know they are your nemeses, then how can you win? But who cares? #Spoiler: when you die, we're fairly certain there aren't a bunch of tickets you take over to the Skee-Ball prize counter to cash in after you beat everyone else at the "I accumulated money" game.

Okay, we can't guarantee that this doesn't happen. (Truthfully, we haven't yet been to heaven, but we have been to Vermont, and people who live there never tire of telling you how close to heaven it is—and more importantly, there's no place to claim your "I made more money than Bob from accounting" prize anywhere in Vermont.)

What we can tell you is that there are significant benefits to accumulating "enough" and then pausing the accumulation game to spend money on the things that make you happy *today*. People without goals either spend everything or save far too much, depending on which game they're inclined to play. People with goals are able to balance having fun today—which brings joy to your life right now—with making sure they'll have enough left for fun tomorrow.

2. *How do I find the "best" investments?*

The real issue is that it's impossible to define the word "best." What's "best" changes as you pursue your goals. Take the following chart we've reproduced here, which may be giving you flashbacks to high school chemistry class. (No, it's not actually the periodic table. We wanted to put a joke here about it, but then we realized we're not quite in our element. #BaDumTss.) It is a list of different types of investments and how they compare in different years. The asset classes are listed with the best-performing ones at the top and the worst-performing at the bottom.

Here's the interesting thing: what's "best" has changed a lot over time, and what's "best" in one year isn't necessarily what's "best" in the next. There are many factors at work here, but without needing a PhD in this stuff, let's just say that "the best investment is in the eye of the beholder."

Asset Class Returns

	2006	2007	2008	2009	2010	2011	2012	2013	2014	2015	2016	2017	2018	2019	2020
1	REIT 35.1%	EM 39.8%	HG Bnd 5.2%	EM 79.0%	REIT 28.0%	REIT 8.3%	REIT 19.7%	Sm Cap 38.8%	REIT 28.0%	REIT 2.8%	Sm Cap 21.3%	EM 37.8%	Cash 1.8%	Lg Cap 31.5%	Sm Cap 20.0%
2	EM 32.6%	Int'l Stk 11.6%	Cash 1.4%	HY Bnd 57.5%	Sm Cap 26.9%	HG Bnd 7.8%	EM 18.6%	Lg Cap 32.4%	Lg Cap 13.7%	Lg Cap 1.4%	HY Bnd 17.5%	Int'l 25.6%	HG Bnd 0.0%	REIT 28.7%	EM 18.7%
3	Int'l Stk 26.9%	AA 7.6%	AA -22.4%	Int'l Stk 32.5%	EM 19.2%	HY Bnd 4.4%	Int'l Stk 17.9%	Int'l Stk 23.3%	AA 6.9%	HG Bnd 0.6%	Lg Cap 12.0%	Lg Cap 21.8%	HY Bnd -2.3%	Sm Cap 25.5%	Lg Cap 18.4%
4	Sm Cap 18.4%	HG Bnd 7.0%	HY Bnd -26.4%	REIT 28.0%	HY Bnd 15.2%	Lg Cap 2.1%	Sm Cap 16.4%	AA 11.5%	HG Bnd 6.0%	Cash 0.1%	EM 11.6%	Sm Cap 14.7%	REIT -4.0%	Int'l Stk 22.7%	AA 9.8%
5	AA 16.7%	Lg Cap 5.5%	Sm Cap -33.8%	Sm Cap 27.2%	Lg Cap 15.1%	AA 0.3%	Lg Cap 16.0%	HY Bnd 7.4%	Sm Cap 4.9%	Int'l Stk -0.4%	REIT 8.6%	AA 14.6%	Lg Cap -4.4%	EM 18.9%	Int'l Stk 8.3%
6	Lg Cap 15.8%	Cash 4.4%	Lg Cap -37.0%	Lg Cap 26.5%	AA 13.5%	Cash 0.1%	HY Bnd 15.6%	REIT 2.9%	HY Bnd 2.5%	AA -1.3%	AA 7.2%	REIT 8.7%	AA -5.6%	AA 18.9%	HY Bnd 7.5%
7	HY Bnd 11.8%	HY Bnd 2.2%	REIT -37.7%	AA 24.6%	Int'l Stk 8.2%	Sm Cap -4.2%	AA 12.2%	Cash 0.1%	Cash 0.0%	Sm Cap -4.4%	HG Bnd 2.7%	HY Band 7.5%	Sm Cap -11.0%	HY Bnd 14.4%	HG Bnd 6.1%
8	Cash 4.7%	Sm Cap -1.6%	Int'l Stk -43.1%	HG Bnd 5.9%	HG Bnd 6.5%	Int'l Stk -11.7%	HG Bnd 4.2%	HG Bnd -2.0%	EM -1.8%	HY Bnd -4.6%	Int'l Stk 1.5%	HG Bnd 3.5%	Int'l Stk -13.4%	HG Bnd 8.7%	Cash 0.6%
9	HG Bnd 4.3%	REIT -15.7%	EM -53.2%	Cash 0.2%	Cash 0.2%	EM -18.2%	Cash 0.1%	EM -2.3%	Int'l Stk -4.5%	EM -14.6%	Cash 0.3%	Cash 1.0%	EM -14.3%	Cash 2.2%	REIT -5.1%

Abbr.	Asset Class - Index	Annual	Best	Worst
Lg Cap	Large Cap Stocks - S&P 500 Index	11.39%	32.4%	-37.0%
Sm Cap	Small Cap Stocks - Russell 2000 Index	10.61%	38.8%	-33.8%
Int'l Stk	International Developed Stocks - MSCI EAFE Index	7.03%	32.5%	-43.1%
EM	Emerging Market Stocks - MSCI Emerging Markets Index	11.45%	79.0%	-53.2%
REIT	REITs - FTSE NAREIT All Equity Index	9.09%	35.1%	-37.7%
HG Bnd	High Grade Bonds - Barclay's U.S. Aggregate Bond	4.43%	8.7%	-2.0%
HY Bnd	High Yield Bonds - BofAML U.S. High Yield Master II Index	8.68%	57.5%	-26.4%
Cash	Cash - 3 Month Treasury Bill Rate	1.15%	4.7%	0.0%
AA	Asset Allocation Portfolio*	7.63%	24.6%	-22.4%

Past performance does not guarantee future returns. The historical performance shows changes in market trends across several asset classes over the past fifteen years. Returns represent total annual returns (reinvestment of all distributions) and does not include fees and expenses. The investments you choose should reflect your financial goals and risk tolerance. For assistance, talk to a financial professional. All data are as of 12/31/20.

*Asset Allocation Porfolio is made up of 15% large-cap stocks, 15% international stocks, 10% small-cap stocks, 10% emerging market stocks, 10% REITs, and 40% high-grade bonds and annual rebalancing.

So how do we know what's "best"?

Joe grew up in farm country, so he's going to hit you with a home-grown metaphor: investments are like crops.[1] There is always a specific growing season. You can't plant corn in July and harvest it in August. Why? The corn wouldn't be ready yet. Also, if—after a late September planting—you left the stalks to grow to full height, the Michigan winter would kill your corn before it matured. Farmers plant corn in the spring and harvest it in late summer because that strategy has proven to work.

Investments also have growing seasons. For instance, stocks have a pretty long one. If you invest in stocks and want your money sooner than ten years from now, it's like pulling corn out right after you planted it. On the other side, there are investments with short growing seasons. Investing in a guaranteed fund for a far-off future date is like planting quick-growing radishes and expecting the harvest to be there for your grandchildren. It ain't gonna happen. You'd almost be better off planting dirt. Again: "best" depends on what you need. The best investment is the one that meets your goal.

Which brings us back to goal setting. While we find these other approaches fascinating, all your technical problems are solved by the simple act of setting goals—or, if you want us to turn up the "nerd meter": you need to determine your timeframe and return needs so you can predict which type of investment is best for your situation. Once we know that a goal is fifteen years away, we can easily find "crops" to plant for that "season."

Knowing your goals is the most effective way to research, because you're going deep only with those investments that matter to your goals. You're more likely to learn and retain information if you're going to use it immediately, and goal setting is the way to achieve your mission.

But, as we've already said, we won't start with the anemic directive to write down your goals—because everyone else does. No, there's a

---

1 *Don't be intimidated by the farm talk. Joe had to explain how corn worked to Emily, despite the fact that she has lived her entire adult life in Ohio, Indiana, and Wisconsin, so we are prepared to go slowly with this metaphor.*

bigger, more helpful approach that few people implement, but it makes a world of difference. Ready for the amazing first-chapter *wow* that's going to rock the rest of this book? Brace yourselves:

Timeline Your Goals

Joe: I know, right? Thank you. I loved it, too, but Emily wasn't 100 percent on board at first because she didn't know where the hell I was going with this whole timeline thing. However, once I explained how absolutely magical this concept was, she agreed: this is clearly the first of many reasons this will be the best book you've ever read about money, if not the greatest work of English prose ever put to paper. Pulitzer committee, we await your call.

So what does it mean to "timeline your goals," and why does it rock? Excellent question.

You make far better decisions when you (1) take goal setting seriously (even though it's cliché), and (2) play your goals off one another. Here's how it works:

1. Take out a piece of paper, and draw a line like this across it.

_____

2. Then draw yourself (or you and your partner/spouse, or you and your pets, or whoever you are navigating this bizarre game called life with) on the far left.

3. Now think about your first goal. Maybe that's retirement. Place that as a point on your line.

4. Place ages below everything you've drawn so far.

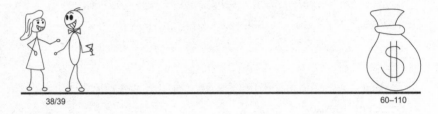

38/39   60–110

5. Fill in other goals.

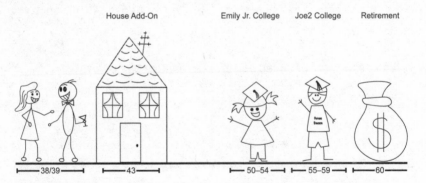

House Add-On   Emily Jr. College   Joe2 College   Retirement

├── 38/39 ──┤ ├── 43 ──┤   ├── 50–54 ──┤ ├── 55–59 ──┤ ├── 60 ──┤

6. Sit back and plan.

Have you ever wondered how your goals intersect with one another? Don't worry if your answer is "Um, intersect?" For instance, if college overlaps for family members—which Joe experienced when his twins both started college at the same time—you can count on lots of stress. Knowing ahead of time how you'll feel in these crunch periods is also a key to figuring out how you'll cope with them.

As you peer at our examples, I'm sure you can already spot plenty of potential issues that you'll need to address. First, as soon as Emily Jr. finishes college, there's only one year to prep for Joe2's school. That could be a problem if you don't plan ahead. Plus, there's then only one year after Joe2 graduates (*if* he spends only four years in college) to get your butts retired.

From the Financial-Planning Trenches

Joe recalls, "I've been in some meetings with clients, and while drawing out this timeline, I was the first to notice that a kid's college was going to fall right in the middle of Mom's retirement celebration. Deal breaker? Not always. Important to know ahead of time? Absolutely."

Timelining your goals makes weighing your options easier because you can visualize them. Without a visual reference, most of us simply look at whatever major financial tollbooth is next on the road of life. It's easy to feel like your kids' college just snuck up on you if you were busy looking no further than the last item in line.

Here is where we apply some *exciting math*—two words we don't often get to celebrate together. Every goal comes down to a simple equation:

A savings × B return = C goal

Let's take a house addition as an example. You know you need to start with a budget for your kick-ass sunroom with a built-in climbing wall. Even though you're years out from being ready to hire a contractor, figure out how much you need to save between now and then.

You might be tempted to ask if you can afford your addition. But let's save that question for later. For now, you're dreaming big and decide that $20,000 will be enough to fund the room.

Now repeat this process for the education goals. Let's say you haven't started saving for college. How much of the kids' college expenses do you wish to pay? Pick a few schools and find current pricing. Let's say you need $35,000 per year × 4 years per child, if you want to pay for the whole shebang—little buggers should be grateful—then factor in that the price of higher education is increasing by about 7 percent per year.

Finally, calculate how much money you'll need at retirement to make that big dream come true. Maybe $2.5 million is going to do the trick, and you've already put aside $350,000, you good little saver, you. (Does $2.5 million sound like a lot of money? It *is* a big stack of Benjamins, but unfortunately, cash won't go as far in the future as it does now. More on that later.)

Putting It All Together

Now, looking at your timeline again and applying the "A savings × B return = C goal" equation, you're able to work the goals backward:

- Home addition goal ($20,000 in four years): You'll need to save $400 a month times a 2 percent return
- College goals ($280,000 in about fifteen years): You need $800 per month times a 7 percent return
- Retirement goal ($2.5 million in twenty-two years): It'll take $800 per month times an 8 percent return

You've built yourself a set of goals that cost $2,000 a month. That's on top of what you might already be sending to retirement or other savings goals. What if you can't afford that? It's time to hyperventilate.

Or not. We prefer not, because this is where the magic starts. Panicking is for non-planners, and we're planning our asses off. It's time to play with the numbers, and boy, do you have lots of options.

First, you can make the numbers work by increasing your income. Studies show that if you ask your boss for a raise, you'll probably get it. But asking for a raise isn't the only way to make more money. You can also start a side gig. Once you have more cash to work with, you may just need to lock in your goals by saving every cent of these new funds. We'll discuss earning more in Chapter 3.

Alternatively, investing your money can help you grow it over time. Matching your timelined goals with the right kind of investment can help ensure you'll have the money you need. A savvy strategy can help you feel confident that your Benjamins will work on stacking themselves in preparation for your goals. We'll discuss how to invest in Chapter 6 and Chapter 11.

In addition to the "make more money" and "make savvy investments" options, we still have many other courses of action available. Feast your eyes on these:

First, you can reduce a goal or push it back. Retire at 60? Maybe 62 is good enough. Should you pay for all of the kids' college? Maybe you can pay three-quarters and they figure out the last quarter. Or maybe you decide that you'll help them find jobs while they're in high school to cover some college costs ahead of time. Finally, looking at all the goals, the home addition is the least important to you, so you decide that it can wait.

See what you did there? While all of those technical books told you to write down your goals and then decide which is most important, timelining your goals accomplished all of that, but in a way that makes more sense. Plus, it's easy and fun. Third, we thought of it, which probably makes it even more brilliant.

But we're not finished. Here's the encore: You *still* have yet another option. You could also take more risk with your investments. (If you do this, you're threatening your ability to reach your goals because you're getting aggressive with your "growing season," so proceed with caution.)

Joe's Mom on the Magic of Timelining Your Goals

There is beauty in simplicity, isn't there? Planning anything becomes simple with this timeline idea, because now you know how long it will take until the bread is done . . . or the crops are ripe, or whatever analogy they want to use in this damned book. You also know if you don't have enough money to make your goals work "as is," which can help you plan for that big raise I've been telling you all along you deserve and that your boss should have given you last November. But whatever. It's not your fault she doesn't recognize greatness.

You didn't start with some silly risk-assessment quiz or a ten-question survey about your feelings around investments, either, did you? While every good mother knows that *feelings* are important, I've always said, "Buck up! It takes some risk to reach your goals, doesn't it?" Knowing what risks you might have to take is the first step, and then you can ask yourself:

"Do I have it within me to take that risk?"
"How do I feel about this?"
"Do I keep in mind how bad leather chaps feel after 140 miles of rough riding?"
"Can I refrain from making big decisions while feeling panicked?"

Don't spend so much time worrying about risk, honey. Spend more time doing the simple math to timeline goals and you'll quickly see how the future might look if only you'd let yourself dream.

So Why Is This Important?

Whether you're just starting out or already enjoying retirement, if there's anything you still want to do with your time and money, timelining your goals will make all the difference.

Joe talked about this strategy with his friend and fellow podcaster Paula Pant on her show *Afford Anything* when they answered listener questions together. While the rest of our show excerpts are from *Stacking Benjamins*, we really enjoyed this case study on a not-so-traditional use of timelining and the fabulous conversation it spurred with Paula.

IT DEPENDS ON THE PURPOSE OF THE MONEY: A DISCUSSION WITH PAULA PANT

Caller: Hi, Paula. It's Ingrid. This question is actually for my mother. She's in her late sixties and will be retiring this year. All of her assets are wrapped up in her property.

She's about to sell her property and will net about a million dollars. So I'm just wondering what she can do with this lump sum of money. I know she can't stick it all in an IRA. So does she use a taxable brokerage account? What would you do if this was your retirement? I don't even know where to start.

Paula: Ingrid, thank you for the question! [I had a similar] question with my own parents. About a year ago, at the age of seventy-eight, my parents got about $250,000 from the sale of something, so they were faced with the question of what to do with a large lump sum when you are already at traditional retirement age.

The answer we came up with is that it very much depends on the purpose of that money. In your mom's case, how much of that million does she plan on using for her own retirement needs? And the answer might be that all of it is going toward her retirement portfolio. And, you know, I don't know your mom's finances. It might be the case that she has a teacher's pension or a military pension or some other relatively stable source of income.

If that's the case, she might not need all of the million as her retirement portfolio. If so, maybe a portion of that million might be money that she wants to give to charity or money that she wants to leave as a legacy. And so that $1 million may or may not be divided up into different slices based on her goals.

The investment that you put [the money] in would be a reflection of the timeline of that goal. So if, for example, there's a portion of that million dollars that she wants to put into an endowment, let's say that she wants to create her own private 501(c)(3)—a private non-operating foundation—and create an endowment, the investment of that endowment, because it's supposed to live on in perpetuity, would be allocated differently than the other slice of that million that would be used for her own living expenses in retirement.

So that's where I would start the conversation.

Joe: I love that we're starting with this one, because this is the most basic question: Where do I start when investing money?

I see people get this wrong all the time, and it starts exactly with what you're talking about: that investments have the same type of "in the ground" planting timeframes that corn has. I grew up in West Michigan and it was all cornfields.

When you plant corn, you don't plant in the fall, because it dies in the winter, right? You don't wait till three weeks after planting and yank it out.

It's the same with investments. Knowing when that timeframe is that your investment historically has been "ripe" is key to answering "Where is the perfect place to invest the money?"

Here's the bad news: because we don't know when this woman needs the money, we can't give her an exact answer. But what we can do is share the way I think about investments, which you nailed, Paula. She starts off by drawing out this timeline of big events she has coming up.

For example, she has this stream of money she may need every month or not. And if she does need money soon, we're going to want to have some money in a short-term "growing season" bucket for those things. We want to leave that money out of the market. So the first question is, how much money is she going to need for the next five years?

Then if she's got big events coming up in her timeline, how far away are those? And if you're thinking about going back to school or buying a rental property, you may not have ever thought about the fact that those two things might affect each other or might happen on top of each other.

When you lay goals out on a timeline and you see how your goals kind of not only contrast with each other, but how far away they are, you can number one, set priorities, number two, figure out which investments historically have done the thing that you need, and then third, set up a much more coherent strategy, how you go about it.

Paula and Joe's advice in a nutshell: To determine where to put your money, you first have to figure out what you want to do and when.

Chapter 1 Benjamin Badge:
Timelining Achievements

If you want your money to take you places, first ask yourself where the heck you're going—and when! Timelining your goals allows you to make the best choices for your money both now and in the future.

Check off each of the following achievements you have completed toward your Benjamin Badge after reading this chapter:

❑ List your goals in timeline format. Bonus points if you add sweet illustrations and/or flame decals.

❑ Calculate "A savings × B return = C goal" for everything on your timeline.

❑ Working backward, massage your goals until you can either reach all of them in some fashion, maybe pushing back less important goals or finding new ways to save for them.

❑ Highlight any shortages you can't yet meet. Use the rest of this guide to help you either find more income, save more money, or invest more wisely to reach your goals. Come back to this chapter when you've finished the book and complete your goal planning.

❑ Slowly put on your sunglasses while the breeze blows in your hair, confident in your sense of being one cool cat who's got this covered.

Date You Completed the Chapter 1 Badge	Parent Signature (Putting your mom's John Hancock on your Benjamin stacking makes it official)

2

Setting Up Your Money Dashboard

TOOLS YOU'LL NEED:

- A smartphone, the internet, or (for you Luddites) a piece of paper and a pencil
- Your spouse, significant other, roommate, best friend, or other accountability partner
- Mini drink umbrellas (a necessity for financial-planning parties)

Let's get the bad news out of the way: you're going to need a budget.

Before you start assuring us that you already have one, make sure you haven't fallen victim to a novice mistake: believing that a smartphone app marking every penny you spent on your last seventeen lattes is the same thing as having a budget.

It's a common error, because truckloads of financial advice focus on knowing how much you spend. But believing that you're covered just because you categorize your expenses in rainbow-colored pie charts is confusing two similar but distinct ideas: tracking and budgeting.

Tracking vs. Budgeting
So if tracking ain't budgeting and budgeting ain't tracking, then what's the difference?

Let's turn to a super-serious example that more financial books should lean on: video games. The differences between budgeting and tracking were all laid out in the early computer game *Oregon Trail*. Our 8-bit pioneer ancestors lived and died to teach us why cars are superior to covered wagons, which is why we solemnly remember them and will always cherish and respect their digital memory.

Those green-pixeled pioneers also showed us the way when it comes to budgeting. Consider the gameplay each time you booted up that Commodore 64:

- The pioneers would parcel out food and water so there was enough for the entire trip, or at least until the next town.
- They'd squirrel away money so that they had enough to purchase supplies later.
- They planned how they'd raise more money to move further toward their goal.
- They'd sometimes die of dysentery. (That has nothing to do with this example or topic, but it's important to avoid dysentery.)

> ### Joe's Mom on Budgeting Missteps
>
> **Mistakes have a long and storied history. Thomas Jeffer-
> son famously kept detailed log books of his every expense,
> thinking that he was being financially responsible. Except
> he was up to his eyeballs in debt (or "yppe to ye eyeballes in
> arrears" back in the day) and his family had to sell everything
> to settle it after he died. Emily and Joe have both fallen victim
> as well. In Joe's case, he thought he had a budget because
> he'd installed the popular Mint app on his phone. Ol' Tommy
> Jeff would have loved Mint—so much tracking and no hand
> cramps or inky fingers. But like Jefferson, Joe never looked
> at his numbers or took corrective action. They were all neatly
> tracked as he comfortably spent himself into more debt.**

See how the first three activities—parceling, squirreling, and planning—are forward-looking? That's a budget. Budgeting is simply the act of plotting your resources ahead of time so that you aren't taken by surprise when you run out prematurely.

Tracking, on the other hand, is all about looking backward. When our third president sat himself down to record all of his extravagant purchases, Jefferson knew precisely how much he had overspent. If you're not a student of history, you may not know that he still whipped out the early 1800s version of the credit card on a regular basis for important and necessary items like wine and plants, while always obsessively writing down each expense. Thank goodness online shopping didn't exist at the time; drunken nights watching HGTV followed by one-click purchases would have sunk him even faster.

The pioneers on the Oregon Trail also tracked their mistakes. Here's how they did it *and* learned from it: They'd write about their journey in diaries or in letters sent via the pony express to Aunt Jane back home. They'd learn through the tactile act of writing these letters, often realizing their mistakes as they penned them. Maybe that snake-oil salesman wasn't to be trusted. Maybe they should have waited until spring to embark. Maybe little Jimmy should have learned how to swim before jumping in the lake. They wrote, reviewed, and learned.

It's the same for you. Tracking your expenses can be helpful because it tells a story that you can learn from—*if you actually review it.*

Budgets and Tracking: Road Maps for a Lifetime of Goals

Which is better, tracking or budgeting? That's like trying to compare Captain Kirk and Mr. Spock. There is no clear winner, and we think they're better together. (That said, Joe is all about the OG Kirk and Spock, while Emily is Team Pine and Quinto. She is clearly wrong.) If budgets tell you where you're going and tracking tells you where you've been, both together deliver a 360-degree view of your financial landscape.

Let's start by figuring out your budget, shall we? A budget is based on the goals that you timelined back in Chapter 1. To start, let's pick one goal now—an easy one that you can attack on the spot, and hopefully one that you've already included on your timeline from the previous chapter.

Your Goal _____

(Examples: visit Mount Rushmore, pay for a calligraphy class, hire a house cleaner, or create an actual Death Star—but this time with shielded exhaust ports so that no single X-wing pilot could destroy the entire thing. Come on, who was responsible for that oversight?)

1. *My goal will cost $_____.*

2. *Currently I've allocated $_____ toward my goal.*

3. *My resources are growing at _____ percent, so they'll be worth $_____ when I reach the goal.*

What Does Your Goal Cost?

We love the little bit of homework it takes to figure out what your goal will cost. It's cool because when you dig in and start researching prices, all of a sudden, your brain starts moving.

For instance, you might learn that the quadanium steel necessary for a working Death Star is prohibitively expensive, but that durasteel from Nag Ubdur is an inexpensive alternative that also looks stylish when you're destroying entire planets. Or you might realize that cutting costs by forgoing the shields over the exhaust ports really does make good economic sense if you absolutely *must* go with the quadanium steel.

See how easy that was? We haven't yet begun to track or budget, but our plan is already at work. Sweet job.

Reaching Your Goal

Is there a difference between the amount of money you need for your goal and the amount you've set aside? Let's find out using some simple math.

1. Will I have enough money to reach this goal on time based on what I have already allocated? Yes/No

2. If not, how much am I short of what I will need? $_____

3. If I will not have enough money to reach my goal on time, do I have other resources I can add to my stack today to help me reach my goal? Yes/No

4. If I do have other resources to add, what are they? _____

_____

5. If I do not have additional resources to reach my goal, how much more would I need to save per month to reach it? $_____

There you have it. You've now set a goal and figured out how much you need to save each month to reach it.

What If There Isn't Enough Money?

Often, you won't have enough to reach your goals. As our friend Paula Pant writes (and says frequently on *Stacking Benjamins*), "You can afford anything, just not everything." It's all a matter of budgets.

To know where the additional funds will come from, we have to understand where we're starting. By looking at where we've been, it's much easier to say, "How do I change?" That means exactly what you think it means:

It's time to build a time machine. (Duh!)

I know you're excited. So are we. Without further ado . . .

Joe and Emily's Do-It-Yourself Money-Tracking Time Machine

Having a money-tracking time machine is the best way to understand your spending patterns and create a budget. And it's much more efficient to go back in time than it is to just try to remember how much you spent in the past. That's because relying on your memory is like digging through the trash to track every single meal you ate last week. You might be reminded about that regrettable midnight run to the border for a Gordita Supreme and Code Red Mountain Dew, but you won't come close to figuring out *everything*.

There's a better way, and as we mentioned at the top of the chapter, it was the part both Jefferson and Joe were already doing well. If you track as you go, you'll see just where the heck your money went. Expense tracking is your time machine.

If you don't track yet, don't worry. Most institutions have done it for you. Your bank keeps records of your spending, and so do your credit card companies. You can get a fairly complete picture except for any cash you spent. (With cash, you'll have to look through the "trash" of your memory.)

But unlike Jefferson and Joe, who never looked back at their numbers, you will use this information to make habit changes. Some people track time to see how they spend it. We'll teach you to track dollars in a similar way to see how they flow.

Financial Technology (FinTech) and Tracking

Here are a few of our favorite FinTech apps for tracking expenses:

1. YOUR BANKING APP: Many banks now offer robust budget and tracking tools. Check out yours before trying a third-party platform that may or may not easily work with your bank's interface.

2. MARCUS INSIGHTS: We were big fans of a tool called Clarity Money, which was purchased by Goldman Sachs. Good news: Goldman rolled the best features into their own product, Marcus Insights. The upsides are a clean interface, lots of tools, easy-to-digest first screens, and simplified budget categories. The downside? While there's a lot under the hood, sometimes it's difficult to grab details.

3. MINT: One of the oldest and most used budget-tracking apps, Mint has it all, from overspending alerts to customizable categories. But it can be tricky to find what you want because there are so many options. Plus, the app will market you pretty hard to consolidate loans or open accounts with their partner companies. Remember: free is never really free.

4. TILLERHQ: Tiller is as simple or as complex as you want it to be, because it's a Google Sheet or Microsoft Excel spreadsheet, but with the added benefit of being able to automatically plug in numbers from your investment accounts and your bank. Don't like an interface? Change it. Don't care for a budget category? Swap it for something you like better or merge it with another. Tiller can truly do whatever you want it to do. But: Tiller is a monthly subscription product, so you will be paying for this additional power.

5. YNAB: Cult favorite You Need a Budget includes robust tools and is actually a complete system. Based on the popular envelope-style of budgeting, YNAB teaches users to give every dollar a mission *before* you start the month. Then you work through your money and delete dollars until a category is empty. Like Tiller, YNAB is a subscription service.

Trends in Tracking

One of the benefits of tracking is that it can help you identify trends that would otherwise pass under your radar. Here are some of the ways that tracking can help budgeters do that:

1. Identify surprises before they surprise you. So many expenses sneak up on us, like the kids' friends' birthday parties, a work colleague coming through town whom you take to dinner, or the Detroit Lions finally winning a game and you have to host a neighborhood party so Jim Simpson will stop complaining that you never do anything together anymore. (Uh, just us?) What area of life should you allocate more resources toward? Tweak wherever your budget doesn't work.

2. Determine strengths and weaknesses. Where are you spending without receiving your money's worth? Cable TV? Your cell plan? That Chia Pet collection? By looking through your expenses, you can turn to your budget and try to drill them down to an acceptable number.

3. Discretionary spending. How much does the "fun" in your life cost? How can you make cuts in some areas so that you can spend more money or time on those things or experiences that bring you joy— like going to live-action role-playing conventions, or taking an *obscene* number of photos of the world's largest ball of twine?

Finding More Benjamins

Tracking can help you identify all the places where dolla dolla bills are slipping through your fingers. But if you'd like to make sure you've found every last budget leak, we've included the Finding Benjamins worksheet tool on the *Stacked* webpage at StackingBenjamins.com/STACKED. This is the tool Joe used in his financial-planning practice to ensure that his clients looked everywhere for money. It includes a long list of all the places, both obvious and obscure, you may be able to find a few more

Georges, Alexanders, Andrews, or even Benjamins. Check the
boxes and knock off a couple each day.

How Tracking Can Help Solve Your Money Problems

"But I *know* how I spend my money!" we can hear you saying. "I know
what my bills are, for heaven's sake."

Those are good points, hypothetical reader who is inserting herself into our book. You probably are perfectly aware of your bills
and obligations.

But . . .

If you find yourself falling short, even just once in a while, then
some of your dollars are sneaking off. Sure, you know the biggest
expenses. The rent check. Electric bill. Clothes. Care and feeding of
your ocelot. What we're looking for isn't that easy. We're looking for
money falling through the cracks.

Here's the thing: if you find a small crack in one wall, you don't
necessarily need to replace the whole house. (Unless it's haunted, of
course.) You just need to fix it. Think of it as spackling for your budget.
The three-step process is this:

1. Find the leak.

*2. Think of a strategy to not just plug the leak, but ensure it never leaks
again.*

3. Implement the new strategy.

Step two is the most important part. By tracking, you're able to
identify what's leaking so you can figure out a way to automate the
fix. Automation allows you to set up systems to consistently create
wins without having to think about them, and also to control problems with your budget.

An Example of Automation at Work to Fix Leaks

Joe seemed to keep booking budget-busting vacations. His budget, which was sound otherwise, seemed to disintegrate whenever his family took off on a road trip. The solution?

1. Budgeting 20 percent more money for vacations. They had clearly been underestimating their costs.
2. Creating a zero-sum envelope system for vacations. Using savings account "buckets" for the expensive parts (the flight, hotel rooms, big meals), he systematically saved money for specific events to prepay for them. One week he'd pay for the hotel, another, the rental car.

   By automating his savings into a separate account for vacations and by expanding his budget by 20 percent, he stopped having budget issues at vacation time.

FinTech FTW

FinTech tools can also make saving money easier. Most of these apps are offered by banks as part of their mobile banking, but there may be some independent FinTech apps providing the same or similar options. Here are a few features you should explore:

- **Roundups:** This cool feature will round up your bills to a predetermined number and automatically save the rest of the cash into your savings account. Let's say you've chosen $5 incremental "roundups." When you use your debit card to buy your next double-shot, extra-nerdy, triple-whip frappe-wappo thingy, a bill that's $7.50 will round to $10.00, putting the additional $2.50 automatically in your savings account.
- **Tip Yourself:** One current bank gives you a higher interest rate on your money if you work out. Another will allow you to add cash to

a virtual tip jar just like you'd tip a waiter. Did you do the dishes without Mom asking? Tip yourself $5. Nice work!

- **Bucket Savings:** Some savings accounts now will let you subdivide a single savings account into several different "buckets" so that you can save for a vacation, that new dishwasher, and your emergency fund in one place without having to open ten accounts.

Budgeting Change (Not the Kind That Lives in Your Pocket)

You're tracking your spending like stone-cold redheaded Tommy Jeff and you've got your Death Star down payment plan in place. It's Miller time!

Not quite, I'm afraid.

A budget is a process, not a single task. Even if you automate all your spending, saving, and money tracking, you can't just make a budget once and call it a day. Your financial life ebbs and flows, and so your budget needs to adjust with it. You need to consistently go over what you've spent in the past and reassess if you're on track to meet your future goals.

Tracking and budgeting need to become a regular part of your life if you want to keep your finances secure.

Your Changing Budget and You

MOM – I SPENT SO MUCH MONEY AT THE STORE THAT MY VOICE CRACKED IS THERE SOMETHING WRONG WITH ME?

OF COURSE NOT. DEAR IT'S JUST YOUR CHANGING BUDGET IT HAPPENS TO EVERYONE

Your budget won't stay the same forever. It will change and grow (and sprout hair in unexpected places) right along with you. While it can feel alarming to see your budget changing before your eyes, there are a number of things you can do to make the transition smoother and less embarrassing.

1. Challenges. With a budget, it's easy to challenge yourself to eat at restaurants less, spend less on weak points (movies, video games, and books are common vulnerabilities), or spend no money at all for a given amount of time.

Some helpful challenges we've seen:

Financial Fasting: Coined by the *Washington Post* financial writer Michelle Singletary, a financial fast works like a physical fast, where you take in only the bare minimum you need to get by. (Think about Thom the office IT guy downing pamplemousse LaCroix during his intermittent fasts. Thom may not be chowing down on cookies or sandwiches—which he tells you ad nauseam— but he makes sure to stay hydrated.) Embarking on a financial fast means cutting out all unnecessary consumption. Yours can last as long as you like, although Singletary recommends twenty-one days. With the exception of bills, gas, and groceries, you will refrain from spending any money whatsoever. Not only does this help you identify any leaks (the three-night-a-week bingo habit apparently isn't helping your bottom line), but it also forces you to get creative with everything from your leftovers to your free time.

Specific-purchase challenges: We all have spending categories where we tend to go overboard. Joe is constantly purchasing hair spray, styling gel, hair dryers, curling irons, and straighteners, even though his bathroom is already full to bursting with these products. Emily has never met a new pen and/or blank notebook that she didn't want to bring home to live in harmony with the other unused

1813- 8270

pens and blank notebooks that she is stockpiling for some sort of stationery singularity. Challenging yourself to stop spending on these favorite items for a set period of time can help save money and recognize when your purchases are not going to meet any needs beyond momentary pleasure. No matter which budget line item tempts you to spend, challenge yourself to make like a surgeon and cut it out for six months—or longer.

Restaurant sharing: Splitting meals is fun (you always want to taste what he's having anyway), and it's better for your waistline. But don't forget to leave a nice tip.

Save your $5 bills: Every time you come across a five-spot, stash that bad boy in savings instead of buying yourself a latte. Treating $5 bills as something to save reframes your view of them and makes it more likely you'll keep your savings growing. Saving Lincolns means you focus on what you plan to do with the bill (save it with others of its kind) rather than on what you could buy with it. That means it would "hurt" even more to spend that fiver, because you can't let it join the party with the rest of its fellows.

2. Games. The best way to make budgeting fun is to make a game of it. Emily has a friend (hi, Stacia!) whose family creates a holiday gift challenge every year. Each year, there is a hard dollar limit for spending and a theme that each giver is required to follow. Some notable examples include the year every Christmas gift had to come from a truck stop, the year of the hospital gift shop, the As Seen on TV year, and the game year. This makes for a fun, frugal, and surprisingly meaningful gift exchange.

Other games could include challenging your significant other to find the most frugal dinner recipes or the most efficient route for running errands. Keeping track of your low-cost dishes and fuel-efficient trips on a whiteboard can amp up the fun.

The Saul-Sehy Family Utility Game
(aka Electricity Jumanji)

When Joe was a financial advisor, back when his twins were still wee bairns of seven or so, he'd sometimes arrive home after a long day of work to find every light in the house on, plus both televisions. Guess how many people were watching them? That's right. None.

So, rather than yell, "Do you think money grows on trees?" in the ancient Dad tradition, Joe came up with a game. He created a simple graph of their utility spending. Every month when the utility bill came, the whole family would look at it together and plot a point showing how much they'd spent the previous thirty days. They'd set a goal amount for the following month and then celebrate with make-your-own pizza night if they met the goal.

Joe's entire clan began talking about ways to cut back so the graph would show big gains. Not only could they shut off the television when they weren't watching, but maybe they could limit TV time altogether? Within weeks, when Joe would leave a light on inadvertently in a room after he'd left, his twins would scold him: "Dad, we're trying to win the challenge!" What had started as a sore spot became a lot of fun for everyone.

3. Zero-sum budgeting. Some programs like YNAB encourage users to determine where every dollar is going before the month even begins. That way, the entire budget is allocated and then divvied out envelope-style throughout the month.

Why People Struggle with Budgeting

While a few Benjamin stackers built their impressive stacks by becoming fantastic budgeters, we'll admit that most people have a tough time of it at first. And the reason isn't because of spreadsheet phobia. Most commonly, stackers will struggle for one of three reasons:

1. They don't check the budget against their plan and neglect to ask them-selves the question "Where the hell am I going with this?" That means they miss easy opportunities to spot trends or build momentum when they're winning, or to avoid frustration when they're falling behind. Budgeting is a process, not a single event. Make it part of your daily routine.

2. They get caught up in life. The fantasyland called More Time doesn't exist. Successful budgeting means *making* time for it. You make time for important tasks. This is important enough that you have to priori-tize budgeting to reach your goals.

3. They don't get buy-in from their partner. In a lot of relationships, it can seem easier to just not mention money, since it seems to provoke one of the hiss-at-each-other-through-your-teeth-at-the-PTA-meeting "discussions" that nobody ever walks away from unscathed. We'll tell ourselves, "I'm sure it'll go away." But problems won't magically disappear by avoiding them. Trust us. We've got a combined ninety-three years of experience in problem avoidance and never has a single one of them magically disappeared.

Joe used to have this third problem. Budget feuds happened fairly regularly at the Saul-Sehy house. Enter **the budget meeting.**

What Is a Budget Meeting?

Just like a major corporation, any people in a relationship who share money need to also have regular budget meetings. (Unlike corporate budget meetings, however, beer or wine drinking is encouraged, as is snogging the CFO.)

In short, you and your partner regularly get together to discuss your financial status, including everything from whether you're on track to meet your goals to how you can reduce your monthly ocelot-feeding budget. So how do you implement one in your house?

Saying "Let's get together and talk about money" sounds about as romantic as suggesting couples' root canals. But it is possible to have a fun budget meeting with your one and only.

First, mind these principles to make these meetings a success:

- More often beats sporadic. We advocate for once a week.
- Meeting over food or drinks is more fun—although we recommend saving the high-proof adult beverages for post-meeting fun. Your ability to math may depend upon this.
- Keeping the meetings short makes it more likely you'll keep doing them.

So now you know (1) that you need regular budget meetings and (2) how to set yourself up for success. But what exactly will you talk about? To avoid an at-home re-creation of that nightmare where you show up for a big presentation at work and realize you forgot to prepare (or wear pants—but maybe that's just our nightmare), have an agenda for your budget meeting with your beloved.

THE AGENDA
- Review bills and bank accounts for the last week. (Everyone reviews all of the bank transactions. Do not divide and conquer to save time. The value here is in everyone seeing the numbers *together*.)
- Assign to-dos if something doesn't look quite right. We've found so much money while diving deeper into questionable phone and utility bills, not to mention via canceling subscriptions.
- Review investments. If it's the six-month mark, check your milestones—are you on pace to reach your timelined goals?
- Talk about upcoming expenses for the next week.
- Talk about big-picture goals and events on the horizon.

That's it! Simple, fast, and easy. It should take no longer than ten to twenty minutes and should also be light in tone most of the time.

HERE'S WHY WE LIKE BUDGET MEETINGS:
- Having quick money chats is the key to winning with your cash.
- Couples who talk about their money get busy more often.[2]
- We're money nerds and think this is fun. Try it. You can be just like us! #BigDreams

What to Do When You Can't Get the Budget Meeting to Work
Sometimes even the best plans and most romantic of agendas don't work out. Either life gets in the way or your partner isn't on the same page. Buck up, reader. We can help you pull it together. Here is what to do when your budget meetings just aren't working:

- Try meetings every other week instead of weekly.
- Meet at different times of day to budget.
- Experiment with different budgeting tools and apps. Have fun exploring.
- Begin meetings with a book club session. Sometimes sharing a read about money habits or stories is a great way to dive deeper into your financial picture.
- Tie your budget meetings to something you both love to do. Have sushi-and-spreadsheet night, board-game-and-budget night, movie-and-money night, or some other combination of things you like with the thing you need to do.
- Set celebrations and milestones. One way to make sure you continue to meet is to celebrate wins. Hell, celebrate the fact that you're still meeting after a week, a month, or even three days. Just don't celebrate by buying a big-screen television. On credit.

------

2 *Your results may vary.*

What to Do When Your Spouse/Significant Other/ Accountability Partner Isn't on Board

Sometimes your partner isn't as into personal finance as you are. (We know, right? Wild—but it happens.) Pushing harder is never a good solution. Your partner will become resistant and maybe even defensive, at which point the game is lost.

While every relationship is different, and there is no magic bullet, we recommend the following course of action.

1. Keep it aspirational. Focus on things you'd like to achieve or the money you'd like to save. Emily brought her husband on board for money conversations by asking him to name the top ten places he wanted to travel. A deep dive into the details of a trip to see the twenty-four-hour Le Mans endurance race in France later, and they were well on their way to budgeting as a team.

2. Start small. Downloading the same app together might be a huge win.

3. Celebrate victories. Sure, they may not be as often as you'd like, but at least you're moving.

4. Maintain your enthusiasm. Making major strides but you still can't get them to talk about money? As a wise man working at the carnival once told us after we'd spent fifty-six bucks trying to clear all the milk jugs, "Keep your eye on the prize." Don't get discouraged if they aren't into it as much as you are or as quickly. They might just be waiting for a little more proof before rolling into action.

5. Ask questions. Don't just bring "fixes" and "adjustments" to the table. Ask your partner, "What do you want? What are you hopeful for? How would you like to proceed?"

Remember this: if you own the success for both of you, you'll only get halfway to your goal. By sharing the ownership, you'll also be much more likely to achieve the win you're hoping for.

So Why Is This Important?

A bad budget feels like bars on the windows. A good budget helps you keep the heartbeat of your financial health. But a great budget? That's where the magic happens.

Let's take a look at how our friend Tiffany "The Budgetnista" Aliche budgets. Tiffany's award-winning work has helped over one million women worldwide save more than $200 million, pay off over $100 million of debt, and build a solid financial foundation. Her community of Dream Catchers is huge and so supportive of one another, and they're all led by this resilient, charismatic woman you're about to meet who first, before anything, had to believe she could get herself out of debt.

She sat down for an episode of the *Stacking Benjamins* podcast and spoke about how she got into debt and how her budget saved her.

MAKING THE LIFE YOU WANT
THROUGH BUDGETING: AN INTERVIEW WITH
THE BUDGETNISTA, TIFFANY ALICHE

Joe: Did you get into $30,000 of debt in one week?

Tiffany: Oh, man. Try like three days.

Joe: That's a great three days.

Tiffany: *I know! I wish I had something to show for it. It was just credit card debt.*

It was an—air quotes—"friend of mine." I told him I wanted to learn how to invest, and he said, "Oh, you've gotta use other people's money." I didn't know what that meant. What he meant was, open up some credit cards and get a cash advance.

Joe: *Oh no . . .*

Tiffany: *I had never heard of a cash advance before. I was in my mid-twenties, and I said, "Okay!" And so I took the money off [the credit card]. I invested it with him, and he promptly stole it. So three days later I was just like, "Hello? Hello? Hello?" and he was gone.*

Joe: *Wow. So did you pay off that [debt] quickly, or did you make some mistakes?*

Tiffany: *No, I made some mistakes. The first year I refused to acknowledge it was my debt. "It was his fault!" That's what I'd tell myself every morning, filled with anger. Yeah, and at first, you're in shock, and then I'd do the angry texts and calls, and then it was the crying, and then it was "I'm resigned to this life of debt."*

And then, finally, I took responsibility and promptly lost my job three days later.

Joe: *Oh no.*

Tiffany: *Yes! It was the height of the [2008] recession and I worked for a nonprofit-based school and we lost our funding. So literally three days later, after me saying, "Okay, Tiffany, you make enough to pay this off. Let's just start paying it off," and three days later no job, and I was like, "Just great." So I ended up moving back home.*

Joe: *Wow. Well, how did you pay it off? Was it cutting your living expenses or what?*

Tiffany: *I cut everything. I didn't have to pay for food; I didn't have to pay for lodging because I'd moved back home with my parents. I think I put my student loans in deferment and I really didn't have a whole lot of bills now that I didn't have a condo to take care of. I didn't have to pay my light bill or water bill because the person that lived there did that. So, I was living very simply. I would say my life probably cost me, like at the time, maybe under $2,000 a month, and I think my unemployment check was like maybe $2,000 every two weeks or something like that. So I was really living super simply and just using that money to pay down debt.*

Joe: *What are the biggest mistakes you find people make when they're trying to get out of debt?*

Tiffany: *Thinking that it's going to happen overnight. It took me two and a half years. Another one is being so down on themselves. We're so terrible to ourselves. The voices in our head and the way we talk to ourselves . . . you would never let anyone speak to you like that, I hope. But you know, it takes time. It took you a lot of time to get into the situation. It's going to take time to come out.*

Joe: *It's not the problem. It's how you look at the problem.*

Tiffany: *Exactly. I truly believe that. When I talk about budgets, people are like, "Oh, God, budgets," but I love budget day. My budget doesn't tell me, "No." My budget tells me, "Yes." If you look to your budget for the no, that's what you're going to get.*

My budget always says, "Yes, if." I want to go to Thailand for my birthday in October. "Yes, you can go to Thailand, if you make these different choices." Thinking about things differently really changes everything.

Joe: *How does your budget work?*

Tiffany: *It's a little different than when I was a schoolteacher. So I know how much I need to make a month just to make my life happen. As soon as I* *get paid anything, I take that money. I allocate it. I set aside 20 percent for retirement. I set aside 30 percent for taxes. I set aside 10 percent to donate and give back, and really the rest I use to live off of. If there's excess left over, I put some into a business or my personal savings account to put toward next month's bills.*

Joe: *Where do you find the money for Thailand? Do you then back down the living expenses . . . or do you try to do more work and earn more income to make that happen?*

Tiffany: *Let's just say I get a big check. Like, say that a big client pays me $10,000.*

Joe: *Woo-hoo!*

Tiffany: *Right?! I don't need $10,000 to make my life work. So there's money left over. I might put 5 percent into my travel account. I might put 5 percent into my house account. So when there's excess, I have other smaller accounts that I only give to when there's excess.*

Joe: *Do you keep separate bank accounts, or are they separate on a piece of paper?*

Tiffany: *No, definitely separate bank accounts. I feel like it's kind of like your grandma's envelope system, but instead of envelopes, I like to have online-only bank accounts for savings. The way it works is that I open up different bank accounts and you can name them. When I pull up my screen, it says, "Travel," or it says, "Give." One says, "Me." I have the "Me" account for fun stuff. So if I put enough money in there, I could do whatever it is I want without guilt. That's how I keep track of excess money.*

Joe: *You said one thing earlier that I want to go back to. You know how much it takes to keep the lights on. That was a big aha for me. How much do I need, the minimum, to live? That's a huge number to know.*

Tiffany: *It is! I call it your "financial baseline." What is the bare minimum you've got to make, just to make it work? One, it lets you know, if you start* *your own business, what do you have to make in order to make it work, or two, if you hate your job and your boss is a total butthead, what do you have to make at your next job? What's the bare minimum you've got to negotiate to make it so you can move?*

Joe: *What are the easiest places you find people could cut but they don't?*

Tiffany: *Basic things like cable, of course, everybody knows that . . . but even eating out. Groceries, for sure . . . entertainment. I find people spend a whole lot of money on grooming. So you can still get your hair cut, but there might be a less expensive way to do so. It's just the excess spending. I call it "cash spending." Things that you usually use your debit card for—or cash for—that's where you have the most control.*

I don't believe in over-sacrifice. People think that because I'm the Budgetnista that I don't do anything. That's not true. I've just learned to save where I can so I can splurge where I want.

Tiffany's advice in a nutshell: Save where you can so you can splurge where you want.

Chapter 2 Benjamin Badge: Money Dashboard Achievements

You must take care of the money you already have to become a world-class Benjamin stacker. In passing these achievements, you've learned simple money rules and how to keep your Benjamins healthy and strong.

Check off each of the following achievements you have completed toward your Benjamin Badge after reading this chapter:

❏ Track your expenses for a week.
❏ Set up a budget for future expenses and check it a week later against reality.

❏ Set up a budget meeting with a spouse/friend/accountability partner/friendly man in a "FREE CANDY" truck/wandering clown.[3]

❏ Find and plug a budget leak. Automatically transfer the difference to savings to lock in your win.

❏ Engage in a budget challenge. If you win, check this off *twice*!

Date You Completed the Chapter 2 Badge	Parent Signature (Putting your mom's John Hancock on your Benjamin stacking makes it official)

---

3 *Two of these options have not been endorsed by the publisher.*

2A

Budgeting Tetris

TOOLS YOU'LL NEED:
- Your lucky pencil (the one with the Troll topper)
- Colored pencils, markers, crayons, or highlighters in a variety of festive colors
- A ruler or T square
- Your budget (remember—the one you made in the last chapter?)

One of the things that they don't teach you in school is that money is just like *Tetris*. In fact, Emily was only able to unearth this uncanny similarity after years of procrastination wherein she fit pixelated colored blocks into corresponding empty spaces (and no, Emily's mom, that is *not* a euphemism). There is no better modern comparison.

*The Money-*Tetris *Matrix*
How exactly is the game that barely beats out Solitaire as an effective way to look busy at work similar to the life-and-death game that is money? Well, consider the following:

- Like *Tetris*, **budgeting is all about allocating scarce resources in the most efficient way possible.** With *Tetris*, you're trying to allocate limited space, while with budgeting, you're trying to allocate limited money.

- **Like *Tetris*, budgeting feels easy when you have few obligations and bills.** When you have a clear floor and slowly falling blocks in *Tetris*, it's a breeze to place your blocks in the optimal spots. And when you have plenty of income to cover the few bills you have coming in, it feels like child's play to make and stick to a budget.
- **Like *Tetris*, handling your financial obligations is a never-ending task.** In traditional *Tetris*, there is no end point where you have won the game and the blocks stop falling. Similarly, your bills will never stop coming. In both cases, it's up to you to work within your current framework to deal with the blocks and bills that continue to come while also navigating the blocks and bills already cluttering up the "game."
- **Like *Tetris*, less-than-ideal budgeting decisions you make early on can keep biting you in the rear end over the long term.** Set a T-shaped piece point-side down in the center of the open floor in *Tetris*, and spend several rounds trying to work around that impossible-to-clear shape. Ignore some bills for a month or two, and spend several months or years trying to pay off the mistake and repair your credit.
- **And like *Tetris*, sometimes you pin your hopes on something outside your control.** While playing *Tetris*, we've all tried to create a four-row block with just a single missing line in the hopes that an I-shaped block will magically appear to allow you to complete four rows at once. (Fun fact: this move is *called* a "Tetris.") More often than not, you wait in vain, watching the game get more and more cluttered as the non-I-blocks keep falling, until you have to make a less-perfect fit just to keep things moving. Waiting for money that you don't personally have control over to take care of your financial obligations can have the same effect. Sometimes the money comes on time and you clear those bills like a *Tetris* boss. Sometimes you wait and wait while your bills pile up around you, making a big mess that you will struggle to fix.

The Folly of Waiting for an I-Block

Emily experienced the financial version of this in 2019. She received a payout from a lawsuit at about the same time she owed a large payment. While she had enough money in her Vanguard taxable investment account to cover the payment, she wanted to use the lawsuit settlement money to make the payment, since withdrawing the money from Vanguard meant losing out on growth until she was able to replace it.

Emily knew that an I-block was on its way in the form of her lawsuit payout, and she was trying to protect her other money—just like nimble-fingered *Tetris* aficionados know that an I-block will eventually appear, allowing them to complete four rows. But counting on it can mean making a mess.

In Emily's case, the defendant in the lawsuit dragged her feet. She waited until the deadline to send the check to Emily's lawyer, who then put the money in the law office's escrow account before cutting a check to Emily, which was then sent via certified mail but misdelivered. And then when Emily finally got the check in her hot little hands, her bank put a hold on the money for a week.

While waiting for that I-block of settlement money to make her one large payment, other financial obligations were piling up. Finally, Emily realized that she needed to access the money in her Vanguard account rather than continue to wait for the "perfect" piece. Using the money from Vanguard was a little messy, but it caused less mess to accept that imperfect solution than to wait around for the perfect one.

Anticipating the Future and Employing the Easy Spin

In some newfangled versions of *Tetris*, new blocks don't just appear at the top of the board. Instead, you are shown which shapes are coming next so there are no surprises. To succeed in *Tetris*, you need to drop your blocks in ways that can be completed with forthcoming blocks. Your current moves can prepare you for the future.

This is similar to money management. If you are simply paying bills as they come without thinking about how you will afford next month's bills, you may overwhelm yourself in the future. Setting aside some of this month's money for next month's bills will ensure that no financial emergencies will destroy your momentum. That way you're not scrambling to pay for future bills, even if they are a surprise.

The advanced level of planning ahead is creating an entire emergency fund. This is like giving yourself a *Tetris* "easy spin." The blocks fall faster and faster the longer you play. But some versions of the game give you a way to slow a block while you decide where it should go. The easy spin, which pauses the descent of the block when you rotate it, gives you a chance to think strategically instead of simply reacting.

While many *Tetris* purists are horrified by the easy spin, this move offers a kind of breathing room that is similar to having an emergency fund. If you are living paycheck to paycheck, an unanticipated expense can make it impossible to pay all your bills. Suddenly, it will feel like the bills are coming faster than you can deal with them. But an emergency fund lets you pay an unexpected expense without harming your monthly budget.

Understanding the Shape of Your Monthly Finances

Thinking of your budget as a big game of *Tetris* can give you a clearer sense of what your monthly financial needs are. Recording your regular bills (remember doing that in the previous chapter?) helps you know the shape of your budget. Your recurring bills are like the blocks already piled up when you start *Tetris* halfway through. Your rent or mortgage, your student loan, your car payment, your credit card bill, your utilities, and other repeating bills are the financial "blocks" that you need to work around.

If you take the time to plan ahead, having these bills does not need to cause you stress. You can even work to make some of them disappear with some careful strategizing.

For instance, Emily's first job after college netted her about $1,000 per month. Her rent was over $500 per month, and she was paying $200 per month to her student loans, while carrying over $2,400 in credit card debt. But instead of stressing about her budget, Emily would try to figure out how to make it all fit together, jotting down all her monthly expenses and then "playing" with the non-fixed numbers to calculate how she could stay within her budget or even get ahead. Knowing the shape of your fixed expenses can help you make good decisions with your discretionary spending.

Your Budgeting Tetris *Board*

You can make an actual *Tetris* board of your fixed expenses to help you visualize how to allocate your discretionary spending. Assume each of the following squares is equal to $100, draw a line at your monthly income, and create your fixed-expenses *Tetris* board:

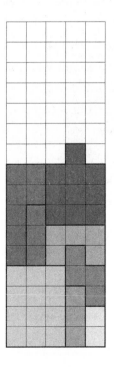

Once you have allocated all of your fixed expenses on your *Tetris* board, you can better see how much money is left in your monthly income for discretionary expenses.

So Why Is This Important?

Treating your budget like a colorful game that you can win makes the whole process more fun and less nerve-wracking. Games offer a two-for-one deal when it comes to motivation: you feel personal, internal satisfaction for completing a task, and you get external rewards that someone else (i.e., the game itself) gives you for leveling up. The first is known as intrinsic motivation, and the second is known as extrinsic motivation. Games feel good because you get both.

For instance, you might spend an afternoon playing *Grand Theft Auto* both because of the game's extrinsic motivation of rewarding you for completing the missions and because of your intrinsic motivation to have some fun destroying buildings, running over pedestrians, and outrunning San Andreas police officers.

Understanding how games tap into both extrinsic and intrinsic motivations can help you figure out how to gamify something as traditionally unfun as money management. It also helps you recognize the importance of only doing a little at a time, since you can't level up right away in gaming or in money management.

Kristin Wong, the author of *Get Money: Live the Life You Want, Not Just the Life You Can Afford*, talked with Joe about how gamification can help you feel more in control of your finances.

GAMIFYING YOUR FINANCES:
AN INTERVIEW WITH KRISTIN WONG

Joe: *Why gamification?*

Kristin: *Gamification is a tool that businesses and companies have been using for decades to make otherwise boring tasks a little bit more engaging and motivating. The McDonald's Monopoly sweepstakes is a good example of this. Buying McDonald's french fries is not super exciting. But somehow when buying the fries gets you another piece in a Monopoly game, you want to buy fries because you feel in charge—*

Joe: *—and I'm gonna buy the medium ones because I get the game piece versus the small one, where I don't get a piece.*

Kristin: *Right!*

I thought it was a perfect thing to apply to personal finance because most of us feel completely out of control with our finances. There's a lot of anxiety and stress around our financial life. And so when you gamify something, you take a lot of that anxiety out of it and you feel more empowered and you feel more in control.

I admit . . . this is much harder to do when you are actually struggling and it's not a game. But there's still value in seeing it like a game if you can. When you're really broke and struggling to get by, you don't have time to learn personal finance, but need it more than ever. That's when you most need that mindset and psychological shift, since there are fewer things you do control. Focus on the gamification because it lets you focus on what you can control when you are struggling.

Joe: *What's the first thing that we do, then?*

Kristin: *Focus on one thing at a time. I think there are probably multiple vices you have that you spend money on that you shouldn't. There are lots of times when people are new at personal finance and think, "I need to be a responsible grown-up" . . . they just want to tackle everything! They say, "I've got to stop spending on all this crazy kid stuff!" But you want to just put a limit on it. So focus on one thing at a time, because if you try to do everything at once you're probably going to fail and you're going to feel even worse because you're going to feel as though you've lost at money. So focus on one thing at a time and try to go for that quick win. You might decide, "I'm going to spend a hundred dollars less on restaurants this month," instead of saying, "I'm never going to spend money on restaurants again in my life." One thing at a time, one month at a time.*

Kristin's advice in a nutshell: Focusing on one thing at a time helps you feel in control.

Chapter 2A Benjamin Badge: Budgeting *Tetris* Achievements

Check off each of the following achievements you have completed toward your Benjamin Badge after reading this subchapter:

❑ Create your own Budgeting *Tetris* board and fill in your fixed expenses.
❑ Track your variable expenses with your *Tetris* board.
❑ Work on minimizing your optional fixed expenses by paying off debts and finding cheaper options for necessary expenses.
❑ Use FinTech to help you lower expenses. Load a shopping app extension to your web browser/mobile phone, and let it pleasantly surprise you with deals when you're already planning on making a purchase.

Date You Completed the Chapter 2A Badge	Parent Signature (Putting your mom's John Hancock on your Benjamin stacking makes it official)

3

Increasing Your Income

I find that the harder I work, the more luck I seem to have.
—*THOMAS JEFFERSON*

TOOLS YOU'LL NEED:
- Motivation to learn mad skills
- A winning attitude
- Perseverance

Sometimes during the planning process, you lift your head from the table and realize, with dawning horror, that the roadblocks between you and winning aren't bills or budgets. They're the lack of money in your wallet and the lack of income to fill it. You just don't make enough cash to fund your big, hairy, audacious dreams. Stuff like kids outgrowing the shoes you just bought them or mufflers dragging behind the car can sneak up on you *and* your budget, and then *wham*—the goals are further away than they were the day before.

Let's roll up our sleeves and make more moolah. You may be wondering why we're tackling this *after* we started budgeting. That's a good question, rhetorical device posing as a hypothetical reader. Here's the thing: nothing wrecks mo' money quicker than a fast and loose spending spree. Lots of people make oodles of cash and still declare bankruptcy.

> ### *Joe's Mom on Overspending*
>
> **It isn't just you, dear. Overspending is a huge problem in the USA and, I suspect, much of the world. I saw a T-shirt at the Mystery Spot Historical Landmark and Gravitational Anomaly Gift Shop, and even with my background I thought to myself, "I absolutely must buy it!," which proves again the true mystery spot for most of us is a bank account. Money never seems to find it.**

So plugging budget leaks has to come first. Once you've done that, then you can figure out how to bring in more money. That's right, it's time to make it rain—by increasing your salary or adding a hustle.

Work Nine to Five vs. Do the Hustle

Over time, our minds have changed on this topic. Joe used to think that making more money from your primary job was the answer to most folks' financial woes. In some ways, Joe's not wrong, if he does say so himself. Studies have shown that if you ask your boss for a raise, you're more likely to receive one. Here's the rub, though: most of us never ask. We also don't consider switching jobs to a competing employer for a salary bump, even though many studies show that's also a way to increase your income.

We thought for a long time that focusing on your primary job was the best way to make money because focus = brilliance. Just look at the most successful people in the world. By having a "laser focus" (a term that makes Joe throw up in his mouth a little any time he uses it unironically), you're able to home in on your skills, perfect them, and make lots of money.

But then the artist Austin Kleon appeared on our podcast and said that side projects actually can help us improve in our main jobs, too. They help us disengage, get ten thousand feet away from our primary career, and use problem-solving creativity. The notion that you get your best ideas in the shower is a cliché for a reason: it's often true. To spur more "shower ideas," try spending at least one day a week working on a skill that doesn't necessarily have a direct line to your career. Not only will you develop new strengths, but the time away from the job makes you even better than if you stayed engaged 24/7.

So if the question is "Should you increase your primary income or start a side hustle?," we've learned that the little girl from the meme has the right answer: "Why not both?"

Your Primary Job: Let's Grab a Raise

Study after study shows that if you ask for a raise during normal working conditions (so maybe not during a pandemic, industry downturns, or a zombie apocalypse), your boss will be inclined to give you one. But you have to know how to ask and what to do to ensure that you'll get it.

Mindset: Understanding the Cube

When negotiating, imagine that there is a cube sitting between the participants, representing the things that are important to each. Some sides of the cube are visible to both of you. You both know the general trends of your industry and have a sense of how your specific company is faring.

But there's the side that's facing only one participant. You know what's on yours: you're thinking about how much you deserve more money, what you hope to do with that extra scratch (Mama needs a new pair of platform shoes with goldfish in the heels), and how hard you have worked for the company over the past year.

While stats show that your boss wants to give you a raise, you don't know what's on her side of the cube. She has a set budget and needs to spend dollars where they're most needed. She's concerned about making sure upcoming projects are handled effectively. It's also likely that there aren't enough dollars to go around. So unless you ask, you shouldn't expect your boss to spend them on you. You have to advocate for yourself.

But just as your boss's side of the cube is opaque to you, they have no idea what you're thinking. If you're wondering, "Why can't they see that I'm angry/frustrated/unhappy now?," chances are, you're expecting too much. You need to show them your point of view.

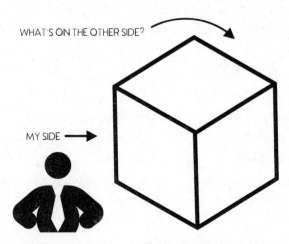

Start by seeking to understand *their* side of the cube, and then take time to clearly draw out your position for them.

A Raise: Your Boss's Side of the Cube

Knowing that your boss has a limited budget and a crunched agenda, how can you create a situation where she wins? It's simple. Ask her to give you more responsibility to help solve her problem. With that increased responsibility, you'll need to be paid more, but that will be a small concession on their end for allowing you to jump in and help. Now your goal isn't just to score a raise; your boss perceives that you're trying to pitch in. This approach takes care of everyone: by giving you more responsibility (with a raise), you can help your boss achieve more.

The Raise Meeting: Bring Facts and Don't Ambush

Empathy plays a big role in a negotiation with your boss. By understanding what she wants, you're more likely to get what you want. First, let's start with this: don't ambush your damned boss. If you've been thinking about a raise for months, don't bring it up at the holiday party. (It's happened to Joe, and it's beyond awkward.) Enjoy the evening, and wait until you're back in normal business hours to stop by your boss's office or send an email.

Put your feet up on your boss's desk to show that you're the real deal. Then say, "Here's how it's gonna be."

Just kidding.

Talk first about your knowledge of the problems on her plate. Ask for more clarification on team goals so that she understands that you want to help. Use as many stats and facts as you can find about how much more successful the company will be by giving you more responsibility. To your boss, it's profits that matter, not just "better products" or happier employees. If you can prove that you'll help the bottom line, your boss is more likely to listen. That's her side of the cube.

There's a good chance—especially in large organizations—that your boss isn't the final decision-maker. While they have a budget, they might have to justify line items to their own boss. Data helps them. What do other firms pay the person taking on your new responsibilities? Arm her with information to help your shared cause.

Here's a recurring theme: if you live your life making things easier for others, life will be easier for you.

Follow-Up: Make It Rain

Alas, sometimes this strategy crashes and burns. Why? You asked for a raise, used facts and figures, became your boss's ally so that when they in turn met with their boss, they could justify the raise or promotion. It all seemed perfect.

But then you didn't deliver.

The most important part of anything in life is to deliver the goods. Bring the noise. Shut down the naysayers. Never make promises you can't keep.

If you do what you promised, you'll find that many doors open in front of you. Your future development conversations will be easier.

Others in the company will know that you're a doer and not a talker. You'll find that you have the benefit of everyone's doubt.

When the Hustle Life Chooses You

So other than asking for a raise, how else could you make a few extra dollars? There are lots of opportunities available, but we truly think that starting a side business can be the most lucrative and fun way to earn extra money. Here's why:

1. The "sharing" economy might not be your friend. If your goal truly is to get Stacked, you might want to take jobs like driving for Uber or food delivery off the table. While over the short term you can make a few bucks, you won't gain many new skills, and the truth is that after things like vehicle depreciation and fuel cost, the amount you pocket is much less than advertised. It's better long-term to invest in creating your own little engine.

If your goal is short-term, then by all means, wipe out that debt, cover the holidays, fund your vacation, or end the bargain with Rumpelstiltskin by driving a few miles and pocketing some quick cash. But if your goal is to continue making money over time on the side, begin building a separate side business.

2. Owning a business isn't as hard as you may think. Before becoming a business owner, Joe thought that all people who owned companies were wealthy and had special knowledge of taxes, business entities, and the secrets of hiring, promoting, or firing. (Joe can neither confirm nor deny that he thought business owners were gifted with a magic decoder ring that helped them navigate the opaque world of entrepreneurship.)

The idea that all business owners are ring-adorned know-it-alls could not be further from the truth. If you own a business, you know that you rarely have all the answers. In fact, business owners will be the first to tell you to become comfortable with never having all the facts when making decisions.

3. Business owners gather new skills faster. Successful business owners look at life as if it's a classroom and their job is to learn as much as possible from as many places as they can. Bill Gates still famously takes a satchel of books whenever he goes to his island hideaway. Starbucks chairperson Mellody Hobson always comes across as conversant on the latest tech and ideas in finance. Business owners study business, which means lifelong learning. Whether your specific company succeeds or not, this will help you immensely with future endeavors.

Side projects can help you become more efficient, develop better systems, and grow in unexpected ways when you pursue a second (or third) stream of income. While there's a danger of spreading yourself too thin, we believe the biggest threat to your ability to earn more money is your lack of diverse skills.

Step 1: Avoiding Common Pitfalls

There are many misconceptions about starting a side business. Here are three Joe saw as an advisor (and business owner):

- **I have to differentiate.** Don't worry about changing the world yet. You probably don't know enough about the field you're about to enter and have a lot of learning to do. Get started.
- **I should pay for expensive courses and training.** Of course you should know what the hell you're doing. But too often people load up on all kinds of expensive and impressive-sounding education, only to wade in far enough to find that this particular side hustle isn't for them. A safer option is to get started and bootstrap the business. Invest just enough money to get rolling, and then as you find success, invest more.

- **I want to operate my side hustle during working hours.** Joe was nearly fired from his primary job early in his career because he was so passionate about his side gig that he continually talked about it at work. Luckily, Joe got off with a stern warning from his boss, but the message was clear. The boss didn't like the fact that Joe was more excited about something other than his business. However, assuming you're smarter than Joe and know that you should focus first on your main job, you'll then carve out the right amount of time before or after work for your side gig.

And for fun, let's throw in a fourth.

- **I need to keep up with the full-timers out of the gate.** Do *not* compare yourself to your competition in the field. Because you're investing less time, you may not move at their pace. That's okay. You have different goals. By sticking with it, as Mom says, you'll win the day in the end.

And how about one more:

- **I need the best equipment.** Not true. Just like more training won't pay off, neither will top-notch tools. Your fledgling business will die quickly if you overspend. Buy equipment at whatever discount you can afford. Here's why this is important: if you're trying to pay off a few bills or afford a vacation, you'll make it that much harder to earn back your investment and reach your goal. If you're after the "big" money, it's worse. While most think that within six or twelve months they'll be successful, it may take you five years before you're harvesting long-term benefits.

And what the heck:

- **I'll know in the first few months whether I'll be successful.** Also not true. Your ability to pivot, learn, and overcome setbacks will guide whether you're a success. You'll need a growth mindset. In fact, we've seen too many good entrepreneurs kill their business *not* because the business was bad but because they weren't able to continue to fight off adversity. They spent too much money too quickly with little result, didn't pivot, and were frustrated by their lack of immediate winning. Phase one is the learning phase of your business. You're exploring the landscape and plotting how to proceed.

In fact, we can draw a map of your beginning stages:

1. Learning phase: What will your business be? What's working? Where are you underpowered? Where should you shift resources? How does your competition stack up?

2. Investment phase: You know your business well enough to know where to invest your time. Now's when you dive into it headfirst.

3. Full-time business phase: If your goal is to make a few extra bucks to pay down debt or build savings a little faster, you probably don't even want to reach this phase. However, there may come a time when you can decide to quit your day job if you choose and pursue this passion without distractions.

Step 2: Getting Started

Once you've chosen your side gig, it's time to execute. The key is not having a great idea. The key is a decent idea and rocking the execution of that idea. I never get excited when I hear someone's brilliant idea because I've seen far more people take a poor idea and make something of it than I have seen people with great ideas get their hands dirty.

Your journey to success begins with a business plan. Business books state that business plans are "supposed to be" monster documents composed of hundreds of pages that nobody ever reads—not even the banker who is usually the one asking for it.

You don't need that type of business plan. You only need to answer these questions:

- What is your product?

  Most people think that a whiz-bang product is essential. But you don't have to have the best mousetrap the world has ever seen. That's the good news. The bad news? Marketing is far more important, and marketing is difficult. While P. T. Barnum is largely seen as a quick-buck artist who didn't have good products, it turns out that he had a talent most others didn't possess: the ability to present his product in a way that made others want to buy it. According to his biographer Robert Wilson—whom we chatted with on *Stacking Benjamins*—Barnum always cared that people felt like they had fun and never felt cheated. Studying marketing will take you far.
- How will you get new customers?
- What type of equipment/funding will you need?

  Michelangelo wasn't awesome because of his paintbrush, and you shouldn't focus on having the best equipment out of the gate.
- What's your competition?

  Please don't tell me you have no competition and your offering is unique. If you're still racking your brain, maybe you need to think more broadly. If your product is innovative, your competition is the existing landscape of legacy services. For the first lightbulb companies, gas lamps were the competitor. Before people were using your product, what were they doing instead? What do you have to convince people to instead use your new (and hopefully improved) product? That is your competition.
- How will you make money?

  There are two keys here. First, don't try to compete on price. Undercutting what you earn because you think it'll attract more business is a surefire road to failure. While you may need to have a few test products or clients to determine your price point, you shouldn't ask what low, low price you can get away with charging and inadvertently put yourself out of business. You should wonder how you can charge more for your current product.

Second, even if you're just trying to make a few bucks on the side, you need to charge enough to cover your overhead and make a profit. Most small business owners are horrible at math. You need to improve your basic skills not only for your side gig but also for your own financial security. (See, Mr. Mims, our editor's tenth-grade math teacher, was right. You do need to use math as an adult.) Here's the deal. If you charge $10 for your doodad, and it costs $7 to make the doodad, you're never going to afford another vacation unless you sell doodads all the doodad day.

Case Study: A Standing Desk

A desk is a desk is a desk . . . but while Joe was purchasing a standing desk recently, the furniture company did everything in their power to lure more money out of his wallet.

Would you like to upgrade the desktop to a nicer wood finish? Would you like some holes in the desk so that wires can easily hang through? How about a power strip for under the desk? Have you bought a chair? They could also, for a small fee, add a light fixture in the corner. You don't want to use the desk in the dark, do you?

Those add-ons raised the amount they made off Joe by 20 percent—and he didn't buy much more than just the desk.

If you aren't making money, is it a side hustle or just a hobby? There's a point at which the business makes sense and below which you're just spinning your wheels. Know the minimum you need to make, and you're going to use your time wisely. Can you sell your service to a bunch of people with less effort and overhead? Maybe you're onto something big.

The Bottom Line

Once you have this "back of the napkin" plan, you're far more ready to start than most businesses. You know what your expenses are, you know how to market, and you have a good idea how much money you'll make.

So Why Is This Important?

While saving on your expenses is an important avenue to Benjamin stacking, making extra cash can often be more fulfilling and life-changing.

Will you ask your boss for a raise, or will you start a side hustle? If you have a side hustle already, will you build systems to make it hum? If you've asked for a raise and failed, will you rethink your strategy and look at your boss's side of the cube?

And finally, we'll drop this like the big tip it is: when you earn more, *lock it in*. Automatically deposit that cash into a savings account for now. We'll talk about what to do with it later in the next section, when we introduce you to the basics of investing.

Much of what we talked about in this chapter involves negotiation. If you're working a side hustle, you'll have to negotiate with both vendors and customers. If you're asking your boss for a raise, that's definitely a negotiation. Let's revisit a conversation Joe had with Mori Taheripour, a negotiations pro who teaches at a little school called Wharton at the University of Pennsylvania. Mori has worked with clients like UPS, Wells Fargo, and the NFL Players Association, and she shared tips on successfully negotiating, well, anything.

LIFE IS A NEGOTIATION: AN INTERVIEW
WITH MORI TAHERIPOUR

Joe: *I'm very curious about how somebody gets interested in negotiating. I'm imagining you, Mori, at sixteen years old, angry after being totally ripped off by a used-car salesperson and wanting to go into negotiation. But I'm sure that's not the real story. How do you get interested in negotiation?*

Mori: *I'm not one of those people that said, "Oh, when I was four, I'd wanted to be a negotiations professor at some point in my life."*

That's not how it happened. I was asked to teach when I was at Wharton. But what I came to realize was that life is a negotiation. And so this may be the most practical skill that we can gain and be better at because we're doing it all the time, every day, all day.

You have to at some point realize that this isn't being ripped off by a used-car salesman. That's not what negotiation is. That's only this tiny sliver of negotiations.

What we do every single day in our daily capacity is negotiation: your dog who doesn't want to come in, even though it's hailing outside; or the kid who doesn't want to go to sleep when you want them to go to sleep. All of these are the negotiations that we have all day, every day.

And so I thought, "This is an extraordinary opportunity for me to play a positive role in something that people do every day." If I could even contribute a little bit to making those conversations more meaningful, to make them less about what you get in the moment, but instead creating value out of these opportunities, that is what I really became passionate about.

Joe: *I think that's fascinating how people misinterpret just the idea of negotiation. What are some other misconceptions people have about skillful negotiating?*

Mori: *That they have to be something that they're not. The word "winning" is one that we've sort of mistaken anyway.*

You have all these things associated with the word "winning," which never is used in my classroom, because oftentimes it's got these inherently masculine attributes associated with it, right? It's like crushing the opponent. If you win, they must lose.

This sort of power and leverage, like those are all the words that are oftentimes associated with the word "winning," whereas you know, you have to redefine what "winning" really means. So I think that's one place to start: What is it that you really want to get out of this conversation?

If it's just a onetime thing, that's actually not as hard. But extracting long-term value, changing these conversations from short-term to indelible opportunities, that's one thing that we don't think enough about. And redefining "winning." You know, you can, by any measure, get some great quantitatively strong outcomes out of negotiation, but if the person who just negotiated with you thinks, "I'd never want to see this person again," was that really winning? How would you feel about yourself?

We think about somebody who's sort of bullying, yelling, and all those sorts of characteristics. Do you enjoy negotiating with somebody like that? I certainly don't.

And because of that, there are people who are oftentimes quite kind. They have a lot of integrity. They value relationships. They're empathetic. Well, who would you rather have a conversation with? If we put more emphasis on those things and held them up as "the winning personality," or the curious person who wants to learn, the person who's empathetic and wants to step into your shoes to understand how you got here to this conversation today, that's what I prefer. That's the person I want to have a conversation with. That's who I want to negotiate with.

Joe: *You tell a great story at the beginning of your book, how early in your career you were helping people, and you were talking to a young kid who wasn't using condoms.*

Mori: *I was young and I moved out to the Bay Area and I wanted to do something in public health and volunteered for this organization. We served really high-risk individuals: prostitutes, drug users, injection drug users, people who had put themselves at risk through their lifestyles.*

I was doing counseling. I met this young man who not only was I trying to teach about safer sex practices, but also counsel him to get tested. He said, "So this AIDS/HIV thing, how long before it kills you?"

And that question alone took me aback. I told him once he gets diagnosed, it could be anywhere from five to seven years, since we were just getting these early treatments.

He said, "That's a really long time. You know, I could come out of my house tomorrow and be shot. So if I can live five to seven years, that's a long time!" I was speechless at that moment. Then I realized how much I've taken for granted about people's lives.

Negotiation is nothing if not about persuasion, right? So for me to persuade this young man, I had to understand his journey. I had to know how he processed the information I was giving him. But it was completely ineffective because I'm thinking, "You want to live forever," and he's thinking seven years is forever.

You are an expert negotiator when you actually think, "I have so much to learn, so I'm going to use this conversation to open my mind, open my heart, and really understand this person better so that when I do want them to see my perspective, I know how to deliver information in a way that they can see it, not the way I intended it to be seen."

Joe: *Your book is called* Bring Yourself: How to Harness the Power of Connection to Negotiate Fearlessly. *If there is a single big idea, what do you think that would be?*

Mori: *The book is called* Bring Yourself, *because I do think it all starts with us. It starts with us when we're preparing to negotiate, and we don't often think about that. It's easy for us to say, "What do I want to buy this car for? What do I want to pay for this house?" But if you step back, even before that, you think, "Who am I? What are my values? Where will I draw the line in the sand that I can't cross, that I can't give up in the course of this conversation? How do I want to treat this person? How do I want people to remember me?" All of that should be done as part of your preparation because you don't want to regret those things. It's those very things that you can't let go of later. That regret just weighs on you. So it starts with you, and then everything else kind of leads from there. What are your goals? What kind of outcomes do you want to achieve, not from this negotiation, but when you put this negotiation as a bigger part of your story, and your journey, and your experience? How do you want people to treat you?*

Who are you authentically? If you're kind, then lead with kindness, like that's who you are. You shouldn't have to be somebody else. And I think when we're ourselves, when we're authentic, when we're so clear about that which makes us who we are, then I think that's pretty much fail-safe because at that point, the outcome doesn't matter as much, right? Maybe you could have done better, but you didn't give up what's most important, which is things like your values and your morals and your ideals. To me, you can't compromise those things, and that's why it's so important.

Mori's advice in a nutshell: Great negotiation is all about knowing who you are and a willingness to learn about the other person.

Chapter 3 Benjamin Badge:
Increasing Your Income Achievements

Whether you increase your income with a side hustle or through embiggening your main income by asking for a raise (double points for both), the process of stacking your Benjamins will go much faster if you have more money coming in.

Check off each of the following achievements you have completed toward your Benjamin Badge after reading this chapter:

☐ Ask your boss for a raise or promotion.
☐ Create a side hustle.
   Who is your competition?
   What is your advantage?
☐ How much extra money did you earn?_____
☐ Lock this extra money in a savings (or investment) account
   automatically!

Date You Completed the Chapter 3 Badge	Parent Signature (Putting your mom's John Hancock on your Benjamin stacking makes it official)

4

Debt, or Driving a Moped Down a Dirt Road to Hell

TOOLS YOU'LL NEED:

- A hamburger today that you'll gladly pay for on Tuesday
- Easy monthly payments for life
- Whatever albatross you're currently wearing around your neck

Back when Emily was an undergrad, credit card issuers set up kiosks on college campuses to give away freebies in exchange for signing up for ~~a lifetime of crushing debt~~ a shiny new credit card.

Many of Emily's classmates were thrilled to sign on the dotted line since they'd get a *free* branded Frisbee, shirt, or even a slice of pizza. That's all it took to begin a lifelong relationship with the enchanted plastic card that allows you to buy now—when you have no money and no sense—and pay later.

While Emily is proud to say that she was never taken in, she was later pulled into the shining but empty world of credit card debt through the power of stationery. When a credit card issuer allowed her to choose which design she would like for her preapproved card, she nearly held out. But when they sweetened the deal with custom stickers, it was all over. This future financial expert—who had always turned up her nose at free stuff—signed up for a card because of the cute stickers and then racked up $2,400 in debt over the following twelve months. Lesson: Want Emily's attention? Wave stickers at her.

Thankfully, in the [redacted] years since Emily's undergraduate studies, the federal government passed the Credit CARD Act of 2009, which made it illegal for credit card issuers to set up shop on college campuses (or even within a thousand feet of campus), glad-hand merchandise in exchange for a card, or market preapproved offers to anyone under the age of twenty-one without their consent.

We wish we could tell you that this law marked the end of college students making ill-thought-out debt decisions with lasting repercussions. And we wish we could tell you that protecting young people (whose brains aren't finished cooking yet) from predatory lending practices was all it took to prevent debt from causing irreparable damage to people's finances—but debt is no fairy-tale world.

Secured vs. Unsecured Debt

Let's start our non–fairy tale with a quick primer on the two types of debt: secured loans and unsecured loans. A secured loan is tied to some sort of collateral. Taking out a loan to finance your car, home, or waterbed means taking on secured debt. If you default on your loan, your suddenly-not-as-friendly neighborhood lender could repossess your car, home, or waterbed in order to recoup some of the financial losses associated with your default.

Unsecured loans don't have anything tangible pledged against the borrowed money. There is nothing a lender can seize to recoup their losses in case of default, because instead of collateral, the lender is extending you a loan or credit based on your credit history and score— and possibly your winning smile. (Unlikely, but worth a try.)

You're likely to pay lower interest on secured debt compared to unsecured debt because the valuable waterbed hedges the lender's risk of default. If you don't pay, you're sleeping on the floor because they took back the item. With no tangible asset behind unsecured debt, the lender assumes more risk and accordingly jacks up the interest rate.

Secured debt includes things like mortgages, auto loans, home equity loans, business loans (where the business itself is the collateral), and the like. Unsecured debt includes personal loans, student loans, and credit cards.

Joe's Mom on Debt: An Important Tool in Your Financial Toolbox

Though debt can cause serious damage, it's important to remember that debt isn't the enemy, like that boy Scott Church back in third grade. Remember him? That's an enemy. No, debt is more like a dangerous tool, like a chainsaw. The chainsaw won't kill you if you know how to wield it like I do, but using it without understanding and respecting its power might leave a boo-boo or two. Someone who knows how to use a chainsaw can clear paths, cut down trees, and menace teenagers who have wandered onto their property without asking nicely. Similarly, you can use debt to pay for expensive items over time or leverage it to improve your finances overall. But just be careful, because debt can be dangerous in the wrong hands. If you don't know how to use the tool, you can destroy everything you have built. Such damage requires quite a bit of cleanup and bleach, and I won't help you mop up any of it. Maybe this analogy got away from me, but you get my point. Joe and Emily are going to introduce you to this handy, potentially damaging tool, so you can treat it and wield it with the respect it deserves, and clean up after any misuse without my having to come in and save you. After all, it's time for *Wheel of Fortune*.

Why Debt Ain't Just a Natural Part of Life

One of the greatest tricks of the last century may have been convincing people that kale is edible, but a close second is the belief that debt is a normal part of life. Like finding new gray hairs every time you look in the mirror or complaining about the weather, we tend to think of accruing debt as a natural part of the aging process. Grow up, start a career, meet a cute somebody with whom you'd like to squabble over Netflix for life—and take on debt so that you'll owe all of your income to lenders, debt collectors, Sallie Mae, and guys with nicknames like "The Weevil" who are a little too interested in your kneecaps. It's the American Way™.

After all, as of 2019, the average American carried over $90,000 in personal debt, which includes mortgages, auto loans, student loans, personal loans, credit cards, and home equity lines of credit. (Sources are unclear on whether debts to the Weevil are included in these calculations.)

But just because debt is pervasive doesn't mean it's something we have to accept. As enlightened Benjamin stackers, we know that it's entirely possible to live debt-free—and eventually mortgage-free—without having to find ourselves a nice yurt off the grid. Living without debt means *you* decide what to do with your income, instead of having to pass it along to your creditors as soon as it hits your bank account. Rather than continuing to work a job you're not super enthused about just so you can keep ahead of your payments, you could take a leap into something unlikely to succeed—like, for instance, starting a podcast from your mom's basement.

Of course, you may be wondering, "Why is debt such a bad thing?" I mean, if a little loan allows you to purchase a diamond-encrusted litter box for your cat even if you haven't saved a dime toward Mr. Kittlesworth's poop box upgrade, isn't it a great idea?

Well, yes and no.

Obviously having the Emperor Litter Box will class up the corner of the laundry room where Mr. K does his business. But what are the long-term costs of owing money?

Debt Is Ruining Your Financial Health

Lenders focus on minimum payments and underemphasize the total cost of your loans over time. These costs are often far higher than you'd expect, since you're paying interest every single month, which can add up over time. Let's peer into one family's household, who have no idea that we're poking our noses into their financial lives like Russian hackers into your Equifax credit report. (What, too soon?)

Eugene Xample and his wife, Esmerelda Xample, and their children, Eowyn and Eustace Xample, are not only nestled around the fireplace as Eugene reads the kids a story and Esmerelda sips from a mug, which her kids think is full of tea—they're also carrying the 2019 national average amount of debt. In fact, they are average in all ways. (They even have the average number of children, at 1.9, after a freak accident involving Eustace, who's fine, just 10 percent shorter.) Being average means that they owe the following:

Mortgage	$203,296
Eugene's auto loan	$13,115
Esmerelda's auto loan	$6,116
Esmerelda's private student loan	$35,640
Credit card	$6,194
Retail card*	$1,155

*This is Eugene's Home Shopping Network card, which Esmerelda doesn't know about. Sadly, hidden debt is also prevalent in the average household.

Each of these debts has a manageable monthly payment amount, which happens to be the only number related to their debt that the Xample family tracks:

Monthly mortgage payment	$1,000
Monthly auto loan payment (Eugene)	$327
Monthly auto loan payment (Esmerelda)	$230
Monthly student loan payment	$418
Monthly credit card minimum payment	$248
Monthly retail card minimum payment	$46

The $2,269 that Eugene and Esmerelda send to their creditors every month feels to them like the total cost of their debts. But it turns out that isn't the case at all. Understanding just how much of that payment is interest can give the Xample family (and you as well, gentle reader) a better understanding of how much their debt costs.

Using the average interest rates on each of these types of debt, let's calculate just how much Eugene and Esmerelda's debt is costing them:

Average mortgage rate	3.94%
Average auto loan rate	5.76%
Average private student loan rate	6.22%
Average credit card rate	18.61%
Average retail card rate	24.89%

Multiplying the amount owed by the interest rate tells you the annual amount of interest:

Annual mortgage interest paid	$8,009.86 (3.94% of $203,296)*
Annual auto loan interest paid (Eugene)	$755.42 (5.76% of $13,115)
Annual auto loan interest paid (Esmerelda)	$352.28 (5.76% of $6,116)
Annual student loan interest paid	$2,216.81 (6.22% of $35,640)
Annual credit card interest paid	$1,152.70 (18.61% of $6,194)
Annual retail card interest paid	$287.48 (24.89% of $1,155)

*Because of amortization tables, this isn't a true amount and should be used only for demonstration purposes. If it's early in the life of their loan, the amount of interest they'll pay is far higher.

Altogether, the Xamples are paying an eye-popping $12,774.55 annually in interest, or $1,064.55 each month. That means that nearly *half* of their monthly payments aren't going to the bottom line. The Xamples (and you, if you're average, too) are paying for stuff multiple times over.

Wanna figure out the cost of your own debt? Wait, don't run away. We know the answer is probably "hell no," since painful truths are painful for a reason. But we learned a long time ago from having passive-aggressive mothers that negative reinforcement works, so knowing just how much your hard-earned money is enriching your creditors can help spur you to close that aching hole in your wallet. You know the one. It's the one Mom's been telling you everyone is staring at. But that's okay, it's your life.

Look up the amount you owe each of your creditors and the interest rate:

Mortgage balance _____ × Interest rate _____ = Annual mortgage interest paid _____

Auto loan balance _____ × Interest rate _____ = Annual auto loan interest paid _____

Student loan balance _____ × Interest rate _____ = Annual student loan interest paid _____

Credit card balance _____ × Interest rate _____ = Annual credit card interest paid _____

Retail card balance _____ × Interest rate _____ = Annual retail card interest paid _____

Home equity line of credit balance _____ × Interest rate _____ = Annual home equity line of credit interest paid

_____

Personal loan balance _____ × Interest rate _____ = Annual personal loan interest paid _____

Add these sums together to calculate your annual interest cost for all your debts. Divide that number by 12 to learn your monthly interest cost.

Is it ugly? Yeah? We'll give you a minute to process. Take your time. Breathe. We've got to scoop the litter box anyway.

[Muzak playing . . .]

All right, ready to move on? Let's dive into the nitty-gritty of paying off your debt.

A Winter Wonderland of Debt Extraction

Hope you've brought along some warm clothes, because for some reason, debt-payoff strategies are decidedly snowy. There are two main strategies on offer: the *debt snowball* and the *debt avalanche.*

Whichever strategy you choose, you need to start by organizing yourself. (That low-pitched moan of satisfaction you heard was Emily's involuntary response to the word "organizing." Feel free to ignore her.)

Gather the following information:

- The name of each creditor, with the exception of your mortgage, from Visa to Sallie Mae to the Weevil. (We'll explain later why we're not including your mortgage in your debt-payoff strategy.)
- Your total balance owed for each debt.
- Your recurring due date for each debt.
- The interest rate you are currently paying and any future rate changes you anticipate.
- The minimum payment for each debt.
- The number of months remaining to pay off each debt.

Now it's time to start a-planning your debt payoff. Here's how.

The Debt Snowball

With all your debts in front of you, start by placing them in order, from smallest balance to largest. In addition, record your minimum payment for each debt and the months remaining until payoff if you continue making minimum payments. Check out how this would look for Eugene and Esmerelda:

Debt	Balance	Minimum Payment	Months to Payoff
HSN credit card	$1,155	$46	36 Months
Auto loan (Esmerelda)	$6,116	$230	29 Months
Credit Card	$6,194	$248	32 Months
Auto loan (Eugene)	$13,115	$327	45 Months
Student loan	$35,640	$418	113 Months

The Xamples send $1,269 per month to their various creditors (minus their mortgage), and Eugene and Esmerelda have decided that they can afford to spend up to $1,500 per month on these debts, meaning they have an additional $231 they can use to crush debts each month.

With the debt-snowball method, Eugene and Esmerelda will start by sending that additional $231 to their lowest-balance debt, while keeping the rest of their payments the same. That means sending $277 per month to the HSN retail card (once Eugene cops to having it), which means this first loan will be paid off in about five months.

Though Eugene wants to high-five everyone after the big win, Esmerelda reminds him that now that they have momentum, it's time to move to the exciting part. Because once the pesky HSN retail card is paid off, they can start sending that additional $277 (on top of the minimum $230 payment) to Esmerelda's auto loan, for a total of $507. *Bam!* See? Exciting. The Xamples are still only sending $1,500 per month to their creditors, but they are strategically whittling down those debts, one by one.

There are now only twenty-four months and a $5,103 balance left in the original payment plan for Esmerelda's car. With that $507 payment going to Esmerelda's auto loan, the Xamples pay off that bad boy in about ten months. Now they're cooking with gas!

With the car out of the way, that entire $507 payment can be rolled over into the credit card payment, meaning now they're sending away $755 per month ($507 more than the minimum payment of $248). The credit card now has a remaining balance of $3,650. By sending $755 per month, the Xamples can eighty-six their credit card in just about five months.

Now that $755 can be rolled over into Eugene's auto loan payment, for a total payment of $1,082. At this point, Eugene's car has only twenty-five payments left and a balance of $7,586. With the $1,082 payment going to his auto loan, the couple can kill it off in about eight months.

Finally, the Xamples can take on their Moby Dick: Sallie (Ms. Mae, if you're nasty). They can send the full $1,500 of their monthly payoff toward Esmerelda's student loans, which has a remaining balance of $28,291. By sending the full $1,500, the couple will slay that mighty beast in only twenty months.

All told, Eugene and Esmerelda are able to say sayonara to debt (minus their mortgage) in about forty-eight months, or four years. Overall, they will pay $71,260.97 over forty-eight months, with $9,040.97 going to interest payments.

You may have noticed that the debt snowball focuses solely on the balance owed, without taking the interest rate into consideration. That means the Xamples may be spending more money here than necessary, since they aren't prioritizing paying off the higher-interest-rate debt first, meaning it's not the most efficient way to pay off debt. But it works for a lot of people because the debt snowball is all about racking up quick emotional victories. Each newly paid-off debt gives you the confidence to keep going to slay the rest of them.

That's where the next snow metaphor comes in.

The Debt Avalanche

As with the snowball, begin your avalanche payoff by ranking your debts in order—but this time, list them from highest to lowest interest rate. You will still want to include the balance, minimum payment, and months remaining until payoff. For Eugene and Esmerelda, it looks like this:

Debt	Interest Rate	Balance	Minimum Payment	Months to Payoff
HSN retail card	24.89%	$1,155	$46	36 Months
Credit card	18.61%	$6,194	$248	32 Months
Student loan	6.22%	$35,640	$418	113 Months
Auto loan (Esmerelda)	5.76%	$6,116	$230	29 Months
Auto loan (Eugene)	5.76%	$13,115	$327	45 Months

So, rewinding to the beginning, Eugene and Esmerelda have $231 above their minimum payment to send to debt each month. As with the debt snowball, the Xamples will start by sending the extra money to the HSN retail card—but for a different reason. With a 24.89% interest rate, that retail card is their most expensive debt.

By sending a total of $277 (the $46 minimum plus the extra $231) to HSN each month, that debt will be paid off in about five months.

Here's where the strategy deviates from the debt snowball. Instead of moving on to the next lowest balance, now the Xamples move on to the *next highest interest rate loan*, which is the credit card and its ugly 18.61% APR. They will send $525 per month to pay down the credit card ($277 plus the minimum payment of $248), which originally had twenty-seven months remaining and a balance of $5,410. With the new $525 payment plan, this debt will be gone-zo in about eleven months.

So far, so good. But the debt avalanche now requires the Xamples to turn their attention to Esmerelda's student loan, since it has the next highest interest rate. At this point, Esmerelda has 97 months remaining on her loan repayment schedule and a remaining balance of $31,297. They will be sending $943 per month to that loan ($525 additional payment plus the minimum payment of $418), which means they will pay off the loan in thirty-seven months, or just over three years. That will shave some serious time off that repayment schedule.

While Eugene and Esmerelda are slogging away at paying off the student loan, they get some good news without changing anything. They've also quietly paid off their cars before reaching the last day of student loan payments. That's because Esmerelda's car only had thirteen months and a balance of $2,672, and Eugene's car only had twenty-eight months and a balance of $8,357 as of the start of their larger payments to the student loan. So Esmerelda's car is paid off within thirteen months, meaning they can start sending this additional $230 to the student loan as well.

At that point, the student loan balance is down to $20,700, and the additional $230 brings the new student loan payment to $1,173. That shaves five months off the repayment plan, meaning the Xamples could be done with their debt in thirty-two months, rather than thirty-seven.

Once Esmerelda's car is paid off and the family can afford to send $1,173 to the student loan, there are only fifteen months left to pay off Eugene's car. That means that once his car is paid off, the couple now plows the full $1,500 to the student loan. At that point, there will be only four months and a $4,050 balance on the student loan, meaning the entire loan will be wiped out a month earlier.

So which method saves you more time? If everything goes exactly right (and when does that happen?), this strategy will take just about the same number of months as the debt snowball. The difference is in how much money it costs overall. In total, the Xamples will pay $70,903.40 over forty-eight months, with $8,683.40 going to interest. In the end, the debt avalanche saves them about $357 in interest payments.

Snowball or Avalanche: Which Is Right for You?

If you spend any time in the personal-finance corner of the internet—or in any of the many personal-finance-themed bars that crop up in major metropolitan areas—you'll often see various "experts" getting spittle-flecked with rage when their preferred payoff method is maligned as suboptimal compared to its snowy cousin.

"You need the psychological motivation provided by small wins!" Davon Rimsay screams, his ears turning purple as he defends his preference for the debt snowball.

"But you're paying more in interest that way!" Sassy Urmon shouts, before smashing a beer bottle in sheer frustration at those who cannot see the clear benefits of the debt avalanche.

At this point, the bartender will throw out both Davon and Sassy, unless it's a Saturday night, in which case the bartender will help tie together their left hands and officiate an arm-wrestling match until one emerges victorious.

Our opinion? Both Davon and Sassy are right. There are benefits to each method. If you need the psychological motivation of small wins that build up over time, then the snowball is the debt-demolition method for you. Remember how long it was going to take to attack that student loan using the debt avalanche? Keeping focused on "extra" payments for three or four years is super tough. Things come up. Holidays arise. As those cars are paid off, the Xamples will imagine new, better machines in their driveway. The debt-snowball method is more likely to keep your eye on the prize. If, on the other hand, it will stick in your craw that you are sending more money to your creditors than absolutely necessary, then get thee to a debt avalanche. You'll save more money, assuming you make it to the end.

Our advice: The method you use is less important than choosing one and following it consistently. There's no need to challenge anyone to an arm-wrestling contest in your defense of one or the other.

Avoiding the Debt Cycle

Your allegiance to one repayment strategy or another means zippo if you slide back into debt. Even after all the exhausting work Eugene and Esmerelda did to kick their debt to the curb, it could all come undone with a single call to reopen their Home Shopping Network card and going to town on the Swarovski-crystal-encrusted-sweater sale.

This is why any discussion of debt needs to include a conversation about what we call "the debt cycle." And like the conversation with your doctor about personal itching, it may start with a look within.

Why'd You Get into Debt to Begin With?

Perhaps it was that easy-to-use credit card that brought all your *Star Wars* figurine dreams to life. Maybe it was the student loan you took on, assuming $150,000 worth of student debt was no big deal because you'd soon be making Stephen King–level money once the big publishers bought your *Pirates of the Caribbean* fan fiction. Or maybe you took on a mortgage that you didn't quite understand or bought more car than you needed. Or maybe debt simply crept up on you over time.

No matter what your journey has been, it's important to look back on the decisions you made that led to your debt to pinpoint how it happened. Recognizing that you're not to be trusted with an $11,000 credit limit and four hours in the Staples highlighter aisle is truly useful information in helping you to end the cycle.

To help you figure out why you got into debt, answer these questions:

- What financial decisions led to my largest debt balances?
- Why did I make those decisions?

- Which choices would I make again, if I had the option? (Those four hours of bliss in Staples will never not be worth it to Emily.)
- Which choices would I change? (Maybe Emily should ask Joe to follow behind her and reshelve the office supplies and slowly remove the credit card from her hand.)

How Can You Avoid Temptation?

Once you have a better sense of why you ended up in debt and you've thought about which choices you regret and which you'd sign up for again, you're in a much better place to start the "interrupting the decisions that might bite you in the butt and send you tumbling back down into the cycle of debt" process.

Some easy ways to nix temptation include:

- Freeze your credit card in a block of ice. This is an old chestnut for a reason.
- Remove your payment information from online retailers.
- Block the websites most likely to trigger a spending binge. This includes things like Pinterest or Wayfair.
- Make your card hard to get out of your wallet by folding it up into a full-size eight-and-a-half-by-eleven-inch sheet of paper. Seriously, you'll get frustrated even thinking about it, and that can nip a spending binge in the bud.
- Get a life-size cardboard cutout of your most disapproving friend or family member, complete with a speech bubble asking, "Do you really *need* that?" that you post somewhere prominent and even take with you to meet with mortgage lenders, to car lots, and, in Emily's case, to Staples.

Don't Forget the Power of Psychology

If you're making enough money to live, then ending the cycle of debt is often about embracing delayed gratification.

When you find yourself stomping your little foot and demanding presents and prizes and sweets and surprises of all shapes and sizes, instead of whipping out the plastic, remind yourself how much fun it is to watch your debt balances plummet. It's far more gratifying than pink macaroons and a million balloons and performing baboons, or anything else that you can buy now and pay for later.

It's likely that your inner Veruca Salt won't believe you. So find ways to help her enjoy the journey:

- **Make yourself a debt-payoff thermometer.** Elementary school teachers know there's something insanely satisfying about coloring in those bad boys and working your way up to debt freedom.
- **Tell your friends about your debt-payoff journey, and ask them to help keep you honest.** They're the ones rolling their eyes at Veruca and also the ones who like you best when you're not overcome with the gimme-gimmes. They'll cheer for you as you reach milestones, and you and I both know that the only thing your inner Veruca likes better than stuff . . . is applause.
- **Find your debt-freedom inspiration.** What big thing do you want from life? Maybe it's a trip to Machu Picchu, or early retirement, or a jelly bean feast. Whatever big thing you want needs to be big enough that it will motivate your Veruca more than those moments of I Want It Now. Find inspiration major enough to keep your eyes on that inspirational prize.

Let's Circle Back to Mortgages (Lest You Think We Forgot About Them)

We didn't include a mortgage in either of our debt-destruction strategies. What's up with that? Isn't a mortgage your biggest debt, and didn't we already establish that debt is hurting your financial health?

Yes, my careful-reader friend who remembers what we wrote two thousand words ago. Mortgages are a type of debt, and a perfect world would see you footloose and debt-free, and that includes your mortgage.

But mortgages are generally not counted in debt-payoff strategies for several reasons:

- **Mortgage interest rates tend to be relatively low.** Mortgage rates have been low for several years and continue to scrape near-historic lows. As of this writing, rates were still below 3 percent for new mortgages for those with good credit. When prioritizing debt payoff by interest rate, this would put the mortgage last on the list if you're following the debt-avalanche method.

  You're just not paying that much to your banker, comparatively speaking, even though a small interest rate on a large amount of money still adds up.

  The counterargument: *Because of the amortization table, new mortgages have huge interest in the first few years as bankers get their money early on. Making early principal payments to your debt can shorten the life of your mortgage tremendously. If mortgage debt is your biggest concern, making extra payments to your principal early on can cut months or years off your loan.*

- **Mortgage balances are pretty darn big.** (Hi there, California homeowners! Indiana says, "*What?*") Since your mortgage balance is likely to be the highest balance of all your debts, getting this bad boy paid off will also be at the bottom of the list for snowball aficionados. It's going to be a while before you have the snowball built up enough to send extra money to your mortgage.

  The counterargument: *Paying off your biggest debt also means you're probably freeing up the most cash flow, which you could be using to save for your goals.*

- **Mortgage interest might be tax deductible.**

One of the most commonly cited reasons for holding on to a mortgage is the fact that Uncle Sam lets some of us deduct the interest paid. That means that every dollar you pay in interest on your mortgage (up to a $750,000 mortgage) reduces your taxable income by the same amount. If you pay $10,000 in mortgage interest in one year, you can reduce your taxable income by $10,000. You can't get that reduction from extra payments you send to the principal.

That said, deciding not to pay off a major debt based on a tax deduction is like adopting a pet rhino based on an offer of free rhino kibble for life. It's a bigger decision than just the mortgage deduction, and becoming a rhino owner has more costs than just food.

The counterargument: *Mortgage interest is now deductible for far fewer people than it was just a few years ago. If you don't prepare your own taxes, check to see if you're deducting this mortgage interest anymore. There's a better-than-good chance you are not.*

The Opportunity Cost of Early Mortgage Payoff

Here's the problem with paying off your mortgage early: this strategy ties up huge sums of money you could be investing. Because long-term investments like stocks have historically earned more than what you are paying in mortgage interest, you could lose out big by paying off your mortgage.

Let's get back to the Xample family. Before them lies a crossroad. In one direction, they begin to send an additional $1,000 per month to their thirty-year mortgage. This doubles their current monthly payment to $2,000. As you'll recall, their mortgage has a balance of $203,296, on which they pay 3.94 percent.

Doubling their monthly payment will pay down the mortgage faster than you can do the Kessel Run. Specifically, Eugene and Esmerelda will have their home paid off in ten years, and that feat will save them over $98,000 in interest payments. That's a lot of Benjamins.

But what about that other path? What if Eugene and Esmerelda leave their mortgage as is and instead sock away their $1,000 per month into an investment with a return of 6 percent per year? At the end of ten years, the Xamples will still owe $159,400 on their mortgage, but their $1,000-per-month investment will have grown to a balance of $162,473.44!

Prioritizing mortgage payoff can also cost you the opportunity to stay liquid with your cash. If you run out of money and have only one payment left, how much of your house does the bank claim? That's right: the whole home. If you keep your money in a place that's easier to access, you'll avoid this issue. That doesn't make nixing your mortgage the wrong choice—it's just another aspect of the decision to consider. Remember: only professional personal finance pundits should get into arm-wrestling matches over these sorts of things.

In many cases, it's a good idea to embrace the joy of financial multitasking. You can increase your monthly payments to your mortgage and both shave some time off your payment schedule and money off your interest payments. At the same time, go ahead and invest some for the long term. Life isn't either/or.

So Why Is This Important?

Debt ain't no natural phenomenon, and it doesn't have to rule your financial life, but it's likely the biggest pitfall you'll encounter on your path to becoming a champion Benjamin stacker. So it behooves you to understand what debt is costing you, how you are tempted into its vicious cycle, and what you can do to kill off your debts once and for all.

Let's check in on how our friend Laura D. Adams, the host of the wildly popular *Money Girl* podcast and author of *Debt-Free Blueprint*, views debt. Laura joined Joe in his mom's basement to talk about how to wash debt right out of your hair:

BUILDING YOUR DEBT-PAYOFF BLUEPRINT:
AN INTERVIEW WITH LAURA D. ADAMS

Joe: *Why is it that so many people make so many awesome decisions about their money at work, and then they come home and forget that all these rules that work really well at work would also work at home?*

Laura: *There are a lot of people that believe that it is just going to work itself out one day. They think, "Yeah, I can have a lot of debt right now. And when I make the big bucks down the road, I'll just pay it all off and everything will work out just fine."*

And that's rarely what happens.

Joe: *If you don't have the skills now, what's going to change so you can pay down debt later? What skills are you going to bring to the table later that you're not using today?*

Laura: *Absolutely. So this began a journey for me to help people understand those messages.*

And some of them are very simple. It's earning more than you spend. It's planning for the future, putting a little bit away consistently over a long period of time. I'm trying to get people to implement these very simple things by kind of knocking them over the head every once in a while with some of these messages.

Joe: Well, you don't knock them over the head. You're very calm and gentle and happy, which I think is why you have so many people that listen to the show. But let's get people out of debt. Let me start here: You talk about tackling debt in the right order. How do we put our debt in the right order to get it done faster?

Laura: When I've talked to people about debt, this is the biggest point of confusion: Where do I even start? I think people get hung up on it. I would say, "Hey, just get started." Do what you can. But if you can do it in the right order, you're going to be much more efficient.

So I like to look at debt in terms of short-term debt and long-term debt. Long-term debts are things like mortgages, or maybe a student loan. They're things you've got to pay over perhaps ten, fifteen years into the future. Those long debts are typically the least worrisome because they're usually fairly inexpensive and they sometimes come with a tax deduction that can make them even cheaper.

That's why I like to focus on short-term debt first.

Joe: So what are those?

Laura: For most of us it's credit card debt, right? And it could be double digits in terms of interest rate. Maybe it's a payday loan. Maybe it's a very expensive auto loan. So those short-term debts are typically costing you the most.

Joe: There's these two methods. One's called the avalanche method, where you look at the interest rate first, and then there's the snowball method, where you put the balances in order. Do you have an opinion about which one of those is better?

Laura: *I tend to tell people to do it mathematically. So I tend to look at the highest interest rates first. However, I would say that if you have a lower-interest-rate debt that is just keeping you up at night . . . you just can't sleep because you've got $1,000 left on your fairly low-interest student loan, I would never deprive you of the joy of knocking that one out. So I do think that it is personal. It is emotional. You can use mathematics as a guide, but let your emotions also take you where they need to go, just to make you happier about your situation.*

Joe: *Know yourself first.*

Laura: *Yeah, absolutely.*

Joe: *I want to ask about some different ways to pay down credit card debt.*

First, what do you think about balance transfers on credit cards? You see these all the time: 0 percent interest for six months. What do you think about those?

Laura: *They can be wise if you truly know that you can pay off the balance in full by the time the promotion ends. What happens often, though, is that the 0 percent offers look so great that we go, "Oh, yes, we're going to transfer everything over here." And then we forget. The offer expires, we still have debt to pay, and the interest rate goes back up, and maybe to an interest rate that's a little higher than before we took the offer to begin with. You end up negating all of the goodness that you were trying to get out of taking that offer in the first place. So if you've got a smart plan, like if it's a twelve-month promotion, you're going to pay one-twelfth of that balance every single month.*

If you can do that, they're the best thing to do.

Joe: *What do you think about changing debt over to a consolidation or a personal loan instead?*

Laura: *That can work, too. You know, the problem there is [if] you get your loan and then go back to the credit card and start spending.*

If you are truly disciplined and you say, "You know what, I'm not going to use that credit card anymore," and you really focus on that thirty-six-month personal loan, that consolidation, they can be a great way to get that debt taken care of and done.

Joe: *Let's talk for a second about staying out of debt in the first place. Where do we start on that front?*

Laura: *I think that a lot of people simply don't know how much they earn. They literally don't know how much they're making or what they're spending. So if you can break it down and really see where your money is going, for a lot of people that is eye-opening. They go, "Whoa! You know, I am spending more than I'm making and that excess is going on the credit card." So if you can truly zero out your money and know where every penny is, that helps.*

"Zero-based budgeting" is what they call it, and you make a home for every bit of your money. Part of that's gotta be savings, part of that's gotta be retirement. You've got to work that into the spending plan. That's typically the only way I know not to go into debt.

Laura's advice in a nutshell: Your debt-payoff plan needs to both make mathematical sense and be personally satisfying.

Chapter 4 Benjamin Badge: Debt-Payoff Achievements

Paying off your debts not only clears your sinuses, it also frees up your budget so you can focus on building your sweet stacks of Benjamins.

Check off each of the following achievements you have completed toward your Benjamin Badge after reading this chapter:

❑ Rank your debts, either in order from smallest to largest balance (for the debt-snowball strategy), or from largest to smallest interest (for the debt-avalanche strategy).

❑ Calculate how much extra money you can send to your debts each month. _____

❑ Systematically eighty-six your debt with that extra money using your chosen payoff strategy.

❑ Make it tougher for you to rerack up your debt by putting barriers in the way of your biggest spending temptations.

CHAPTER 4

DEBT

Date You Completed the Chapter 4 Badge	Parent Signature (Putting your mom's John Hancock on your Benjamin stacking makes it official)

5

Credit, aka One for Me, Three for the Bank

TOOLS YOU'LL NEED:

- Your credit report
- A smartphone or computer
- The belief that you deserve a better score (you do!)
- The underrated ability to ignore your credit score most of the time

Remember *Strange Case of Dr. Jekyll and Mr. Hyde* by Robert Louis Stevenson? Though most people wouldn't notice such well-hidden symbolism, Joe discovered that this classic spooky story is an analogy for debt.

Like the good guy Dr. Jekyll, who drinks a potion that transforms him into the murderous Mr. Hyde, credit is that helpful tool that, because of your hubris, becomes your worst enemy. With credit's help you can:

- Buy clothing, video games, and a new computer . . . that costs many times the purchase price and takes years to pay off.
- Buy a hot car your friends will love . . . that gets repossessed because you didn't make the payments.
- Buy a big, beautiful house . . . that you lose to the bank.

Doesn't credit sound like a blast?

To be fair, it really can be useful. But for many, it just isn't. Credit's like that kind of unstable girl- or boyfriend everyone warns you about, the one you keep telling your friends that they just don't understand. You know that the problem isn't the card, so you can keep carrying it in your pocket—and breaking it out on the reg. What can it possibly hurt?

It can hurt a ton, as Joe well knows. Here's his story of how he learned the hard way.

Joe's Plastic Adventure

I spent my first two years of college at the Citadel, the Military College of South Carolina. Not only did this mean that I got a cool new haircut, but I also couldn't hold a job off campus. That didn't stop me from walking into our student union during the first week of school and applying for an American Express card.

And of course, badaboom-badabing, I was almost immediately approved for my shiny new credit card. Within a couple of weeks, it was in my hand. This clearly told the world that I was an adult now, or so I thought.

The first time we could escape from the high white walls of school, my friends and I headed out to the mall in North Charleston. I bought a sweater at Nordstrom, an eighties-tastic purple sweater with an argyle design around the V-neck, and it wasn't cheap. I had no money, but I proudly flashed the sales clerk my beautiful card. Cha-ching.

Then, we all headed out to Ruby Tuesday. When the waiter presented us with the check, I again flashed my card. I even quipped, "I've got this."

A few weeks later, I saw that someone had sent me a letter. Well, not exactly a letter. It was something I'd never considered, called "the American Express bill."

A bill? What did they mean when they wrote that I'd have to pay for my new sweater (that I couldn't even wear because I was in a military school and wore a uniform everywhere) and my big-man lunch purchase? So, I did what any rational human being would do.

I called my mom.

"Mom," I said. "We have a problem."

"No," she told me. "*You* have a problem."

Within ninety days, my credit was ruined and the card was long gone. I spent the next summer trying to figure out how to pay the collection agency that chased me the rest of the school year.

So while you may carry around a bunch of excuses like I did about how great credit can be, let's agree that if you can afford life without credit, it's better. Without credit, you know that you built it yourself. You owe nobody. You pay zero dollars in interest above the purchase price. There's no reaching back later to pay for fun you've already had or sweaters you've already bought. You're living within your means. That's when you're truly #adulting.

Of course, living completely without credit isn't often possible in the modern world. I've needed to take on mortgages, car loans, and credit cards. The difference is that I learned to think about credit differently.

How Old Joe Used Credit	How New Joe Uses Credit
Credit was my crutch.	Credit is a tool.
Credit was for allowing me to keep up with friends.	Credit allows me to increase my ability to profit.
Credit extended my lifestyle.	Credit expands my reach.

Let's Get Better Credit

Now that you've heard Joe's cautionary tale, it's time to grab *better* credit. Let's start by defining the "New Joe" goals.

Credit is a tool. Joe now uses credit to make large purchases, protect his purchases (travel, rental cars, and big-ticket items are protected by most credit cards), and for convenience. He keeps funds ready to pay his card off *in full* every month.

Credit allows me to increase my ability to profit. In the unlikely event that he's strapped for business cash, Joe will use his card to purchase items to make his investments in his business stronger. He may buy a high-ticket item like a computer with credit, even though he knows he'll owe interest. But he doesn't bet on the future without a plan. He's investing in himself with a clear strategy that details how to pay off the debt. If he can't figure out how to pay the debt, he doesn't take it.

Credit expands my reach. A mortgage is the classic method for using credit to expand your reach. If you could buy a house only once you'd saved up every single dollar of the $350,000 purchase price, then only people with names like Toff Biffington IV could ever afford to own a home before they were old and gray. Being able to qualify for a loan expands your purchasing power.

Understanding How Credit Works

Joe's mindset shift came about after he learned the hows and whys of credit. It's important to understand exactly what credit measures if you want to wield it intelligently.

To start, credit revolves around a credit score, a number between 0 and 800+ that tells creditors how trustworthy you are. Remember that credit scores are just that: a number. Your FICO score and your Vantage-Score (not to mention all the mimic scores from parroting agencies) don't and can't define you, any more than your high school "permanent record" does.

That said, there are bonuses to having great credit. First, your interest rates are lower on nearly everything. If you have a 700+ score, things get really sexy—and when you get to 800+, you get the executive platinum treatment. Companies beg you to use their money, and at a low, low rate. In the few cases where Joe's had to borrow money in recent years, it's always at the lowest rate possible.

Second, you become eligible for the company's biggest reward programs. By paying your debt and accumulating points, you can navigate a system that's designed to trap people. You have good credit, so take advantage of it. Yes, the rewards you earn are built on the backs of people getting into trouble—like College Joe. But by taking advantage of their perks today, he's getting back thousands of the dollars he handed these companies early on.

> ### Joe's Reward Card Success—Or, How to Get Your Own Back Two Drinks at a Time
>
> My wife, Cheryl, and I upgraded our cards, and now whenever we fly, we fly in comfort. We use the airline lounges, feasting on the buffet and enjoying not being crammed into whatever seats we can find near the gate. While we fly coach, we're rarely paying for the flight, and on international flights you'll often find us in business or first-class so that we arrive rested and ready for fun.
>
> I don't say any of this to brag. I paid craploads of money to these companies, and now I'm getting mine back. I try to have two drinks every time I go to the bar at the American Express club in airports just to get even.

So how do they calculate this magical score that can get you free stuff (but only if you don't need it)? Unfortunately, the system is flawed, both on the systemic and individual level. Much smarter folks than us have explained the myriad issues with the credit-scoring system, so we'll just cover the basics of how the system works.

Your credit score is based on five main factors:

1. Do you pay your bills on time? If not, your credit score will get whacked across the knees.

2. How old is your credit? If you've been able to handle credit for twenty years, I'll trust you more than someone who whipped out their first card at Nordstrom and Ruby Tuesday even though they had no job and no income.

3. How much credit do you have available, and how much are you already using? If others have handed you a ton of credit but you haven't used it, creditors like you. You know how to be disciplined and not touch other people's money in an irresponsible way. However, if you have very little credit and it's maxed out, that makes you a bigger risk.

4. What is your credit mix? If you're loaded up with credit cards but no other categories of loans, it's difficult for lenders to see how you spend money and use credit in different situations. They feel more comfortable if you've had both revolving credit (aka credit cards) and installment loans (like auto loans, student loans, or mortgages).

5. Have you applied for much credit lately? If so, that might be a sign of panic. Lenders don't like panic. Early in his career, Joe applied for three credit cards all at once. None of them approved him.

In addition to these five factors that help determine your credit score, you should also remember these two big credit principles:

1. Only apply for credit you're going to use. By "use," we don't mean "max out." That means apply only for cards that you're going to actively carry and use.

2. Pay your bills on time. In a perfect world, you'll pay off your card in full every month to avoid interest. But if you can't do that, you have to make sure you pay what you can (that's at least the minimum payment or above) *on time*. Make even one late payment, and you'll carry a negative mark on your credit for a long time.

Based on these two principles, here are some handy-dandy ways to improve yo' credit:

- **Sign up for automatic payments of the minimum amount on your cards.** For a long time, Joe often forgot to make his minimum payment on time, and the credit card company made sure they got their pound of flesh. Setting up automatic payments fixed that problem.
- **Whenever you get an alert, use this to pay even more.** When Joe's credit card company alerted him that they'd made an automatic minimum payment, he didn't say, "Cool, well now I'm off the hook until next month!" Instead, he tried to immediately make an additional payment to either pay off or significantly pay down his debt.
- **When credit card companies offer you more credit, take it.** But only if you know you can trust yourself. Joe explains: "There was a time that I couldn't do this. If I had more credit, I was going to spend it. I had to learn the hard way. But if a credit card company offers me a larger credit line now? I'll take it. Because I'm never going to use it, my credit goes even higher."
- **Keep your oldest card open.** Joe only recently canceled his oldest card, one he'd had since 1992. The people who'd initially trusted him with a card during his dark days of horrible credit stayed with him for a long, long time. Joe only canceled this card because he now knows his credit is safe. Don't cancel an old card until your credit is like Joe's and you're sure it won't hit a bump. We've seen too many people close old accounts because they didn't use the card, but unless there's a downside like an annual fee, keep it open and it'll help your credit.

Credit's Double-Edged Sword

Sadly, we believe that credit scores are designed as gotchas for most people. In fact, the "solutions" just described can and should all be considered potential traps. Here's why:

- **DO YOU REALLY NEED CREDIT?** Joe told himself he needed it for expenses when he signed on Amex's dotted line back at the Citadel's student union, but he really just wanted a status symbol. What the hell do you need that's so important that you should use someone else's money? We're not saying these purchases don't exist. They just aren't as prevalent as the number of applications would have you believe.

- **INCREASING YOUR CREDIT WILL GIVE YOU MORE POWER.** That may sound like a good thing, but we've all seen *Lord of the Rings*, *Star Wars*, and *Aladdin*. Lesson: Power corrupts. More credit is more power, and until you can handle it, tell the credit companies, "Oh, hell no. Do not raise my credit limit." Extra points if you tell them, "What are you trying to do, turn me into Darth Vader?" At least you'll be memorable.

- **REWARD POINTS? ARE YOU KIDDING ME? DO YOU KNOW HOW THAT GAME WORKS?** Companies offer rewards so you'll *spend more money*. No for-profit company gives away anything for free. Your buddy who can't pay his credit cards on time is paying for your flight upgrade. You don't want to be the person paying for Joe's flight upgrade. He's not going to call and thank you.

How to Fix Your Credit

Maybe your credit doesn't need fixing. You probably also brush your teeth three times a day and are able to honestly say yes when the dentist asks if you've been flossing. However, you still should read this, because everyone needs to keep track of their credit, and many of these steps apply to you, too.

First: Grab Yo' Credit Score

Credit agencies will give you a peek-a-boo at your credit for free once per year. But they won't show you the one thing you and I want to see—your credit score. Jerks.

So, just like when the fridge is empty of delicious foamy beverages but we're still thirsty, we have to create a workaround. We might ask our neighbor Doug if he wants to come enjoy some chips and salsa on the porch with us, since we know he'll ask if he can bring anything and we can ask him to provide the brewskis.

The same principle applies to figuring out your credit score. Many companies and credit cards offer a free peek; ask your own credit card provider(s). If not, the list of sites to look at is vast but always changing—which is why we're not naming any here. (We don't want this book to age like shrimp cocktail left out overnight.) Suffice it to say, free credit score websites are out there. Just stick with companies you've heard of before—so avoid Wacky Bob's Credit Score and Lube—and never give payment information to a credit score website.

By the way, the score you find won't be correct. You are now making a frustrated noise. We know, and not just because we could hear your groan from all the way over here. We feel the same way. Maybe it'll help to walk through the history of how this mess came to be. So how about we have our resident historian tell us why your online free credit score might not be exactly correct.

Joe's Mom on Credit Scores

Back in the day there was one credit score to rule them all. It was called the FICO score. That FICO nonsense is short for Fair Isaac . . . oh, who cares. The point is that until 2006, there was one score and that was it.

Then the credit companies "said" that the score wasn't accurate, so they wanted to create a new one. They called this "new-and-improved" number the VantageScore. Want to know how the VantageScore is different? Look it up. Better yet, Bing it so you get paid to search.[4]

The reason they wanted a new score smells to me like they

---

4 *Microsoft, if you want to sponsor this paragraph, look us up.*

were sick of the FICO people having a monopoly, but once again, that doesn't matter. What matters is that there are now two scores, neither of which is perfect, but both basically work the way Joe and Emily have laid out in this chapter. I'm so proud of them.

And then, seeing how only the credit companies and those Fair Isaac people had all these Benjamins streaming in, the FinTech people during the great online revolution said, "Why can't we offer scores for free?" When the FICO and Vantage-Score people stuck out their hands to get paid for sharing this tech, the FinTechies replied, "We don't need to pay you! We can make up a score that's close!" And the FICO people and VantageScore people shrugged.

And so the FinTech dudes and dudettes made up one that was close but not the same. I call it the "horseshoes and corn-hole score," but you probably won't. And no, I don't know how they did it. Again, I'm not sure why you even want to know.

There are now bunches of scores. None are the same score that your lender will use, probably. But who cares? Your goal, like the goal of any epic hero, is to get close enough to make a difference. You don't need a perfect score, because who the hell knows what perfect is? You just have to be in the general parking lot–ish vicinity of greatness.

Now go clean your room.

There you have it from Mom. That's what you need to know about your credit score. But we're not quite done yet, since you also need to take a look at your credit report.

Remember when we said the credit agencies will let you look at your credit once a year? That would be your credit report. Don't get us started on the fact that they gather information about you constantly and let you take a look at it only annually. It's like a stalker allowing you to look at the photos he's taken of you once a year. What a guy.

But it's important to keep an eye on your credit report. In 2010,

ABC News reported that 79 percent of all credit reports have something wrong, which can majorly ding your score. (That's like your stalker having pictures of other people in your album. The invasion of privacy could at least be *accurate*.) Joe's had to fix five different credit issues with credit agencies. It wasn't fun, but it was worth it, and all the agencies have specific ways you can fight what appears on your report. So get your credit report and contest anything that's wrong. Here's how to dispute inaccuracies with the credit agencies:

* **Experian:** Experian.com/disputes
* **Equifax:** Equifax.com/personal/education/credit/report/how-to-dispute-credit-report-information
* **TransUnion:** Transunion.com/credit-disputes/dispute-your-credit

By knowing where you stand now, you're far more likely to do better in the future. It doesn't matter how wonderful your credit is currently—you can make it better, and by knowing where you are a few times a year, you'll see your score gradually rise. Yeah, the credit agencies may be tracking you like the stalkers they are—why are you obsessed with me, Experian?—but you can show them who's in charge: you.

Second: Create an Action Plan to Pay Down Debt

Here is an unfortunate truth: you can't fix your credit unless you fix the problem that caused you to have bad credit. There's no magic wand, no special incantation, no "weird old trick to fix your credit problems!!!" The solution is rolling up your sleeves and doing the tough stuff: Work at paying down your debt. Pay your damned bills on time. Use the hacks in this book to get your train rolling.

You can do this. Maybe it takes making extra money or setting up minimum payments, but know that you have it inside you to get things rolling.

If You Can't Fix It on Your Own

You might have more of a credit problem than a can-do attitude and a solid action plan can fix. It's not a fun place to be, as Joe can tell you—but it's also not hopeless, either. Rather than bury your head in the sand or decide that you might as well buy another few Nordstrom sweaters and Ruby Tuesday lunches before they cancel your card, here are some concrete strategies for getting help.

Call Your Creditors and Credit Card Agencies

This was the hardest part for Joe: negotiating with creditors. Let's start with a few obvious but intimidating points:

- **Creditors would rather have some of your money than none at all.** Remember that you're in control. Every time creditors tried to take over the situation, they messed it up for Joe. Don't let them do the same for you. Stay in control.
- **Make lowball offers to pay off old debt.** We know you want to pay off the whole thing. We want you to pay off the whole thing. But nobody wins if you aren't finding a way to, well, win. Find out what they'll accept to get their collections department off your back. Don't be ashamed. You paid more than many, and you're going to make them proud that they were generous. If they are generous, pay it forward. Be generous to someone starting out or in the same spot you'd been in.
- **Realize when you're beaten.** If you can't control your debt or your spending, and you can't find a way out, meet with credit counselors before you do something irrevocable. Specifically, we mean letting an attorney talk you into filing for bankruptcy protection.

Joe's Take on Bankruptcy

With bankruptcy, you completely wipe the slate clean—kinda. You also end up with ruined credit for at least seven

years. And you'll regret not trying to pay back the people
you owe. If your creditors look you in the eye and say that
they'll take less, that's one thing. But cutting them out
altogether, detonating not just all the debt that you owe
but also your own ability to get credit in the future? I'm not
a fan. That doesn't mean that filing for bankruptcy isn't the
right decision for you. There have been a few circumstances
when I could see no way around advising someone to seek
out an attorney. But there are plenty of other options available first.

With that out of the way, call your creditors. This is a worthwhile use of time, whether you have credit problems or not.

Here are some questions you should ask:

1. What can I do if I accidentally don't pay a bill on time? Can I call and request to have it not hit my credit report?

2. Can I get autopay set up to pay the minimum if I forget?

3. What protections and benefits does my credit card give me?

4. What's my annual fee? Is there a way to have it waived?

5. What's my interest rate, and is there a way to get that lowered?

You'll hang up feeling empowered and, in many cases, with some fees waived and interest rates lowered. But even if you don't, you should feel fantastic that you took control of debt.

Credit Counseling

If you're in over your head, credit counselors can negotiate with creditors on your behalf and help you secure better terms. Even better, in many cases they'll make it easy for you. They'll take all your money toward debt, pay off the creditors, and leave you with whatever you're allowed to spend. Does that sound like Big Brother? Sure it does. But sometimes, especially when you're trying to get your act together at first, you need someone to get it done. That's what a credit counselor can do.

A note of caution: there are some really dirty credit counselors out there. Find ones that are nonprofit and with a strong track record. Do your homework before letting someone have your money in exchange for a "promise" to pay your creditors.

So Why Is This Important?

Your credit score and history help determine how easily you can build your Benjamin stacks. Understanding how credit works for the credit bureaus and within your own financial psychology will help you make the best decisions for your money.

Farnoosh Torabi, the host of the *So Money* podcast, a credit expert, and the author of the bestseller *When She Makes More*, came down to the basement to talk to Joe about how credit fits into a financial plan.

CREDIT SKELETONS IN YOUR CLOSET:
AN INTERVIEW WITH FARNOOSH TORABI

Joe: *Let's say hello to our good friend Farnoosh Torabi.*

Welcome back to Texarkana.

Farnoosh: *I like what you've done with the place.*

Joe: *Mom makes us clean when you come around.*

Farnoosh: *Is that Febreze that I smell?*

Joe: *I can neither confirm nor deny. But let's quickly change the subject: credit scores. You had this hit you in a very personal way, not paying enough attention to your credit score.*

Farnoosh: *Right. I was—to your point—I was in my early twenties, living in New York City for the first time on my own. I had a full-time job, was making the Benjamins.*

And I started to open up a few credit cards. One in particular was a store credit card. I won't tell you what retailer, but it was one of my favorite stores at the time. And I think I just got overwhelmed with the number of bills that were coming in every month. I wasn't automating anything. That was the first mistake. I ended up forgetting to pay one of the monthly bills from this store credit card. I recognized it quite soon. I think a couple of days went by and I was like, "Oh my gosh, oops!" I went to go pay it. I paid it on the phone so that I could pay it the fastest way. Still, I was past due. That ended up hitting my credit report, which then impacted my credit score.

I didn't really think much about it until a couple years later [when] I went to get a mortgage. The underwriters took issue with my late payment. They brought it up. They said, "What is this? How long ago was this? What happened?"

Joe: *Two years later?*

Farnoosh: *The skeletons in my closet came out. I had to justify that now* *things have changed. This was just a onetime issue. I'm really not a late payer, but it was a real wake-up call. I realized too late the importance of automating your bills and why it helps to be really organized when it comes to managing your payments and your credit cards, because at the end of the day, it can really impact your score if you're not careful.*

Joe: *It seems like missing it by a day wouldn't matter. But when it comes to your credit, the little things do matter.*

Farnoosh: *They do. I feel like we're getting to consumers at a point in their lives when the information about credit health and credit scores is really important. We don't learn this in school. A lot of times we don't learn it at home. And the little things do matter.*

Something as small as paying your bills on time. Even if you miss it by six hours, or a day. It's late, late, late. Just like you can't be a little pregnant. You either are, or you aren't.

Joe: *What tips can you give us that people can implement ASAP?*

Farnoosh: *Well, first, knowledge is key. You can learn your credit score, and you can review your credit report. We can't make any change or make an action plan without really knowing where we stand.*

So know your credit score. It'll allow you to create a personalized plan. We all have a lot of goals that can be affected by credit, whether that's to buy a home or even rent a home. Your prospective landlord will want to review your credit report. Better to get ahead of that before anybody else looks at your report or your score so that you can make the important changes before you apply for that loan or apartment. I wish I had known before applying for that mortgage that one poorly timed payment actually landed on my credit report and impacted my credit score. I would've had more of a readiness to talk about it with the underwriters. I maybe would have just brought it up before they discovered it.

Joe: *What are some healthy habits of people with good credit?*

Farnoosh: *Very good question. In talking to FICO a couple of years ago, what they found is that their best scorers are the ones who are keeping very low debt-to-credit ratios. So they may have a mixture of credit cards, but the balances are very low relative to the limits. In fact, a good ratio is something like 6 percent or 7 percent of total credit that you have. So just to simplify, if you have one credit card that has a $10,000 limit, 7 percent of that is what . . . $700 at any given point in time. That's the average balance that they're carrying. They're also paying their bills on time. They're automating payments. They're not messing with stamps and checkbooks. They are hooking up a checking account to the bills so that they get paid on time and in full every month.*

Joe: *I get what you're saying about paying the full amount, but I love automation for people that can't seem to get their act together. It makes sure that you make a minimum payment. You can hook that up to happen automatically as well.*

Farnoosh: *Absolutely. Paying the full amount every month, I get it, not everybody can do that. It's something to work toward, but paying just the minimum, you can do that, or you can do, like, $10 more than the minimum or 25 percent more than the minimum, and then make that a fixed payment every single month. You will inevitably pay less in interest and you'll get out of debt sooner, even with just a little bit more.*

Joe: *What's another good habit people with great credit scores have?*

Farnoosh: *They've got their ducks in a row. They're talking about their credit scores with their partners. They have transparency around their credit health. They're in the know, and they're not maxing out their credit cards. I mean, that kind of goes hand in hand with keeping a low debt-to-credit ratio, but you know, certainly some months you're spending more than others, but on average, they're not spending to the limits and they're being very careful about how much they're carrying.*

Joe: *Part of being careful I think is being intentional. It sounds like that is what you're talking about. I love this idea of credit moderation. Is there a credit rule that I should never break?*

Farnoosh: *Going back to my story, it's paying your bills on time. That is the largest contributor to your credit health, your credit score, per FICO. It's just one of those variables that means so much to whether you have a top score or an okay score or a not-so-great score. When we get in the habit of being late to pay our bills, that can really take a toll. And it's hard to recover from that. It's not something that you can change overnight.*

Creating some breathing room in your budget in terms of when your bills are due can be helpful.

If all your bills are due on the fifteenth and you don't get paid until the twentieth, that can create some strain on not only your budget but also your bank account. You can sometimes call your creditors, your lenders, all the accounts that you have, and say, "Hey, can we adjust the date of the month that this is due?"

Joe: *In my experience, they're happy to do that. Some people are surprised how readily they'll change the due date.*

Farnoosh: *Yeah, absolutely. "I'm going to automate this so I'm never going to be late, but I would really appreciate doing this the week before or the week after."*

Joe: *Farnoosh Torabi. Thanks for hanging out with us today.*

Farnoosh: *Thank you for having me, and say hi to Mom for me.*

Farnoosh's advice in a nutshell: The same habits that make for good financial health—paying your bills on time and in full, and spending less than your credit limit—also improve your credit health.

Chapter 5 Benjamin Badge:
Credit Achievements

Check off each of the following achievements you have completed toward your Benjamin Badge after reading this chapter:

❑ Request your credit score. There are many online tools that will show you for free, likely including your credit card issuer. Remember, you're allowed to see your credit report three times a year: once each from all three of the reporting agencies. But this doesn't include your score.

❑ Set up automatic payments with your creditors so that at least the minimums are paid each month.

❑ Call your credit card companies and ask the five questions.

Date You Completed the Chapter 5 Badge	Parent Signature (Putting your mom's John Hancock on your Benjamin stacking makes it official)

PART 2

BUILDING A STACK
OF BENJAMINS

Don't stay in bed unless you can make money in bed.
—GEORGE BURNS

6

What to Expect When You're Investing

TOOLS YOU'LL NEED:

- Building blocks (of a healthy financial life)
- Patience for dealing with lack of maturity
- Industrial-grade breast pump (optional)

When we're kids, our parents talk about investing in hushed tones for fear of corrupting our innocent ears. Who among us wasn't told, "Shush when grown folks are talking!" after asking Mom or Dad to explain the term "yield to maturity"? And nearly everyone had their mouth washed out with soap after dropping "large-cap investment" at the dinner table after hearing it from one of the kids whose parents openly discussed exchange-traded funds.

At the risk of people calling us too "open" or "casual" about these matters, we believe nobody should think of investing as incomprehensible, embarrassing, or not fit for discussion in polite company. Now's the time to erase the shame, knock down stereotypes, and build a portfolio, Stackers. We all lose out when we fumble around during our first time opening a brokerage account. We'll teach you to relax and lean into it. It's okay if you're nervous. We've all been there. So while it may sound shocking to hear us say things like "compounding interest" and "bull market" around children, we firmly believe it's time society got over the stigma surrounding this natural process and welcomed dis-cussions of the origins of life(time income).

Even if your parents never sat you down for the "bonds and the bees" talk, there's no reason to let it keep you from becoming a success-ful investor. It starts with an honest and unashamed look at how your money can grow from a tiny egg into a fully formed portfolio that'll provide a lifetime of joy. Here's what you need to know.

The Difference Between Saving and Investing

Just like there's a difference between "gettin' busy" and "making sweet love," it's time we drew a line between the words "saving" and "invest-ing." You'll often hear them used interchangeably, as in, "Everyone ought to be saving for retirement" or "God Invest the Queen." But sav-ing and investing are not the same thing, and it's important to under-stand the distinctions before you cause an international incident while visiting Buckingham Palace.

Saving money is about setting moolah aside for a future purchase— which can include an emergency fund. When you save money, you want it to be easily accessible, face virtually no risk, and incur minimal fees, if any. While it's lovely to earn interest on savings, that is not the raison d'être of saving money. Your savings are your easy-to-reach booty call. You want to know that it will be around when you need it.

Investing is also about setting money aside for the future, but there's a deeper sense of intimacy and connection than with saving alone. It's a long-term relationship that you want to treat with care. While it's an old wives' tale that you'll go blind if you touch your funds too often, investors understand that they're going to leave this stack alone for many years while it's growing to earn its keep.

To completely change metaphors, invested money is like the young-est child in a fairy tale, who goes off to seek their fortune. The money and the young princess are gone from the day-to-day life of the castle, and they may encounter dangers while they're away—including loss of principal or minor maiming by a ravenous inflation or taxation beast. Investors put their faith in their investment's ability to bounce back over time (and the kid's ability to survive, find their fortune, and make their way home). Investors recognize that they simply won't see either their investment or the wandering heir for years at a time.

So unlike saving, investing is about waving goodbye to your money for the foreseeable future, looking for the best possible returns, and letting time and compound interest handle things while you keep the castle nice and warm for the day you can welcome back your world traveler.

This distinction matters for a few reasons. When we refer to the process of accumulating money for retirement purposes as "saving for retirement" instead of "investing for retirement," we make the job sound harder than it is. Saving enough money for a comfortable retirement would be an overwhelming job if the money wasn't also pulling its weight and growing bigger while you wait.

Imagine having to save enough money to live on for thirty years if you were responsible for earning every single dollar your own damn self. We're way too lazy to use or recommend that plan.

Why Invest?

You may be wondering, "Who has the kind of money that they can afford to give up some for a long time, other than people who are already swimming in vaults full of Benjamins?" Hopefully, you.

We all should practice safe investing, not just the top-hat-and-monocle types. That's because investing offers an important benefit that you cannot re-create any other way:

COMPOUND INTEREST, BABY!

Albert Einstein, professional big-brain-haver and hair model, is reported to have said, "Compound interest is the eighth wonder of the world. He who understands it, earns it . . . he who doesn't . . . pays it." (Ivy McFadden, our eagle-eyed proofreader, had to give us the sad news that Einstein never actually said this. And he never said,

"Insanity is doing the same thing over and over and expecting different results," nor "The trains will run on time or it will be your head!," nor even "Don't believe everything you read on the internet.") Compound interest is the process of earning interest on interest. It's like your money had a baby, and that moneybaby then went and also had a baby. How huge is that? Normal money is something you have to trade in hours of your life for in exchange for a few sweet green Benjamins. If you want more? Back to work you go. But compound interest just grows money without you having to lift a finger. It does all the work for you.

Let's say you've saved up $1,000 after weeks of paper cuts in the Dunder Mifflin paper mine. Since you're a smart Benjamin stacker who doesn't want to be mining paper for life, you put that $1,000 into an investment that has historically earned 10 percent per year. (Just FYI: if you whisper the words "historical return" to a sleeping financial professional, they will bolt upright to exclaim, "Past performance is no guarantee of future results," without even fully waking up.) Your $1,000 will grow exponentially, even if you add not one cent more, because of how interest compounds. Let's calculate just how much money you'll have at the end of five years if your investment continues to provide a 10 percent return every year.

The first year's calculation is straightforward: 10 percent of $1,000 is $100, so after one year, you'll have $1,100. To earn that extra hundie at work, it would take at least three hours of hoisting a pickax among the A4 ream caverns. But the interest isn't done making your life easier. In year two, you'll earn 10 percent interest on the full balance of $1,100, not just on your original investment of $1,000. So that means another $110 will be added to the balance, bringing it to $1,210. That's two Benjamins and a sawbuck that you didn't have to work to earn.

And the hits keep coming. In year three, compound interest will make the investment grow to $1,331 ($1,210 × 10 percent = $121, and $1,210 + $121 = $1,331). After four years, your investment will earn $133.10 in interest ($1,331 × 10 percent = $133.10), making the total

$1,464.10 ($1,331 + $133.10 = $1,464.10). And five years after investing your $1,000 stake, you will have a total of $1,610.51 ($1,464.10 × 10 percent = $146.41, and $1,464.10 + $146.41 = $1,610.51).

The thing about compound interest—and the reason why Mr. Einstein was (ALLEGEDLY!) so impressed with it, even though he spent his days doing amazing things like pasting split atoms back together with tiny tweezers and Krazy Glue—is how much heavy lifting the compounding of interest will do to grow your money.

After ten years, that same $1,000 investment (assuming you add nothing more to it and the 10 percent returns remain consistent[5]) will be worth $2,593.74. After twenty years, it will be worth $6,727.50. In thirty years, it will be a cool $17,449.40. At year fifty, you'll be the proud owner of $117,390.85, only $1,000 of which you had to hoist a paper pickax to earn.

Now start with a bigger number like $10,000 and sprinkle some compounding interest honey on it. Or, imagine spreading compounding interest lovingly over an investment that you regularly and continuously add more money to. There's a reason the concept

---

5 *"Past performance is no guarantee of future results, even in fictional scenarios," Joe mumbles in his sleep.*

(ALLEGEDLY!) blew Einstein's mind. The mental shock of this discovery is also how he came to possess his famous hairstyle.

Investment Concerns

Successful investors start with the end in mind, so there are a few issues you need to get clear on before you start. These are risk, time horizon, and liquidity.

Risk

Are you the no-worries, starry-eyed dreamer who thinks, "You gotta spend money to make money, honey," or are you the Chicken Little investor who is ready to stash your whole nest egg in your mattress the moment there's a tiny dip in the market?

Knowing yourself is a big part of winning with investments. If you've got the stomach to watch your money roller coaster on the instability of the market over a longer period of time (see the following section on time horizon), then your risk tolerance will suggest you're comfortable putting your money in more aggressive investments.

But if just thinking about a market drop makes you reach for the Mylanta, you might want more conservative investments. These will offer more potential stability for your principal, but you'll pay for the peace of mind with lower potential returns.

Joe's Mom Weighs the Options

Just like with parenting, no matter what you decide to do, there are sure to be consequences. If your investments are too risky, it could turn out like the time I took the bus to Atlantic City with the knitting club and lost all $15 I brought. That was a bad day. But if your investments are so conservative that you have to invest lots more to make up for the fact that your cash isn't growing, it will be just like that time the kids put on their life vests and sat in the neighbor's boat while it was parked in his driveway. You might stay safe, but you'll never get anywhere, will you?

So which do you choose? This is where timelining your goals, as Joe and Emily brilliantly outlined in Chapter 1, comes in. By starting with "What risks do I need to take?," you'll put together a balanced plan, won't you? No matter, you still should diversify your money so that one investment doesn't dominate the garden. Don't bet your long-term goals on one or two investments, that's what I always say.

Time Horizon

How long till you're going to need this money? The bread you need next year will go into a different kind of investment than dough you can wait on for thirty years. Knowing your time horizon, whether you're trying to scrape together enough money for a down payment on a llama or enough money to retire and travel the world (on a llama), will help you figure out the best type of investment and risk level you need in order to reach all your llama-themed goals. Again, timelining wins the day. Different investments perform better over different timeframes, so knowing when you want the money (another reason to timeline your goals) will help you pick the right investment for the job.

We'll end this right here before Joe starts in on another damned corn analogy.

– Emily

Liquidity

Money is liquid when you can access and spend it. Joe, a lifelong spender, says this is his favorite type of money.

Some investments are more liquid than others. At one end are the investments that you can take your principal out of whenever you please, with no penalties whatsoever. (You'll sometimes even get a lollipop for your efforts, depending on where you've got the money stashed and whether you go in person to collect it.) For instance, money in a checking or savings account is entirely liquid, because you can spend it easily.

On the other end are investments that require time and work to access your money. Think about the equity in your home. To get at that money, you can't just peel off the bathroom for Junior's college. You need to either sell the whole house or take out a loan against your own property.

In between these extremes are investments that are less liquid than checking and savings accounts and more liquid than home equity. These types of investments may allow you to get hold of your money in more of a hurry than you can sell a house, but you will often pay a penalty for being in such a dang rush.

In general, less liquid investments offer the opportunity for more aggressive returns, because otherwise there would be no incentive for you to tie up your money for the long haul. Recognizing the trade-offs between liquid and illiquid investments can help you determine how to invest for your specific goals.

Types of Investments

Okay, so investing in assets that offer compounding interest is the "Einstein-approved" method of preparing for the future. But how exactly do you get started? Calling the Mutual Fund Store and telling the receptionist, "Hey, doll, I'd like a couple of them investments, see?" is likely to get you laughed at, even if there is no such thing as a Mutual Fund Store.

To know how to invest, you need to know what to invest in. While the guidebook for writing these types of manuals says that we should start with the boring stuff (CDs and savings accounts) and work up the ladder, investing in those things are the small-ball decisions. Seriously. When you look at two different money markets today, one may pay 0.25 percent interest and the other a whopping 0.65 percent. While you have more than doubled your return, you still aren't making any money. Save those decisions for a rainy day when there's nothing on television.

We'll start with the investments that are worth worrying about. Here are the most common asset classes (i.e., types of investments, but "asset classes" is more fun to say, especially when you put emphasis on the first syllable like the authors, who have retained the same sense of humor they enjoyed in middle school, do).

Stocks

While we aren't going to recommend buying stocks directly when you're starting out, you need to know how they work, because stocks are the backbone of mutual funds and exchange-traded funds, which are the investments we do think you should try on for size.

Stocks offer investors a neat arrangement. You, the investor, get a chance to own a small slice of a company. As a part owner, you're going to share in the ups and downs of the company. If you bought shares of Amazon stock when the company was little more than a book warehouse run out of Jeff Bezos's garage, you took on the risk that it might have gone under and become a footnote in retail history—but you also got to high-five your rich-ass self when the $1.50-per-share stock you bought in 1997 becomes worth more than $3,300 per share a couple of decades later.

That's (kind of) what stocks are all about. The Amazon example is not the norm. Ford stock was $10 a share in 1987 and is still hovering in the $10 range as we write this.

When you invest in the market, you do so with the expectation that your stocks just might fluctuate a little more than Ford in value. Investors grow their investment by taking advantage of these fluctuations. The most hoped-for way to do this is to buy low and sell high, which can also be called "timing the market." Historically, investors trying to time the market have largely failed, so it's better to just invest immediately and let time *in* the market make you some money.

Alternatively, investors can perform a "short sale," where they sell stocks they don't yet own—which are generally loaned to them by a broker—because they hope the price will go down. Short sellers then buy the stocks at the lower price when the value drops, making a profit from their time-twisted sell-then-buy. The plot of the film *Trading Places* hinged upon a short sale, although we would like to point out that what Dan Aykroyd's and Eddie Murphy's characters did in that movie is hella illegal since they not only had insider information about the orange crop, but also misled the Duke brothers to artificially inflate the prices. Short sales in the real world do not involve clandestine meetings with corporate spies, costume parties on public transportation, gorillas, or Jamie Lee Curtis.

Most investors are aiming for a longer-term investment in a bull market, which means a market that is trending upward. Up markets happen far more often than down ones. Short sales are associated with down-trending bear markets.

Okay, what's with the bull and the bear?

We're glad you asked! No one really knows.

What? That can't be true.

We're afraid so.

Okay, but is there a theory at least?

Indeed there is. The prevailing theory is as follows:

A bull gores its prey (sarcastic gray rabbits wielding red capes, if our early childhood education via cartoon is to be trusted) by thrusting its horns up in the air, while a bear mauls its prey (pic-a-nic baskets, if going by the same source) by swiping its lethal claws downward. So a bull market follows a bull's upward thrust of death, and a bear market follows a bear's downward murder swipe. Pleasant, huh?

Wow.

Yeah. You're welcome.

Mutual Funds

For many years, even as the daughter of a financial planner who hung on her father's every word, Emily found that the words "mutual fund" out of anyone's mouth sounded like the adults in the Charlie Brown universe: all muted trombone and no clear meaning.

If you've also felt a strong desire to take a nap during these conversations, we offer a simple and effective solution: imagine the words "mutual fund" in Samuel L. Jackson's voice. Picture Jules from *Pulp Fiction* shouting, "MUTUAL FUND!" with the intensity and zeal one usually reserves for a couple named Pumpkin and Honey Bunny holding up a diner.

Check out how much better this reads now:

Here's what you need to know about those M____ F___s!

Mu-fus pool money from several different investors and then plow that pooled cash into stocks, bonds, money market accounts, and other assets. Professional money managers operate mutual funds. The MF money managers structure the fund to create income or growth for the MF investors. There are three ways MFs can make money for you: via dividend payments from the stocks owned within the fund, via capital gains when stocks are sold within the fund, and via increased net asset value (NAV) when the value of the assets within the fund increases.

The specific investment strategies and goals for getting you some of these sweet, sweet gains are written up in something known as a prospectus, which is a packet of information that you can either find online or that comes in the mail to investors and that will keep a fire burning for hours (unless you're Emily, who first files it in her filing cabinet in a folder labeled "Investments" before she finally recycles it three to five business years later, when the cabinet is about to collapse under the weight of unread paperwork).

The point is that mutual funds are set up with specific goals and objectives outlined in their prospectuses, so you can find the right MF for your needs.

Why Mutual Funds?

You might be wondering what makes a mutual fund better than just buying the stuff à la carte. Why not just scoop up some stocks, bonds, and other stuff rather than dealing with an *MF* MF manager?

Here's the thing rich people have known forever: being diversified saves your bacon when things go, as Mom says, "tits up" in the financial markets. It's safer to own a lot of different investments rather than just one. Buying some mu-fu investments makes this easy. You can own a whole lotta stocks, bonds, and whatnot without having to invest a big honking chunk of money into each asset class or stock.

For instance, with the T. Rowe Price Growth Stock fund (PRGFX), you'll hypothetically pay $2,500 and get several shares. In each share, you'll buy lots of U.S. stocks that the people at T. Rowe Price think will grow. And within your stock purchase, you'll own pieces of Merck, AT&T, Microsoft, IBM, and many, many others.

To get this kind of diversity with your own money, you'd need a heck of a lot more than $2,500, the fund minimum. And you'd need a lot of time on your hands. Mutual fund managers don't just sit around on the same mix of investments. They are constantly moving in and out of different stocks and bonds to try to maintain a good performance and to hold true to the fund's original goals.

So with a mutual fund, a full-time professional manager handles all of this. The trade-off with mutual funds is, of course, that you have to pay this professional to manage all this for you. Those MF fees might be a real pain in the Samuel L. Jackson—which is why it's important to understand them.

Exchange-Traded Funds, Mutual Funds' Hotter Cousin

Much of the moving around of stocks and bonds within a mutual fund has proven to be pointless. This is where MF's hotter cousin, the exchange-traded fund, comes in. ETFs are made to trade like a security, i.e., you purchase shares just like you're buying Amazon or Ford. But instead of a single stock, you're buying a basket of stocks.

Most of the early ETFs copied the basic indexes, like the S&P 500 (buying the five hundred biggest companies in America), the NASDAQ 100 (one hundred big mostly-tech companies that trade on the NASDAQ exchange), and the Dow Jones Industrials (thirty of the biggest companies in America). By purchasing the ETF, you're buying those stocks, and trades occur only when the underlying index makes a change.

ETFs have become a trendy topic with investors, so financial companies have rolled out funds that mimic a "passive" approach, but sometimes with questionable objectives. Some mimic the indexes of developing economies. Others niche down to sectors that are in the news (like space travel, an actual ETF). Stay away from these "investments" until you know what you're doing—and probably stay away from them even then. We'll talk more about how to set up your diversified portfolio in the Investing 201 chapter.

MF and ETF Fees

Remember those cartoons where the bunny rabbit would hold the mallet over the lion's head and ask where the lion wanted to get hit? He wouldn't ask *if* the lion wanted lumps, just where. That's going to be the same with MFs and ETFs. They're going to get paid—you just have to decide where you want to get hit.

Mutual fund fees come in two flavors: shareholder fees and annual fund operation expenses. Your mutual fund may charge you shareholder fees when you buy or sell the mutual fund in its entirety, but annual fund operation expenses will drain out consistently throughout the year. MFs like to be *paid*. ETFs are the newer, more streamlined investment, so you will pay only the operation expenses. These fees are typically lower in a garden-variety ETF than they are in a mutual fund.

Your prospectus (that paper packet you immediately threw in the fire, or the long PDF you downloaded from the investment website portal but never actually looked at) will disclose what to expect, so you can't exactly say you have *had it* with these mutual fund expenses in this *mutual fund portfolio*! Unlike snakes on a plane, these expenses shouldn't be a surprise.

You can find the information on these fees and expenses in a section in your prospectus cryptically titled "Fees and Expenses." Look for the net annual fund operating expenses, and you'll find the expenses expressed as a percentage. In addition, check to see if there is a section listed as "Investment Adviser and Management Expenses." This will let you know if there is a performance bonus to the investment manager in years when they outperform their benchmark.

Finally, check the turnover cost. Higher turnover—when the manager buys and sells securities more often—can mean additional costs and additional taxes if your fund is in a taxable account and not sheltered in an IRA or Roth IRA. One strategy we love is to organize your higher turnover investments (which can mean additional taxes) into your IRAs and leave the lower turnover investments outside of tax shelters.

The cost of fees is generally worthwhile for investors, provided you are choosing mutual funds with reasonable expense ratios and investment strategies that fit your needs, goals, and timeline. We'll let other books haggle over fees. We're just happy you're investing.

Both index funds and target-date funds can be easy ways to take advantage of the benefits of mutual funds without drowning in MF prospectuses. Another way to check your expenses? Head to a site like Morningstar.com that reports independently on exactly what you're buying, what it costs, and how it's performed against its peers, all in simple-to-understand English. More on Morningstar later.

Index Funds

If you don't have ETFs available in your retirement plan at work, there still may be a good proxy called an index fund. This type of mu-fu, like the ETF, is set up to mirror a specific market index.

Broad market index funds often represent lower risk because they have wide built-in market exposure. They are also lower cost than other types of mutual funds because they do not require hands-on maintenance from a fund manager and they have little turnover within the portfolio. Indexes are the ultimate "set it and forget it" investment for both you and the fund company managing it. The more you wade into the "sexy" new funds and ETFs being offered, the more you should expect to see fees rise.

Because of all these benefits, retirement accounts often use index funds as the core of their investing strategy. Some investors also swear by these funds because those MF managers have a poor track record when it comes to beating the index.

Target-Date Funds

These mutual funds are engineered to back down the risk level in the portfolio as you get closer to your goal so you don't have to. You just have to give them a target date for your goal. A target-date fund is a single MF that's professionally managed and diversified based upon their assumption that you're going to want the money at that date. That means your asset allocation (the amount of money you have invested in stocks versus bonds) gradually becomes more conservative.

For instance, a forty-two-year-old in 2021 with a fund target dated for retirement in 2045 will have more of her investments placed in higher-risk/high-return assets right now, but that asset allocation will gradually shift to lower-risk/higher-stability assets as she gets closer to her retirement.

Target-date funds have been around since the early 1990s, but they have become much more popular in the past fifteen years for two major reasons. First, U.S. legislation in 2006 allowed employers to auto-enroll their employees in defined contribution retirement plans like 401(k)s. Before that, people had to fill out paperwork to invest. Now they could procrastinate forever and the company can automatically sign them up for a small amount. This move created a need for a default plan that would provide appropriate asset allocation and rebalancing even if you never looked at your balance. Target-date funds were a perfect fit for this need.

Second, any investor retiring near the 2008 financial downturn got a horrible shock if they stayed aggressive. Their funds were sometimes half of what they'd been just a few months earlier. They learned about diversification a little too late. Target-date funds offer an attractive alternative to manually rebalancing your asset allocation as you approach retirement.

Why Joe *Hates* Target-Date Funds

Two words: glide path.

(That far off FOOOM you heard was Joe's head exploding.)

The "glide path" is the term for the fund's investment strategy leading up to and past your target retirement date. The glide path describes how your investments in the target-date fund become more conservative over time. Imagine the glide path like a big cruise ship coming in to dock. From the full-speed-ahead momentum in the middle of the ocean to a slower pace as it nears land, the ship's captain is sure to change up the pace as the giant ship approaches the dock.

A poorly planned glide path will look more like a ship disaster in a B movie. If you're too aggressive, the ship crashes into the city, like Sandra Bullock and not–Keanu Reeves in *Speed 2: Cruise Control*. Like Sandra and not–Keanu's runaway cruise ship, a glide path that's too aggressive can potentially cause destruction if your investments are too risky too close to when you need them.

We wish that were usually the problem, but it isn't. Far more likely is that your glide path will be too conservative (for many, it's because they worry about another 2008-esque crash). Some target-date funds have a glide path that becomes static as of your target retirement date, meaning your money is no longer invested in any potentially higher-risk/high-return assets as of your retirement date. Since you are theoretically going to be retired for several decades, being that overconservative could lead to you running out of money. That would be like turning off the ship's engines while you're still in the middle of the ocean.

In a perfect world, your glide path would look like the disaster at the end of *The Incredibles 2*, when the boat is full steam ahead until it stops at the edge of the city in a perfect landing. It's exactly where everyone needs to be, and there are zero casualties or damage to the city. But there is no way to call up your target-date fund manager and request the Elastigirl "just right" glide path. That's why it's smart to either choose a target-date fund that has a date a couple of years after you plan to retire, or have a separate investment for long-term growth outside the target-date fund.

That's not the only problem with target-date funds. Because most investors in these funds pay no attention to the underlying investment, many companies treat their target-date funds like the equivalent of the Sunday brunch at your favorite restaurant: they stick in everything that doesn't sell in a "salad." They're cleaning out the back closets, meaning horrible fee structures and managers overseeing managers overseeing bad products. That can mean fees on top of fees on top of investments you don't want. No thank you.

FinTech to the Rescue (or Not): Robo-Advisors

If you have no interest in learning how to diversify your money, apps called robo-advisors[6] can do it for you. As you add money to the app, you're automatically invested among many different investments so you won't have to worry about losing it all in a market crash.

The thing is, you probably don't need this much diversification. Even worse? Some of these accounts are beginning to sneak in "proprietary" funds that look suspiciously like they've been designed to make the creators some extra money. Invest in robo-advisors at your own risk and expense. We're not huge fans, but they're available and can be decent if you aren't going to take the time to do anything better.

Bonds

Investing in bonds has less to do with international intrigue or martinis than one might like, but it can be a relatively safe (albeit slow) way to grow your stack.

Your mutual funds or ETFs may include bonds, which is the most common way to be a bond investor. Alternatively, you can directly invest in bonds in one of two ways: as the first owner who gets to take off the plastic and breathe in the new-bond smell, or as a secondary investor, who buys a used bond off another investor. But few of us have any need to purchase individual bonds either way. That's because a bond is a version of an IOU, except instead of a slip of paper with the letters "IOU" written in ketchup, a bond is issued by a company or a government, which means there's more of a guarantee of repayment (plus interest) than you can count on from your buddy Shifty Steve. When you purchase a bond, you loan a specified amount of money for

---

6 *Joe just said something we can't print in this book. Why? Because whoever decided that these "money diversifiers" are "advisors" is a damn dirty liar. The "advisor" here doesn't exist. But the "robo" part of the equation can be useful.*

a specified number of years in return for interest on the investment, which is paid periodically, typically twice a year.

Unlike stocks, bond investors don't own part of the company or government that issued the bond, since the money is nothing more than a loan. There's an upside and a downside to this lack of ownership. The upside is that assuming the company doesn't start pushing daisies, bonds should still pay out both interest and the face value, even when the bond issuer isn't doing well. That means bonds are relatively stable investments. The downside, however, is that bond investors are usually going to sit on the sidelines and miss out on the company's growth spurt. Less risk means fewer rewards.

Bonds have two big benefits, even considering the fact that major growth isn't necessarily reflected in your bond holdings:

1. Periodic interest payments give you a steady and virtually guaranteed income stream.

2. Bonds can help protect you from market dips, falls, drops, double drops, tunnels, headchoppers, cobra rolls, inclined loops, barrel rolls, or other heart-stopping roller coaster–like money movement that may be fun when you are strapped into a candy-colored ride with your high school BFF but tends to be much more worrisome when it's your money playing chicken with gravity.

And here's a bonus: if someone asks you what you're invested in, you can respond, "Bonds. James Bonds." Hilarious. For one of you.

Bond Vocabulary

The world of bonds features many terms that seem like words you already know but mean something specific in this context. Let's review a few so you don't embarrass yourself at your next cocktail party:

- **Coupon:** If you're thinking of the little square you cut from the newspaper to save 10¢ on Charmin, this ain't it. For maximum confusion, "coupon" is what the bond world calls the interest rate paid by the bond.

- **Face Value:** This was the amount the bond was worth at the time of issue. Bonds generally have a face value of $1,000. You may also hear this referred to as the "par value" because finance types want to make sure would-be investors are as confused as possible. But not to worry—that's why you have this book.

- **Yield:** This is not what you do when pedestrians have the right of way. Nope, the yield is the calculation of how much interest you'll earn while taking into account the fluctuation of the bond's value if it is sold on the secondary market. Generally, you can calculate a bond's yield by dividing the coupon by the bond's current price.

How to Choose Bonds

If you have a long time horizon and can stomach the stock market's gyrations, many in the financial-advising community will tell you to largely forego bonds altogether, or to invest in them sparingly. Changes in overall interest rates (thanks, Federal Reserve!) can affect how far above inflation your bond's coupon falls. If you have a bond with a maturity date far in the future, there's more risk that rates will change between now and then, making your bond's growth less impressive. This is why bonds with longer maturities also tend to have higher yields, since that will make the bond more devastatingly attractive to potential investors (a Daniel Craig bond, for instance), whereas a bond with a long maturity and a low yield would be far less attractive (like a George Lazenby bond).

The relationship between a bond's maturity and its yield is known as the yield curve, and you'll often find shapely yield curves in the centerfolds of economic magazines. (We only read those magazines for the articles.)

Real Estate

Over long periods of time, real estate and the S&P 500 have similar results, but how they get there is entirely different. Stocks are liquid:

you can sell your shares and have the money in your hand quickly. Real estate can take months to sell, and then there are often intermediaries between you and your cash.

Score one for stocks. But counter that with the fact that stock markets are a roller-coaster ride, while the real estate market rises and falls much more slowly. When it craters, though, it can be devastating.

The best way for a casual investor to purchase real estate is through a real estate investment trust (REIT). REITs are like mutual funds or ETFs, but with real estate properties at the core. You can own many different pieces of land, enjoy liquidity similar to that of the stock market, and diversify your portfolio. REIT funds are attractive because they offer competitive dividends and still rise in value—on average—more than bonds. REITs aren't just "better bonds," though. You assume more risk of loss with real estate than you do with a bond, so it's always important to remember the immortal advice of "caveat emptor."[7]

The Importance of Diversifying

As a teenager, Emily joined an after-school club known as Envirothon. She and four other friends who didn't get cast in the school play learned about five different aspects of the local Maryland environment (Soils, Forestry, Aquatics, Wildlife, and a topic that changed from year to year), and then competed with other teams in an academic fight to the death to show off their environmentaling skills.

Not. Nerdy. At. All.

Not only are we proud to report that Emily's team won the regional competition two out of three years, but they also finished number one in the state in the Aquatic Ecology portion in 1994. She still has the T-shirt proving it.

---

7 *This literally means "empty your caboose" in Latin, but we generally use it in its metaphorical sense of "buyer beware."*

Sadly, all Emily can recall from those halcyon days is a concept called "biodiversity," which can help determine the health of an ecosystem. When lots of different plants and critters, from the microscopic to the enormous, live in harmony, you can bet your sweet bippy that you've found yourself an ecologically healthy environment.

Financial health also rests on a similar level of diversity. Having only one type of investment in your portfolio is bad news, even if that type of investment is currently going gangbusters and people think you're some sort of investing genius (*ahem*, Bitcoiners). That's because without diversity, there's nothing to pick up the investing slack if your single type of investment decides to make like a submarine and dive.

Your investment portfolio will be a healthy environment for your Benjamin stacks if you diversify. When you're wondering what kinds of investments to pursue, find a balanced diet of several of them, because that's the best way to ensure that your money is well protected and positioned for growth. In Chapter 11, we'll tackle some strategies to help you start.

Where Will You Hold All These Investments?

You're going to want to open a brokerage account. To buy mutual funds, exchange-traded funds, stocks, or other investments, you'll need this account to trade. There are a bazillion brokerage accounts to choose from, but don't worry about choosing the "best" one. Look for an account that:

- Is a name brand that you've heard of and that has been around for a while. This isn't a spot where you want to have money in an app that may or may not go out of business.

- Gives you lots of research opportunities. Some accounts are bare-bones and come with few to no tools. If you decide to nerd out into your account, you want good tools.

- Offers free trades.

- Is transparent about how they manage their money.

Take a look at your brokerage account's marketing. Are they all about planning and long-term goals? That's probably for you. Is it about stock market trading and getting rich quick? We'd stay away.

Making More from Your Cash

Well, that's it for investments! Time to move on to the next chapter.

What's that? You want to know about bank products and getting more money from your cash reserves?

Okay, if you insist. Even though this is a hard game with a low yield, we're in. Follow us to the corner of the park where people waste their time turning 0.50 percent into 0.65 percent. (It's right next to the spot in the park where you'll hear people whisper, "Psst! Wanna buy a watch?")

Certificates of Deposit

Certificates of deposit (CDs to their friends) are investments offered by banks. When you purchase one of these bad boys, you agree to hand over your money for a specific term to the institution, which then lends out the moolah to someone else in the form of a loan. What you receive in return is a guaranteed interest rate for the term of the CD investment, so you'll know before you invest how fast your money will grow with the CD.

Since CDs are offered by banks, that means they are insured by the Federal Deposit Insurance Corporation (FDIC) up to $250,000. So even if the bank holding your CD goes belly up, your money will be safe.

Each CD has a maturity date, which is the date on which the CD term ends. (Not to be confused with the time when you started sprouting hair in embarrassing places.) At that point, the bank returns your initial deposit along with the interest you earned during that term. Most CDs have terms from about six months to five years, with longer terms usually offering higher rates.

Here are the downsides:

1. Your money is tied up for the term of the CD. Though it's possible to break a CD early, your bank slaps you with a penalty, usually in the form of lost interest.

2. Interest on CDs tends to be low. Low, locked-in rates mean your investment may not even keep up with inflation. The rates offered by banks are tied to the interest rates set by the Federal Reserve. As of 2020, the Fed's rates are at a number best described as "Triple Fart Minus."[8] So CD rates are slightly less exciting than that person you dated in high school who collected mollusk-themed postage stamps. (That said, there have been times in the past when CD rates reached dizzying heights, as in 1980, when you could buy a three-month CD with a whopping return of 18.65 percent. However, that rate came with a side order of double-digit inflation, which was an eye-watering 13.5 percent, so your growth was mostly eaten up by a rapidly increasing cost of stayin' alive.)

Climbing the CD Ladder

A CD ladder is a strategy where you purchase a few CDs of varying maturity dates, so that all your money isn't tied up in a single maturity, giving you the best balance between high interest rates and liquidity.

For instance, if you had $5,000 to invest in CDs, you could decide to put all $5,000 into a five-year CD, since it has the highest current rate available. As we write this, that rate is a decidedly non-dizzying 1.35 percent. But what if in year two or three of owning your five-year CD, the Fed raised rates and banks started offering 2 percent or 3 per-

---

8 *Also known as between 0 percent and 0.25 percent.*

cent or 18.31415 percent rates (a money nerd can dream)? Worse yet, what if you need some of the cash in year three? Then you'd either be stuck with the lackluster 1.35 percent while all around you new CD investors are popping champagne or you'd pay a penalty on all your money when you maybe need only a portion.

To solve both of these problems, instead of putting all the money in a five-year CD, you invest $1,000 each into a one-year-, two-year-, three-year-, four-year-, and five-year-term CD. Though your shorter-term CDs will have lower rates (0.80 percent for a one-year CD as of this writing, sob!), you'll get the best of both worlds: you get to earn the highest APYs and you maintain liquidity as your shorter-term CDs mature, meaning you can take advantage of rising rates.

Money Market Account (MMA)

Banks and Ultimate Fighting Championship rings are the two places where you can regularly find MMAs, although it's a good idea not to mix them up. Money market accounts are a savings product that double as a checking account, and their interest rates are much more generous compared to that of traditional savings accounts. Mixed martial artists, on the other hand, are terrifyingly fit individuals who can crack walnuts with their thighs. You can find MMAs at both traditional and online banks, unless you're talking about the other kind of MMAs, in which case you are less likely to run into them at a bank, though it is not unheard of.

MMAs are like CDs, in that their interest rates are set based on the Federal Reserve rate. As of this writing, the best MMA rates are 0.70 percent, according to the rate aggregator Bankrate, and to even get that sweet 0.70 percent rate, you'll need to fork over $250,000 or more.

Unlike CDs, the interest rates on MMAs rise and fall as the Fed adjusts interest rates. Your rate is not locked in forever, so when rates increase overall, your bank is likely to raise your MMA rate.

In short, you can't count on MMAs to make you rich. The rates on money market accounts are too low to count on for impressive financial growth. MMAs are a nice place to stash savings that you'd like to keep liquid and growing faster than inflation. For instance, if you're saving up for a down payment for a house, an MMA could be a great place to park your cash. Since it is a banking product, it is FDIC insured up to $250,000, so you know your money is secure.

And though it is a type of savings account, it comes with checking account features, such as paper checks (remember those?), ATM access, debit cards, and even online banking. But like a savings account, money market accounts are limited to a combined total of six withdrawals or transfers per calendar month per account by federal law. That said, the gub'mint doesn't impose any limits on ATM withdrawals or official checks mailed directly to you from MMAs.

Of course, if you tend to get the gimme gimmes around big piles of money that you can easily access, an MMA may not be right for you.

Treasury Bills

A treasury bill (T-bill) is a short-term investment offered by Uncle Sam. The term is usually less than one year and typically three months, and the bills are generally sold in denominations of $1,000. Like a CD, you know going into a T-bill investment just how much you will earn from the purchase.

T-bills are backed by the full faith and credit of the U.S. government, which means they are about as secure as an investment can get. (Please, no political jokes here, we're trying to write a personal finance book.) Short of Godzilla's latest enemy making landfall and swallowing up every single government official, or twelve independent meteors hitting all twelve of the regional banks making up the Federal Reserve System, you can feel confident that the government is not going to renege on a T-bill. Most people buying individual T-bills will buy through TreasuryDirect or through their online broker.

So Why Is This Important?

Investing is the best way to make sure your stacks of Benjamins take care of themselves—and you. Why work forever when your invested money can do some of the important heavy lifting? And while the world of investing may not always be discussed in polite society, understanding the specific mechanics behind this miraculous feat is all part of growing into the mature and prepared Benjamin stacker you are meant to be.

Friend of the show Bola Sokunbi has plenty to say about how to get started as a rookie investor. As the creator of Clever Girl Finance, she knows a thing or two about the best way to get your money to work for you. She headed down to Joe's mom's basement to talk about the importance of investing:

A LOOK INTO THE BASICS: AN INTERVIEW WITH BOLA SOKUNBI, CREATOR OF CLEVER GIRL FINANCE

Joe: I'd like to go through some phrases that are misconceptions that people have, and you tell me what's wrong with each of these.

The first one: "Investing is too hard."

Bola: *It's not too hard. You've got to try it first. Then you've got to educate yourself to make it simple for yourself.*

Joe: *And when you say, "Educate yourself," what do you mean? Do you mean becoming an engineer at this and knowing every little thing?*

Bola: *No! It's really easy, picking up a 101 book. Listen, I was a girl sitting on the New York subway reading* Investing for Dummies, *and people would look at me like I was a fool.*

And I'm thinking, "No, you *are the dummy, because I'm the one reading about investing for dummies at all."*

It's about learning how it works, starting with the basics. And as you learn, you start to craft a plan that makes sense for you and your own unique financial situation.

Joe: *Next misconception: "Investing is only for rich people. They have money to burn, and I don't."*

Bola: *People say that a lot. They also say, "I'm going to wait until I earn more money to invest," like investing is this thing that is exclusively for the elite. But when you really look at the elites, when you exclude those who are the trust fund babies, a lot of these wealthy people made their money from investing. At one point they weren't "elite." So investing is not just for the rich. Investing is for anybody. And when you start investing, you put yourself on the pathway to becoming rich—and not just for yourself. It's for your family, for your children, for your community to transition generational wealth. You start now with what you can. That's the best way to learn, so you're not losing $10,000. You're losing fifty bucks when you're making your mistakes.*

Joe: *Tell me about the rule of 72. It's a cool little mathematical trick.*

Bola: *The rule of 72 is a super basic investing and growth rule. It shows you how much time it'll take for your investment to double when you* *multiply the timeline by 72. It's not just effective on your investments, but your debt as well.*

Joe: *Okay, let's say that you invested in index funds [and] that index fund received 8 percent over time. So we take 8 percent, we divide it into 72. That means every nine years your money's going to double. So let's say at twenty-five years old, you invest five hundred bucks.*

If you're saving it for retirement, we'll pretend you'll need that money in your mid-sixties. That's not $500 anymore. It's going to double time and again. So, eight into 72 means that your money doubles every nine years. So if you do that at twenty-five, it's going to double when you're thirty-four, it's going to double when you're forty-three, it's going to double when you're fifty-two, and it's going to double again when you're sixty-one.

And if you decide this money isn't needed until after seventy, it's going to get another double. So it'll double four times by sixty-one, and five times by seventy, if you leave it. So you aren't talking about $500 anymore. It's $1,000 with the first double, $2,000 with the second, $4,000 with the third, and at age sixty-one, that $500 is now $8,000. If you leave it until seventy, you've turned that $500 into $16,000.

Bola: *And keep in mind that doubling is based on your interest rate, right? You haven't gotten a dividend either here. Which if you get a good dividend, that's a big deal because you can add that on top of that amount.*

Joe: *Okay. Last misconception. People say that investing feels like gambling.*

Bola: *It feels like gambling if you don't know what you're doing. If you're getting investing advice from your favorite influencer on Instagram without really researching, what is the investment? Why are you investing? It is a gamble, then. Any time you put your money in something you don't understand, it is a gamble. But when you do your research, it becomes less of a gamble and you can make more confident decisions. So you feel you have an understanding of this investment before you put your money into it.*

Just because everybody says, "Buy this stock!" doesn't mean you should buy it. You want to minimize the feeling of gambling and instead build up that feeling of confidence as an investor.

Joe: *You point out that these indexes are based on the economy. So really, it's not voodoo. If the economy does well, your index should do well.*

Bola: *Yeah. And if the economy isn't doing well, then we have a lot of other problems, like a pandemic.*

Joe: *You mentioned that there are only two ways really to make money.*

Bola: *Either you can work forty hours a week, or you can put your money to work for you. You're doing whatever and your money's hard at work, earning more money for you.*

Joe: *If you're putting your money in a bank account, money's never going to make money for you. So you're going to have to work for every single dollar.*

Bola: *Yeah, it's funny watching people chase these interest rates.*

"Oh, this bank is 1 percent. No, this bank is doing 1.1 percent." Remember: inflation is 2.5 percent! Unless the bank account is beating inflation, at the end of the day, I'm losing money the longer I have it in that bank account.

And it's fine if you want to have that money safe for short-term goals like having a baby, getting married, buying a house. But long-term, your money should not be in a bank account. You want to put that money to work for you by investing: investing in the stock market, being in business, investing in real estate.

You want to invest that money.

Bola's advice in a nutshell: The skills necessary for savvy investing are within everyone's reach and will help you grow your money.

Chapter 6 Benjamin Badge:
Investing 101 Achievements

Check off each of the following achievements you have completed toward your Benjamin Badge after reading this chapter:

❏ Prepare to begin investing by opening a brokerage account.
❏ Draw up a list of the investments in this chapter you should explore further because they meet your timeline goals from Chapter 1.
❏ Don't dwell on it, but move your emergency funds to a more efficient, higher-interest strategy.

Date You Completed the Chapter 6 Badge	Parent Signature (Putting your mom's John Hancock on your Benjamin stacking makes it official)

7

Taking Action, or "Let's Actually Do Something Here!"

TOOLS YOU'LL NEED:
- A Magic 8 Ball (for guidance in making the tough decisions)
- A "Jump to Conclusions" mat
- Paralyzing fear of making the wrong choice, with a side of second-guessing previously settled decisions

When Emily was eight years old, her father took her to Toys Я Us (of blessed memory) to pick out a new plaything. Little Emily waffled between two equally exciting options: the Snoopy Sno Cone Maker, and a toy whose specifics have been lost to the mists of time but that for the purposes of this story we'll call the HOT THANG.

For a period of time that became increasingly irritating to Emily's father—who was truly regretting his decision to take her to Toys Я Us (peace be upon it)—this future financial expert who tells people how to make better decisions wandered the aisles between the Fighting Ace's Sno Cone machine and the HOT THANG.

When Mr. Guy finally insisted, through gritted teeth, that she had to make a decision immediately or go home with no toy, Emily opted for the HOT THANG.

This is a decision that still haunts Emily to this day.

She has no memory whatsoever of the HOT THANG, but she can

name the details of the Sno Cone Maker with startling precision. From the jaunty red roof of Snoopy's doghouse-cum-Sno-Cone-maker to the decals of Sally and Charlie adorning the front of the doghouse to the snowman-shaped syrup holder—which featured a satisfied-looking Woodstock—to the pièce de résistance: Snoopy himself seated happily atop the ice-pushing device sticking out of the roof. Every aspect of this adorable toy is burned into her brain.

This Snoopy regret was Emily's first foray into the anxiety-inducing field of decision-making, and she still carries the mental scars of her fear of making a Wrong Decision. When she sees anyone paralyzed by the number of choices available within their 401(k) or unable to let go of their regret about selling their Amazon stock at the same time they got rid of their Pets.com shares, she nods with sympathetic recognition, reexperiencing the pain of that long-ago trip to Toys Я Us (blessings to its everlasting memory).

If you want to do something with your money, you need to dive into *why* making a choice can feel so hard. Only then can you learn to let go of the Sno Cone Makers that got away and embrace the opportunities you have, at Toys Я Us (whose memory will bless our children's children) or elsewhere.

Understanding the Awful Power of Opportunity Cost

Making a decision can feel like torture because of something economists call "opportunity cost." Opportunity cost is the value of whatever you give up when you make any decision.

* If you move to New York after graduation, you can't also move to Paris.
* If you decide to marry Betty, you can't also marry Veronica (unless you live in a place with some loose matrimonial laws and you feel confident neither lady will think you a complete Jughead for suggesting it).

* If you buy bacon-flavored ice cream with a $5 bill, you can't use that same $5 bill to buy a bottle of water to wash the taste out of your mouth.

The opportunity cost of New York, Betty, or baco-cream is not being able to choose something else with the same resources. You can always decide to relocate to Paris, divorce Betty and marry Veronica, or use another $5 bill to purchase something (anything!) to get that taste out of your mouth, but you are using new resources (time, wedding planning, money) to change your decision.

Emily and her husband watched opportunity cost occur in real time when their five-year-old son decided to spend some of his allowance money on a new Batman toy. As he prepared to make the purchase, he suddenly got teary-eyed at the loss of the money from his piggy bank and froze. Should he buy the Batman? He wanted the Batman! But buying the Batman meant the money was gone, never to return. He wanted the money! But he wanted the Batman! But he wanted the money!

That day, Emily's son learned an important lesson: he might have gained an awesome new action figure, but he lost the money—and the possibilities it represented—by doing so. You'll have to wait for his book to see if he regrets that decision.

Misvaluing Opportunity Costs: Overvalue vs. Undervalue (the Devil's Conundrum)

Opportunity costs are a fact of life. Were we human beings able to make rational decisions with the emotionless grace of a Vulcan, then opportunity cost would simply be a piece of information we could use to make a decision. We would sigh and admit that we cannot use the same resources twice, and then we'd buckle down and determine the cost-benefit analysis of each option. We'd then logically make the decision that would bring us the greatest satisfaction or utility.

But we are not logical creatures. We want to have our cake and eat it, too. So we find ourselves misvaluing opportunity costs with frightening regularity. We struggle to recognize what we lose in opportunity costs by either taking too much time deciding or by jumping in too quickly. Both lead to poor choices. Our bad decisions are predictable, common—and hard to recognize when they are happening. Here's how it looks.

Overvaluing Opportunity Costs: Analysis Paralysis

Emily's son spent ten minutes after he made his purchase waffling between returning the toy or keeping it. Though there were only two choices available, he kept second-guessing. Would he be happier with Batman or with a fatter piggy bank? How could he possibly decide such an important question!? Meanwhile, we sit with our benefits book open and can't choose a life insurance or 401(k) asset allocation.

As tough as this kind of decision-making/second-guessing has always been, it's only gotten worse. Nearly everything we do involves a dizzying menu of options, with potential for choosing the "wrong" one. Too many choices make it harder to choose, and when we do, we tend to enjoy it less because we imagine all the things we didn't go with.

This sounds counterintuitive, since we tend to prize having choices. But anyone who has scrolled through Netflix for thirty minutes only to sit through a sitcom that they've seen four times already can attest to the paralyzing nature of possibility. According to Barry Schwartz, the author of *The Paradox of Choice*, the abundance of choices we face in modern society often leads to unrealistic expectations, second-guessing, paralysis, anxiety, and stress. In other words, we often make *no decision* because we overvalue the opportunity costs each alternative represents.

And while going home with no toy would have made for a miserable eight-year-old Emily, and rewatching *Parks and Rec* while reciting Ron Swanson's dialogue line-for-line may make for a boring evening, they are relatively minor pitfalls of deciding not to decide. The stakes are much higher with financial decisions. When it comes to things like choosing your 401(k) asset allocation or figuring out which insurance package you need during open enrollment, making no decision is the *worst decision*. Pretty much anything would be better than nothing here, since no choice leaves your retirement nest egg sitting in cash instead of invested or leaves you stuck with the default insurance coverage that doesn't meet your needs.

Again, it's perfectly natural: You know that choosing that asset allocation or insurance package is a priority, but it's also confusing and stressful. So, you decide to wait—and make no decision at all. This is the definition of analysis paralysis, stemming from the feeling that there truly is one solution, and you could lose out if you choose anything other than this platonic ideal. But chasing perfection is the way madness (and lost compounding interest and loss of coverage for your halitosis treatments) lies.

How to Overcome Analysis Paralysis

To figure out some ways to break through analysis paralysis, we thought for a long time and then thought some more. (Kidding!) Here are some tried-and-true strategies to get unstuck.

Limit Your Research Time

Part of the reason why we freeze when faced with a major decision is because the thought of becoming smart enough to recognize the ideal option is paralyzing. Who has time to get a degree in economics to fully understand their 401(k)?

But you don't need to become the foremost authority in any subject. You just need to find an option that will work well enough for your needs. So set limits. Tell yourself you will make the best decision you can after one hour of research. If, after you've completed your hour, you still don't feel like you know enough, then extend your research by another hour, but no more. That time limit will help you gather the information you need without falling down rabbit holes or skipping the research altogether because it's just too much.

The 3-Then-5 Rule

Similarly, you can limit yourself by the number of options you consider. Start with three alternatives that seem like a reasonable fit and compare them in detail. After you figure out which of the three is best, then look at up to five more options to compare with your first winner. If one of the five new options is better than the best of the original three, choose that one. If not, go back to the best of the three.

Using this strategy will keep you from overdoing the research-and-paralysis stage while still allowing you to do your due diligence. You'll feel confident that even if you don't pick the perfect choice (as if there could be such a thing), you've got a top option.

Undervaluing Opportunity Costs: Jumping at Free Stuff

The other side of the paralysis coin is the "quick draw." This happens because opportunity costs dress up like time wasters, so we undervalue them as unworthy of more than a moment's consideration.

The biggest culprit? The word "FREE!" Even to a diehard minimalist, something about "FREE!" short-circuits our brains. We can't seem to recognize that there are other costs to consider when we hear it—like the opportunity cost of space in our dressers and cabinets. The behavioral economist Dan Ariely explains this inability to see opportunity costs when things are financially free in his book *Predictably Irrational*:

> Most transactions have an upside [benefit] and a downside [opportunity cost], but when something is free, we forget the downside. Free gives us such an emotional charge that we perceive what is being offered as immensely more valuable than it really is. Why? I think it's because humans are intrinsically afraid

of loss. The real allure of free is tied to this fear. There's no visible possibility of loss when we choose a free item. (It's free!) But suppose we chose the item that's *not* free. Uh-oh, now there's a risk of having made a poor decision—the possibility of a loss.

Other than making it impossible to close your T-shirt drawer, the downside of allowing free items to make their way into your home comes with a relatively low opportunity cost. But there can be much bigger consequences to undervaluing opportunity costs. For instance, why do hard-sell annuity or insurance presentations focus on the fact that you will pay nothing out of pocket? By taking away the up-front cost of a product or service, the ~~shark~~ salesperson reduces the likelihood that their ~~marks~~ customers will think through any negative opportunity costs over time.

Here's some irony: whether we overvalue or undervalue opportunity costs, we're trying to stave off regret in a way that's guaranteed to make us feel regretful. Our future selves will wish our current selves had just made a damned decision because it would have been better than doing nothing, or our future selves will wish our current selves would have stopped to think for a second before jumping on the "no out of pocket cost" lifetime annuity because it costs a hell of a lot more than it seemed like it would when the nice woman sold it to you.

How to Overcome Snap Judgments

Here are some ideas we came up with off the cuff. (Kidding again.)

Don't Take Free Stuff You Wouldn't Buy

Combatting our tendency to undervalue opportunity costs if the word "free" is attached is pretty easy. Ask yourself, "Would I spend money on this?" Look objectively at the T-shirt, mug, squeeze ball, or once-in-a-lifetime opportunity to guarantee yourself income for life. Would you get dressed, brush your teeth, get in the car, drive to a store/insurance agent's office, locate the item, take it to the counter/sit across the agent's desk, whip out your wallet, and hand over your hard-earned Benjamins, all in exchange for the item that someone is offering you for "free"?

If the answer is a resounding no, then more good news: you don't need to snap up the free thing. You'll probably never think about it again, which is a hell of a lot better than kicking yourself later on for accepting something for free that you wouldn't pay for.

Sunk Costs: When You're in a Hole, Stop Digging

The other side of the opportunity cost coin is the problem of sunk costs, which are costs that you cannot recoup. For example, let's say you buy nonrefundable Engelbert Humperdinck concert tickets but come down with a terrible case of "getting an invitation to something more fun" on the day of the show. The cost of those nonrefundable tickets is "sunk," meaning that money is just as gone as if it never existed, so it really doesn't matter what you decide to do.

But most of us will show up to the concert just because we've already bought the tickets. You don't want to waste the money you've spent, even though you'd rather be somewhere else.

> #### Joe's Mom on Sunk Costs
> One of my favorite underused adages is a great reminder of why we need to beware the sunk-cost fallacy:
> It's no use crying over spilled Humperdincks.

Of course, refusing to give up on a lost cause can affect more than just your evening concert plans. Sunk costs are weighed poorly when we look at investments that didn't pan out (and that we should sell), career choices that have us dreading Monday mornings, and even relationships that aren't working out.

Overcoming "But I Can't Quit Now!"

In any decision, from the financial (selling an investment that's not going to make back your stake) to the life-changing (changing your career or relationship) to the quotidian (missing a concert of Humperdinckian proportions), smart Benjamin stackers don't factor sunk costs into future choices. Avoid letting sunk costs sink your thinking, too.

Instead, look at a decision as if you're an amnesiac tourist, unconnected to the earlier version of you who made the "wrong" choice. This allows you to ask yourself what you want right now (as opposed to yesterday). Instead of going to a concert because you spent good money on it, the person who pulled out their wallet was a stranger whose choices have no bearing on your current options. You have amnesia, and that means all you know is what you want right now.

We especially like this line of thinking because too many of us are wrapped up in old narratives about our lives. The past doesn't equal the future. You can change anything the moment you decide to.

As Nike says, *Just Do It!*

So Why Is This Important?

Benjamin stacking requires a number of important decisions, and that can be terrifying if you're the type of person who has ever tried to rent socks. Understanding why decision-making is difficult is the first step in figuring out how to make better ones, as is recognizing the nonexistence of perfect decisions.

The behavioral economist Dan Ariely is an expert in this topic. Burned badly on over 70 percent of his body as a child, he became interested in pain and why we make bad decisions, especially during times of crisis, such as our recent pandemic. He's not only counseled some of the biggest and best-known financial companies, but he's founded a couple of powerhouses of his own. We caught up with Dan to ask him about how to make better decisions not just during a pandemic but in regular ol' daily life.

IMAGINARY FRIENDS AND HABITUATION:
AN INTERVIEW WITH DAN ARIELY

Joe: *How were you through the pandemic, man?*

Dan: *It's very, very tough in many ways, because I deal with human decision-making. I'm looking to see failure. And when I'm successful, I'm exposed to a lot of terrible things. At the same time, on the good side, I feel incredibly useful when times are tough.*

Now's the time when you see clearly that we need to understand human nature in a much, much deeper way, so I'm in high demand. I feel very useful, but I'm exposed to lots of pain.

Joe: *I want to dive into decision-making here during this rough time for people. As I think back on your books and your TED Talks and the times that I've heard you speak elsewhere, there's this underlying theme of friction. How do we get rid of that friction to make the timely decisions we need to make? Because I don't think it's about not having the right information.*

Dan: *No, it comes from making a decision under stress. It comes from being depleted and not having energy to deal with a decision. And there's* *lots of ways to try and fix it. But one way that is helpful in general is by first giving advice to somebody else in your situation.*

So imagine you have a good friend who is in your situation. Think to yourself, "What would you tell them?" The reason this is good is you take what we call the outside perspective. So imagine you're saying, "Okay, imaginary friend, how much money is coming in every month, and are you sure that this will keep on coming? And what will you do if less is going to come in? What are you spending? Let's go over your credit card." Then, you could try to give this friend advice. The thing is that when we make decisions for ourselves, we use both cognition and emotions. When we give advice to other people, we're much more cold and calculated and we see things in a more objective way. So the strategy is to give advice to somebody in our shoes and then go ahead and then take that advice.

Another thing that we need to do is have an action plan in case things get worse. So while it's tempting to say, "Right now I'm managing, let me just continue like this. I don't want to think about it." [Thinking about it is] unpleasant. But what if things get worse? You can say, "Let me wait until things get worse and then I'll deal with it."

[But] if things get worse, now you're under stress, and under stress is not the right time to make decisions. A good thing to do is have an action plan, then say, "Okay, here's what I'm doing." For example, if things aren't getting better, three months later, I'm going to do X, Y, and Z. And if I lose my job, these are the things I need to do. And the moment you have this alternative action plan in your back pocket, things are easier. Things are simpler.

And then maybe another piece of advice, there's this notion called depletion. Depletion is the idea that when we have full energy, like first thing in the morning, we're able to be more rational, but as the day goes on and we get more and more tired, it's harder for us to think and easier for us to fall for temptation.

Let's then try and make the most important decisions first thing in the morning. It's not a fun way to start the day, but it is the best time in the day to try it.

Joe: *Like we have only so much life in the battery, so to speak.*

Dan: *That's right. You start the day with a bit more energy.*

Joe: *There was a concept that you introduced me to recently that I think we're all fighting against right now. You called it habituation. You mentioned it with respect to the crisis, but I'm also guessing that habituation applies to our money in general. Can you explain habituation and how we fight against that?*

Dan: *So, first of all, just to be clear, a lot of these concepts are not good or bad. They're just there, and they have good sides and bad sides. So habituation is basically that we get used to it. And again, I'll give myself as an example. You know, I was really badly injured. I'm kind of used to it. Am I used to it a hundred percent? No. But let's say when I got injured, you would ask me then how bad would it be if you got burned over 70 percent of your body, and you've had this amount of pain for this amount of years, and then have to keep on with this disability, I would say that it would be terrible. But the reality is that life became really terrible and then it slowly got better.*

I got used to it. I'm not the same as a non-injured version of Dan, but I got used to lots of elements like this. Habituation has the good side there. We get used to bad things. For example, in the world of spending, we just get into a repertoire of spending without thinking about the quality of life that we get from that. Money is not about spending money; it's about buying joy.

You want to buy the most joy you can with the least amount of money, right? We want money for retirement. We want to enjoy now. How much money do we spend for how much joy? But if you look at your daily expenses, you would probably find places where you are spending too much and not getting much joy from it.

For example, for me, giving up television was wonderful. And not only am I not paying for television; I discovered life is better. But you know, there are other things like that during COVID-19. We all probably are eating out less and cooking more. I am getting really good at omelets. COVID-19 forced us to change lots of our habits.

Which of those are we happy with? Imagine [in 2019] I came to you and said, "Joe, would you mind for the next three months not to eat out?" And I said, "How will it be if you didn't do that for three months?" You would say, "Oh, it will be terrible. I'm not willing to try it."

All of the sudden we were forced to do all kinds of things differently. And now it's a really interesting time to evaluate. From all the things we did differently, which ones were good and which ones were bad? Our brain basically wants to do things that are repeated demands, that take the least amount of energy and the least amount of thinking.

In the past you've said to yourself, "I did this before. I only make good decisions. Therefore, that must be a good decision. Let me do it again. No need to rethink." So we end up with all kinds of processes that we never thought would be there for a long time. Now we cut them.

Just for fun, go back after we finish our discussion today and look at your credit cards from November of 2019. Which of those habits were good ones, and which ones are not? But at the moment when you were in it, it was very hard to get out. But we got out of some of those during COVID, which turned out to be a good time to evaluate.

Dan's advice in a nutshell: Changing the way you look at problems can help you reduce stress, make better decisions, and identify which of your choices are habitual rather than beneficial.

Chapter 7 Benjamin Badge:
Taking Action Achievements

Check off each of the following achievements you have completed toward your Benjamin Badge after reading this chapter:

❏ Identify your enemy.
  Do you suffer from too much analysis?
  Do you snap to judgment too soon?
  Do you spend too much time chasing sunk cost?
❏ Place blocks in your way to avoid making these mistakes. What blocks did you set up? _____

Date You Completed the Chapter 7 Badge	Parent Signature (Putting your mom's John Hancock on your Benjamin stacking makes it official)

PART 3

HOLDING ON TO BENJAMINS

(WITHOUT BURYING THEM IN THE BACKYARD)

Joe: Would Transformers buy life insurance or car insurance?

Emily: . . .

8

The Condom Broke and Other Risk-Management Horror Stories

TOOLS YOU'LL NEED:

- A better condom
- Some common sense
- The desire to live your life without wearing a helmet everywhere

Insurance is all about preparing for an uncertain future. All it took was one bright idea for us to recognize its benefits. In some ye olde village, the locals were wondering how to manage the risk of their houses burning down because houses were constantly catching fire. Then one guy, whom we'll call Earl, said, "Hey, I have an idea! How about if we plan ahead? We'll each put money aside to pay for things if something happens."

Everyone thought that was a fantastic idea, even if Earl wasn't the smartest knife in the drawer and also not a snappy dresser. None of that mattered, because Earl had a Good Point.

What the villagers and Earl did not know was that he had invented a key concept: the emergency fund. Having an emergency fund is the first step in managing your risk.

Self-Insurance, aka the Emergency Fund

The first and most likely risk you will face is that you'll have an emergency you can't afford. Like the time Emily ran up a $350 cell phone bill as a newly minted adult because she thought the three hundred minutes her contract offered her were weekly rather than monthly. She'd only just started working on the Barnes & Noble smelting floor and had no way to pay.

The best defense against life's pitfalls is to build an emergency fund for unexpected problems and keep the money somewhere accessible—in a bank account. Yes, even though that means your emergency money won't be growing.

The Wrong Argument About Emergency Funds

We often hear this argument against emergency funds: "That's cash sitting and not earning any money," they'll tell you. "You're watching your money deteriorate in front of your eyes," they'll say.

You know what? They're not wrong. But they're missing the point.

Emergency funds aren't about maximizing your interest rates. If your money is all invested when the market takes a tumble (and we're not talking about a little bump-on-the-head downturn, but the ultimate in worst-case crashes), then what will you do for cash?

Broke professors will tell you, "That's easy, Joe! I go to my huge lines of credit." Well, that might make sense, except for the main reasons that you might need money: job loss, disability, or other income-limiting life event. If you need cash quickly, and you either don't have a job or are burning through cash, using debt products will only land you with an even bigger problem.

There's only one correct argument about emergency funds: Have one. Period. While some money nerds with too much time on their hands will tell you that you'll rarely use it, we'd posit that these are pod-people who have never made a financial mistake or nearly fainted after opening their Verizon bill. Imperfect people need emergency funds—which means you need an emergency fund.

The right amount of money in an emergency fund is enough to keep your family afloat while you figure out life. If you lose your job, how long will it take you to find a new one? If you're disabled, how long until the policy starts paying? If your disability income won't cover it all, how much will you need? The common wisdom (based on much financial nerdery) is that an ideal emergency fund is equal to three to six months' worth of expenses.

Additionally, an emergency fund can save money on insurance because you can do the following:

* Raise the deductibles on your auto and homeowner's policies
* Invest your other savings more aggressively
* Buy less disability insurance
* Buy less life insurance
* Forego policies on your kids and pets, if you wish

Emergency funds don't pay based on the interest rate. They pay because of the amount they save you from forking over money to insurance companies and losing interest in funds you had to rob when something went wrong.

> ### You Probably Need Less Than You Think You Do
>
> **If you're doing the math and thinking, "Holy cow, I make $75,000 per year! How the hell am I ever going to save up six months' worth of that?"**
>
> **Consider: There's a big difference between three to six months' *expenses* and three to six months' *income*. Here's another case where frugal people win big. You don't need to cover what you'll make, only what you'll spend.**
>
> **Doesn't that feel better?**

Insurance and the Law of Large Numbers

Insurance is a way to pool your risk with other people, so you can take advantage of the law of large numbers. We didn't always understand the law of large numbers. (Fun fact: Our remote ancestors couldn't count higher than the five fingers on their hand. This got awkward when trying to cater holiday office parties. There was never enough shrimp cocktail.) But it was something we eventually figured out, after learning the downside of the emergency fund.

See, in ye olde village, things didn't work out when they tried it Earl's way. Edna had *just* started putting money away for an emergency when her damned nephew Caden shot out the TV and set the house on fire. The whole place went up in flames. Edna didn't have enough money saved to replace Caden's BB gun—which was lost in the blaze—let alone pay for a new house.

"Earl," Edna said. "Your idea is stupid."

But Earl knew that his idea wasn't stupid. He just needed to revise it.

"I have a better idea," Earl said. He pretended not to see Edna roll her eyes. "Instead of saving separately," he explained, "we should all save together into one barrel in the middle of town. That way, if something bad happens to someone's house, the community barrel will have enough money to cover it."

"I don't want to share a bucket with Edna. Her damned kid shot out the TV," said Rose. Everyone murmured in agreement.

Earl swooped in to defend Edna, because he knew it was his chance to crawl back into her good graces. "You and I know Edna won't let Caden do that again. Plus, what's the chance something will happen to more than one of us within a short time? The probability is low. By saving together, we'll make sure money is available for everyone."

People still murmured, but nobody wanted to seem ungrateful. Earl's idea made sense.

So they all began saving money into the same barrel. They worked out a few more kinks, like the fact that Rose, it turned out, liked to "rob the kitty," as she called it, for her weekly Friday foamy beverage. That forced them to find someone to monitor the bucket. His name was Phillip, and after a while he demanded to be paid. So everyone put a little more money in the bucket and Phillip was allowed from time to time to scoop a little out for himself for his trouble.

Some complained that they had taken far fewer risks than others. Edna had her history of trouble, so everyone agreed she should put in more. Earl lived in a small tent, so he put in just a few bucks. People were happy in ye olde village, except for Caden, who was annoyed he never got a replacement BB gun.

This possibly apocryphal anecdote can teach us a lot. First, Edna's experience makes it clear why you buy into insurance with other people, pooling your risk. You know there is money available when you need it, even if you personally don't have enough.

Second, like Phillip in the story, a company running the insurance program provides an essential service. That protects the customers from bad actors (like Rose) so they can feel confident the money will be there for them. Yes, the company makes a profit, but the arrangement is still beneficial to the insured parties.

Joe's Mom on Why You're Not Being Ripped Off by Your Insurance Company

Insurance companies have their problems (and boy howdy do they), but stealing your money is not one of them, despite what you may have been led to believe on that damned Tweeter you're always staring at. Here's why:

Insurance companies are monitored and licensed by individual states. With all that oversight, it's hard to get away with a scam.

Think about how many companies sell insurance these days! They have to fight for your business. They do that by either lowering prices or giving you more benefits for the same price. It works down at the farmer's market and with disability coverage.

If you think you're getting ripped off by an insurance company, you're probably either 1) using your insurance wrong, or 2) being ripped off by the salesman who's using the insurance wrong. If there's a commission at stake, a bad apple just might be your problem.

Also, if you are high risk (like Edna in this ridiculous story the kids are sharing), insurance companies will raise your rates. This isn't to rip you off, but because it's only fair to the people who don't shoot out TVs.

Finally, there are other factors involved—like how Earl pays less because he lives in a tent. Knowing what factors may affect your premium (the amount you're paying in) is a huge part of winning when it comes to insurance.

Now let's get into the things you need to protect.

Evaluating Insurances

We start with this question: "What would happen if . . . ?"

When we widen the question from "What insurance should I buy?" to this better question of "What would happen if . . . ?," we take away the push for unnecessary coverage. Sure, we're going to use insurance, but the whole idea is to cover all those things that might go wrong and you can't cover yourself. So let's keep first things first and think about what we can pay for with our own cash.

Once you have your emergency fund in place, know which insurances are most critical to have. Insurance companies (with their wee, beady eyes) charge more for policies that they think you're going to use more often. They charge less for policies they think are a waste of money for you. So what does that mean?

You should look at expensive insurances and ignore cheap ones.

"Wait a minute, Joe and Emily!" you exclaim angrily. "You expect me to believe that we are going to want to look mostly at the insurances that we can't afford?"

No, person we made up for yet another story in this book. What we're saying is that *the issues these policies address represent the biggest threats to your well-being.* That is, insurance companies know what claims they're most likely to have to pay. They do *a lot* of market research. That's why you want to focus on the expensive issues first. Like:

- Suffering a disability
- Being in a car wreck
- Dying
- Something happening to your home, whether you rent or own

We know that you may stay up late worried about the possibility of a hurricane, flood, tornado, or rhino sneak-attack—and possibly rightfully so—but those are regional risks, while these four represent the biggest risks globally.

The #1 Activity You Need to Think About When It Comes to Risk Management

Of these four biggies, the biggie-est threat to you and anyone you support is that you won't be able to earn an income. So protecting yourself against the chance that your paycheck may go away is job numero uno.

We've talked about how to insure against losing your job: have an emergency fund covering three to six months' worth of expenses. That's because in 2020, it took an average of twenty weeks to find a new job after a layoff, according to the Bureau of Labor Statistics. Your joblessness is not permanent, so you just need to bridge the gap until you find the next gig.

Next: the statistics on the likelihood of becoming disabled are perhaps worse than you might expect. (It turns out we're way shittier skiers than we imagine.) Check out these stats from the United Nations:

- One billion people in the world live with a disability.

- That means one in seven people have a disability.
- Having a disability increases your income need by one-third.

And more from Wheelchair Pride:

- Almost 13 percent of the U.S. population is affected by disabilities.
- Only 36 percent of working-age people with disabilities have a job.
- People with disabilities earn significantly less than people without disabilities ($22,047 vs. $33,476).
- People with disabilities are more likely to live in poverty than people without disabilities (20.9 percent vs. 13.1 percent).

When Joe was a financial planner, people were excited to talk about life insurance—well, maybe not excited, but at least *open* to the topic—but exactly zero times did anyone want to talk about the fact that maybe something bad could happen to them where they didn't die. But this attitude is optimistic and, sadly, unrealistic.

How to Cover the Threat of Disability

If you've accumulated enough money, you may not need to do anything. If your Benjamin stacks are sizable enough that you don't need to work, then don't worry about the economic toll of disability—unless you pay for a full-time aide or require daily assistance.

Depending on your spouse's job, you may be able to rely on their income, if it will cover any increase in expenses. But:

1. Don't assume your spouse will earn more money in the coming years. If they are taking care of your butt, the chance of raises and promotions are probably reduced.

2. There's even a good chance your spouse's income will sink, especially if they're paid an hourly wage. Factor that into your plan.

Our last tip is to look into disability coverage at work. Most people have disability insurance associated with their jobs, but they don't think about what type or how much coverage they have. In many cases, when clients told Joe, "I have that covered through work," Joe asked, "How much do you have?" only to be met with a blank stare. Hunt down the paperwork or your password to find out exactly what is covered and at what cost.

There are a few kinds of disability insurance out there:

- **Short-term disability** covers you if you're unable to work for about six to twelve months. Here's the deal with short-term disability coverage: If you have an emergency fund, you may not need it. If you're paying for it and you have an emergency fund that is enough to cover the same period, you can stop paying those premiums and self-cover.
- **Long-term disability** typically offers benefit period options of two years, five years, ten years, or until retirement age (usually sixty-five or sixty-seven).

How Does Your Long-Term Disability Insurance Stack Up?

To get a sense of how helpful your disability insurance will be in the event you need it, you just have to answer these two questions:

1. How much is the benefit you'll receive?

2. Is there a cap on the benefit? As an example: many coverages say they'll give you 60 percent of your pay, but then they slip "up to $1,000 a month" in the fine print. Uh . . . that isn't 60 percent for someone earning $85k per year, now, is it? Sneaky, sneaky.

There are other, even nerdier questions, but our goal isn't to get a PhD in disability insurance—it's to have the right coverage.

So now, and this is the exciting part, let's figure out how much money we'll need. To reiterate for the forty-seventh time: Don't ask how much insurance you need to buy. Calculate how much money you'll need to cover your expenses. Then figure out how to cover it.

If you become disabled, some expenses will sink and others will increase. Remember the previously mentioned stat: the average person sees their income needs go up by a third. Let's pretend that we're going to be unable to work and require assistance forever.

Though you can purchase disability insurance on your own, the first place to start shopping for policies is at work—if you're eligible to buy more there—since the chuckleheads you work for are subsidizing the price. However, remember that the average person stays at any one employer for only 4.1 years, according to the Bureau of Labor Statistics, so it's not a bad idea to look outside work and purchase a portable policy as well—or take your existing policy when you change jobs, if they'll let you, which most will.

Some disability insurance features you should look for:

- **Own-occupation coverage.** This provides money if you're disabled and aren't able to perform your specific job. Without this provision, disability insurance companies may insist that you take a minimum-wage job if you're healthy enough to work. Read your contract carefully. Own-occupation coverage gives you the ability to only take work that's meaningful to you.
- **Inflation protection.** Hopefully you don't need to use your disability coverage at all, but if you end up needing it, let's also pray that it's a long, long time from now. If that's the case and you haven't protected against the threat of prices rising (another #spoiler: they will), your coverage isn't going to be worth much.
- **Long-term protection.** We shouldn't need to say this, but *you want a policy that will pay a benefit for as long as possible.* Don't buy a one-year or three-year policy, unless you're sure the miracle cure will arrive right at the time your benefits run out.

Chapter 8 Benjamin Sub-Badge: Disability Insurance Achievements

Check off each of the following achievements you have completed toward your Benjamin Sub-Badge after reading this section:

❑ Calculate how much money you would have coming in if you become disabled—either from accumulated assets, your spouse's income, or via disability coverage you have through work.
❑ Create a disability budget based on that income.
❑ Find appropriate insurance to fill the gap between the money you can count on if you were disabled and the money you'd need to live comfortably.

Date You Completed the Chapter 8 Sub-Badge	Parent Signature (Putting your mom's John Hancock on your Benjamin stacking makes it official)

Auto Insurance

Don't be surprised if you find yourself buying more insurance when we're done. Unfortunately, the statistics show that there's a good chance someone else's bad day can also wreck yours. Until you have an emergency fund, don't mess around with your auto coverage to save a few bucks. This is one of the top places people cut corners, and it's also the place where they most often get burned.

When it comes to car insurance, ask: "How likely is the insurance company going to be to pay my claim?" There are two things you'll want when you make an auto insurance claim: for the claim to be paid immediately and without a bunch of questions that try to discourage you from getting money for a new car.

The statistics of getting that claim paid quickly are against you. So start with your emergency fund. If you have a reserve that's large enough to afford a new car, then you can opt for less insurance. If you don't have a reserve, you'll opt for more. Again, your emergency fund saves you money, even though you settled for a low interest rate.

There are many types of auto insurance coverage, but let's cover the basic two: full coverage versus personal liability and property damage (PLPD) policies.

Full-coverage policies are like that friend who holds your hair back after a too-long night at the bar. It takes care of everything and handles all the situations you can imagine.

Personal liability and damage is more like that friend who waits for the bill to come, pretends they have to hit the restroom, and never comes back. It'll get you out of a legal bind, but that doesn't help out much when it comes to replacing your asset.

You can see how not asking the right questions gets people in trouble. They'll ask an agent, "How much do you charge?" Full coverage is more expensive (by a lot), so it seems logical and reasonable for people to opt for PLPD, not understanding that they just compared an apple to an orange. Or better yet, they compared an apple to a dump truck that's barreling right toward them.

When you ask for a quote, the company will list you several line items that appear in most full and PLPD coverages. Here's an overview:

- **Bodily injury liability:** This protects against you causing harm to someone else. If you're found to have injured or (heaven forfend) killed someone, it covers those events.
- **Property damage liability:** This protects against the damage to another auto, if you're found to be liable.
- **Personal injury:** This covers anyone in the car if there's a problem. This is usually "no fault" coverage, meaning that even if you aren't the guilty party, it'll help pay for hospital bills, and even lost wages in some cases.

Next up are the biggies that appear only in full-coverage policies:

- **Collision coverage:** No matter what you hit, this pays.
- **Comprehensive coverage:** This covers all the other stuff that happens, whether it's fires, floods, or alien invasions. Think of it as "everything but collision."

Finally, you may or may not see these coverages on your policy:

- **Uninsured motorist:** Do you know how many people drive but don't have insurance? Yeah, you don't want to know—but it's ugly. Because of that, uninsured motorist coverage picks up the tab if you have a run-in with an uninsured idiot.
- **Towing/rental car:** If you have no emergency fund, then this one might make sense. Your car is in the shop for a month? How are you going to get to work? However, if you have a solid reserve, you can eliminate this coverage first.

FinTech and Auto Coverage

You can score big auto insurance discounts if you're okay with them playing Big Brother. Some companies offer incentives, like much better rates, if you install a device that lets them "watch" you drive. Just know that you're helping them secure lots of data about you and other drivers.

Our vote here is always no (stick it to the man), but we also know that this is a quixotic mission: sooner or later, like Mark Zuckerberg, they're going to have all our information anyway. Hell, why not give it to them right now? We're not hiding anything anyway. (But that voice inside us still says, "You'll never catch me, copper!!!")

Homeowner's Insurance

You can proactively avoid homeowner horror stories with just a few lifestyle moves:

- Make a video of your house with your belongings. Include as many product serial numbers as possible.
- Keep your deductible low until you have a decent cash reserve. Then raise this deductible.
- Look to bundle coverages. Companies want your business, and they will often give you an easy discount if you sign up for both home and auto coverage.

Chapter 8 Benjamin Sub-Badge: Auto and Homeowner's Insurance Achievements

Check off each of the following achievements you have completed toward your Benjamin Sub-Badge after reading this section:

❑ Call your insurance company and ask about your home and auto policies. Can you change your deductible or any of the covenants to give you better coverage and maybe save money?

❑ Ask about discounts. Are there any available that you aren't receiving?

❑ Will bundling home and auto save you money?

❑ Call three competitors. Can they offer you the same coverage for a better rate? Also ask them about bundling.

Date You Completed the Chapter 8 Sub-Badge	Parent Signature (Putting your mom's John Hancock on your Benjamin stacking makes it official)

What Happens If I Die (Check That, "What Happens When *I Die*?")[9]

Rather than jumping into your life insurance needs, we start with the same question we ask with all insurance: "What happens when I die?"

Specifically, you need to answer these two questions:

---

9 *We know that you are personally planning on living forever. However, it's always best to plan for the worst, no matter how remote the possibility. So while you're working on achieving immortality via an experiment using a few rubber bands, a liquid lunch, and a particle accelerator, please do make sure you read this section carefully and follow our suggestions. Just in case.*

1. Who depends on me for money? How much do they need? How long do they need money?

2. What resources will be available to my family when I die? Don't forget to include Social Security benefits that may be available for surviving spouses and any workplace benefits.

If you have enough resources, you can skip this whole chapter (unless you're rolling in dough, to the tune of more than $11 million, at which point you should look at life insurance for estate-planning purposes). But if you, like most people, find yourself a little short, well, it's time to nerd out.

To calculate how much money a person will need over their whole life, use one of the many calculators online to determine how much life insurance you'll need today. Don't use one of the many ridiculous rules of thumb—like the one that claims the amount you need is based solely on your age or the one that says you should always tell your mother-in-law how she looks in those jeans.

We want to go over how this stuff works for a reason: our extensive frustration when it comes to insurance is caused by the shortcuts everyone uses. Is life insurance hard? Sure. But can you learn it? Yes, you can. In fact, it's a lot of fun and will give you a crapload of ahas (both "crapload" and "ahas" are technical terms). So let's do this.

There are two answers you're hoping to find when calculating your insurance need:

- How much insurance you need (yet another #shocker); and
- How long you'll need it.

For both of these questions, you'll need to learn how insurances are priced to make a good decision. There's no such thing as an insurance store, but just go with it. You walk up to the register and say, "I'll take one hundred of these $1,000 blocks, please, because I'm a baller."

The clerk is going to ask your birthday. Why? Those blocks of insurance are sold based on your age, as priced by math nerds known as actuaries. (Actuaries are gentle creatures that are easy to tame. Just offer them a Werther's Original caramel and casually mutter "statistics" and "probability" and they will cheerfully calculate your life expectancy.) If you're young, actuaries know that you'll probably pay for that insurance for a long time.

The bad news is that actuaries don't care that we just gave them candy. Just like Joe's crush in eighth grade only cared about David Sampson, who was on the baseball team and had the fluffy seventies hair that Joe could never pull off, actuaries only care about "the math" and not how nice we're being to them. And the math says that with every birthday you celebrate, you're a little more likely to die. This is why actuaries are not invited to a lot of birthday parties.

Joe's Mom on Testing the Upper Limit

How about this: with most policies, if you still have it in force on your one hundredth birthday, the insurer just sends you a check with a note that reads, "Well, shit. We guess you win."

Okay, they don't send that note, even though it would be epic marketing, wouldn't it? But the rest is true—although some insurance companies wait until you've reached 110 or 121 before sending you the money and a "Congratulations for outrunning the grim reaper!" note. My goal is to outlive all those bastards.

Let's first look at term coverage, a popular choice because it's the least expensive. You're buying insurance for a predetermined length of time (the "term"). You pick a term (usually ten, fifteen, twenty, or thirty years) and pay a level fee for the insurance over the entire time. That way, you aren't paying a lot in those last few years, when you're more likely to die.

You can also buy term insurance in decreasing amounts, so that it slowly provides less coverage. As the price increases on every block, you're shedding them, so the amount you're paying stays level. This is also a solid option if you're sure you're going to accumulate assets and therefore need less coverage.

> ### *Joe on FinTech and Insurance*
>
> **When I was an advisor, helping clients fill out applications took forever, and invariably we'd miss something super vital (read: not at all important) and the insurance company would delay their decision. This area was ripe for a FinTech overhaul. Now, companies are offering insurance with a fraction of the questions, much less underwriting, and still giving you solid coverage. Some even offer decisions after a less-than-five-minute application process. That's progress.**

Term insurance is simple: your rate is based on your age and the size of the death benefit. If it's level term, you'll also pay the same rate for that entire time.

Permanent insurance, aka "whole life," is where things get tricky. Whole-life insurance is a product that's guaranteed to last . . . your whole life. (You're welcome. Let me lift that for you.)

These types of policies are called "bundled" insurance, meaning that you can't see their inner workings. So let's undress this thing. There's nothing shameful about seeing a life insurance policy in the altogether. Yes, we'll be examining the dangly bits, but that's how we learn and get over our embarrassment.

Here's how it works:

First, remember those actuaries who just care about math (and hard candies)? The actuaries realized that term insurance became pricey when people reached between sixty and seventy years old. If insurance was going to be around for someone's whole life, how were they ever going to afford it?

The solution was a concept called "cash value." Let's say you have a $10,000 whole-life policy and the current cost of your insurance is only $25 per month because you are a young, robust, healthy individual who doesn't make a habit of falling out of high windows while smoking a pack a day. However, the insurance company may ask you to pay $100 per month, with the remainder squirreled away in cash. Because you now have $75 per month going into the cash value, two things happen. First, that money can help subsidize or completely pay your premium later in life when you are at higher risk of dying and therefore a $10,000 policy would cost you more than $100 per month. Second, you are building accumulated cash that will be part of your death benefit.

Want to nerd out on the details? Check this out: Over time, let's say you have $1,000 in your "cash value." The insurance company, in most cases, is going to return this money along with enough insurance proceeds to equal what you bought. If that number is $10,000, the death benefit will be composed of $9,000 of the insurance company's money and $1,000 of your own money back.

That means the best way to save on permanent life insurance is to send as much money as possible to your policy. (We know. It sounds bonkers. But stick with us.) The more money you pay in the form of premiums, the more goes into your cash value, thereby reducing the cost of the insurance part. Since you can access your cash value if you need it, buying permanent insurance this way sets aside funds for your future needs while also protecting your family from the economic fallout of your eventual demise.

Joe and Emily may not agree with the need for permanent insurance, but if you're going to buy it, sock as much money into that cash value portion as you possibly can. Cash value was originally meant to make permanent life insurance affordable. But over the years, insurance companies have worked on ways to make their policies competitive so the cash value can grow more quickly.

They also decoupled the cash value from the insurance cost, so that you can see what's going on in the guts of your policy. These are universal life policies, which are permanent policies that combine expensive one-year term insurance that is renewed annually with a separate cash value. The insurance company will ask you to pay at least the cost of insurance, but you can add more to the cash value.

Over time, a product emerged inside universal life policies: the ability to buy funds similar to mutual funds. Now you could have a wide range of investments inside of your policy, giving you more freedom to hopefully make your policy less expensive over time, or even use it as an investment. Those, if you need to know, are called variable universal life policies.

Life Insurance Takeaways

- If you need life insurance short-term, or until you are sixty to sixty-five, term insurance is less expensive. However, there's a huge chance the insurance won't be around when you die (that's a good thing) because you're likely to be older than your mid-sixties when you buy the farm.
- If you're feeling stingy, whole-life insurance is the only way to buy life insurance with a guaranteed death benefit. However, you're going to pay dearly for those guarantees.
- Universal life and its offspring decouple your insurances, giving people "in the middle" or who want the possibility of "investing" their insurance the ability to do this. Should you? Probably not. But if you want a permanent policy with more competitive, variable rates than a whole-life policy, it's more promising.

And one more point: Are life insurance companies ripping you off? Maybe, but we doubt it. First, we have to circle back to our original story about what insurance really is: a bunch of people sharing risk.

However, some insurance agents add in optional provisions called "riders," which are special types of insurance you can buy, like the add-ons they talk you into at the car dealership. The leather seat upgrades may have been worth every penny in your El Camino, but in most cases, you just want the basics.

The Missing Insurance

Five out of five doctors agree that death is the least healthy state of being, so why haven't we discussed health insurance? While being able to pay for your healthcare is an essential part of a balanced diet (not to mention budget), health coverage is quickly evolving, multifaceted, and complex enough to require a whole separate book. We're considering this for the inevitable sequel after our sold-out world tour for this book.

So Why Is This Important?

Hopefully we saved you a bunch of money on insurance. Even better, hopefully you now have a cohesive risk-management strategy. Proper risk management has the same takeaway as that classic three bears story: not too much, not too little, but *just right*.

One of Joe's favorite parts of hosting *Stacking Benjamins* is facilitating the weekly roundtable episodes. He loves chatting with three people with diverse backgrounds and interests, and the discussion often goes in unexpected directions. To dig a little deeper into life insurance, we had a roundtable discussion with Sandy Smith, a former human resources professional and the creator of the Elevate conference, which promotes and supports influencers of color; Ty Roberts, the brain behind the *Camp FIRE Finance* blog (he's since sold it); and Chris Huntley, president of LifeInsuranceShopping Reviews.com, where he sells term life insurance. Here's part of that conversation.

MY WIFE'S REPLACEMENT HUSBAND:
A DISCUSSION WITH SANDY SMITH,
TY ROBERTS, AND CHRIS HUNTLEY

Joe: *Chris, because you're in the business, you probably hear people talk about reasons why they're not going to buy life insurance all the time.*

Chris: *One excuse is "I've got plenty of assets, so if I check out early, my family can fall back on those now." Another one is "I'm healthy, so it would just be a waste of money."*

And then the third one is just about putting it off. That's obviously the most common.

The first excuse, that I've got plenty of assets, I sort of agree with. If someone has a million dollars in assets and some of it's liquid, then maybe your family doesn't need life insurance to fall back on. They're somewhat self-insured.

But the excuse of "I'm healthy" doesn't work.

You could get hit by a truck tomorrow and you've got maybe ten, twenty, thirty years of income earning potential down the drain. It could be a financial disaster for your family.

Joe: *When you're teaching this to people at work, Sandy, do you find that people have these or different excuses?*

Sandy: *Well, a lot of our people are pretty young. The average age is in the thirties at my office because I'm in FinTech. So they're all thinking, "I'm too young. I really don't need this yet." But I've had to process one employee death every year for the last four years.*

But the most often thing that I hear is, "Oh, I'm too young. I really don't need it right now."

Right . . .

Joe: *If they don't have assets yet, do they need it?*

Sandy: *In my early twenties, I was thinking, "Hey, if I die now, who cares?" Because I've got a ton of student loans and a bunch of credit cards from all the pizza from college. I'm not married. I don't own a home. I don't have any kids. If I dropped dead tomorrow, who's going to pay my student loans? Nobody co-signed for it for me. Right? I'm good to go there. Nobody co-signed on my credit cards, so they don't have to pay a dang thing. They just have to worry about my funeral and I've got enough money in my 401(k) and I'm good to go.*

That was my thought process through my twenties. But as I got later into my twenties, I started thinking, "What if I get married? And what if I want to buy a house? It's so much cheaper for me to buy life insurance now than doing it ten years later."

That's where I started to evolve, in that it was just so much cheaper to get it in my late twenties versus in my thirties. I just got it early, just in case. And now here I am. I'm married. I've got a house and other assets that I need to protect, so I'm happy that I got insurance then versus continuing that line of thinking.

But it's definitely something that I fight with a pretty young staff.

Joe: *We're more insurable when we're younger. We can make sure that before we have things come up, such as maybe medical problems, that we can get the insurance. Is that as important a factor as Sandy's making it, or do you see insurance people overplay that?*

Chris: *It's true. It's cheaper the earlier you get it.*

Not just because life insurance is cheaper when you're younger, but also because ten years from now, who knows what health condition that you'll have? You know, when I was twenty-seven, I got my first policy and I was shocked that I had really high cholesterol. I had no idea, and I actually got penalized and I didn't get the best rate.

And here I was, you know, six foot one, 170 pounds. I've always been in great shape. I thought I was a shoe-in to get the best rate and I didn't.

Joe: *Sandy, you talk about processing employee deaths. Are there times when they probably should have been better covered than they were?*

Sandy: *The one that sticks out in my mind was about two years ago. This gentleman was in his early forties and had started with the company—I kid you not—four weeks before he drops dead of a heart attack. He had just slid into our employer plan, where he was covered, just based on the fact that we offer three times your annual salary as a benefit in life insurance. You don't have to pay for it.*

When his spouse called, they had nothing liquid, really. It was just his paycheck that was coming and this life insurance that I was processing. He had nothing else. Had he not been on the company's life insurance policy, the only cash that she would have had was his final paycheck.

They had a house, but that asset was tied to a huge debt as well. She was a stay-at-home mom. They had kids, and she would not have had the money to pay for a funeral. So even if you have assets, you have to think about liquidity.

People in HR tend to be some of the most insured people who I know, because they just see all these horror stories.

I've had to process a death for a twenty-two-year-old. And then the oldest was a gentleman who was fifty-four. It's still not that old. And all their families needed the money right away just to bury them.

Joe: *Chris, how long does it take beneficiaries to get the money after someone dies?*

Chris: *Typically, once you file the claim, it's within thirty days. The companies have to pay interest after that. However, if the death occurs within the first two years after the policy was issued, then there's typically a contestability period where they're going to look into it. They check that all the questions were answered correctly on the application and there were no misrepresentations or lies about any drug use, smoking use, things like that. In that case, it can take several months, but typically thirty days or less.*

Joe: *Ty, was it on baby number one, or when you started your job, when you decided it was time to get some life insurance?*

Ty: *I always knew that I should get insurance. There were a lot of reasons I didn't; they were all pretty pathetic excuses. No time. No money. I maybe felt like time was on my side.*

But mainly I didn't want my wife's replacement husband to be living the good life 'cause I checked out early.

Joe: *I'm with you. Ha! So how many children did you have before you decided to buy life insurance outside of work?*

Ty: *It's kind of terrible to say, but I had all four kids when I decided. I'm a recent purchaser of life insurance outside of work.*

Joe: *Chris, if Ty had bought insurance with baby number one before he had three more babies—is it better for him at baby number one to buy enough to protect future children, or should he add on more later as his family grows?*

Chris: *It's not so much about the dependents as it is the replacement of income. So we typically will look at insuring seven to ten times your income.*

And you can just add on later if you look at things and you're like, "Wow, maybe seven to ten times my income is not going to cut it anymore." I know I've added on two separate times.

Joe: *But isn't it really important to cover expenses? When we look at a family's capital needs, the needs go up with mouths to feed.*

Chris: *Definitely. I just don't like to overcomplicate the needs analysis. If I'm talking to someone who's not really sophisticated about it, I'll typically just recommend a multiple of income.*

If they're more sophisticated or the engineering types where we'll just talk all day about it and we'll have a blast because it's a couple of insurance nerds in a room together, we'll get granular.

Joe: *Ty, how did you figure out how much was enough for your family?*

Ty: *I don't like the rules of thumb or the multipliers of income, personally.*

Those are a starting-off point for me. What we did was figure out what our financial independence number was, and that's what we went for.

Joe: *Chris, I'm sure in your profession, you see too many people get paralyzed around having the perfect number.*

Chris: *It's like when you're a parent and your child asks, "How are babies made?" You could give them "the talk" all day, which is what it would take to give them a real answer, but that's not really what they need. You could explain insurance all day to someone who asks a simple question about buying, but you'll paralyze them. So I think it's better to give them enough information so they can make a decision.*

Joe: *Sandy, how much insurance do you tell people at work they should buy in your workplace plan?*

Sandy: Since most of our folks tend to be pretty young, I go with the very simple multiplier or covering their debt plus what they think their family might need afterward. As our employees get a little bit older and they're more sophisticated, then I walk through, "What are your assets? What's liquid? How much income do you make? How much time do you think you need to cover? Do you have kids? Do you plan on covering their college?"

For example, the fifty-four-year-old gentleman who passed away—that day his wife was an instant millionaire because he had gone through and done this assessment. Between what he had in his 401(k)—over half a million dollars—plus the company-sponsored life insurance, plus additional life insurance that he bought at work, plus life insurance he had outside of work.

It's a little bit harder for our folks in their twenties because they are still paying for their student loans. They might be thinking about getting married. They might not. I'm also fighting with the Superman syndrome where you think you're going to live forever.

Until they understand the importance of life insurance, then we can go with their needs using a rule of thumb, usually what's going to cover your student loans and your debt and stuff. That's where I start off at. Just very simple so that they're not scared of it, because again, we're talking about their mortality.

Nobody wants to think they're going to die. Nobody does.

Chris: Sandy, most of the group plans I see have a multiple of income of one to three years. Can group plans go beyond three years of income replacement, typically?

Sandy: Oh yeah. For example, there's the group term insurance where we set the number, which is three times your salary up to a maximum of half a million dollars. That's company-provided off the bat. You don't pay a penny for it. And then you have the ability to purchase supplemental life insurance, sold on a dollar value.

And it's a guarantee issue. That's the life insurance where you don't have to go for any kind of health exam or questions. As long as you sign up for it and you pay for it, it's yours.

Anything above the guarantee issue, then you've got to go through an evidence of insurability. It depends what the number is that your company has signed up for. In our case, I think our cap is up to an additional half a million dollars or $750,000. So you have the potential as an employee to have $1.2 to $5 million in life insurance. Just through the company alone.

Joe: *Ty, you also have insurance through work.*

Ty: *I do. We are covered in multiple places. We've got our personal insurance. We have the voluntary plan through my employer, and then I also have a policy where I'm paying through work. But it's not a great policy, and I'll probably need to dump it soon.*

Joe: *Why do you need to dump the one through work? Is your personal insurance plan less expensive?*

Ty: *That's it exactly. I get more with my outside plan for about half the cost. We're going to use the money we save to get insurance on my wife.*

Joe: *Is it often the case that if people can find insurance outside their work, beyond the free stuff that Sandy talked about, it's less expensive on their own than what they can buy through work?*

Chris: *It depends on their health. If they're unhealthy, it's awesome to be in a group plan, because typically there's only a couple of questions. I believe— Sandy, correct me if I'm wrong—that typically it'll just ask you if you smoke or not, and your age, or just a couple of questions for the guarantee issue.*

Sandy: *They're the very simplest questions. Have you had cancer? Do you smoke? Do you have diabetes? Only three or four simple questions.*

Chris: *It's really easy to get through those questions if you do have some* *sort of health history. But for people who are really healthy, they're getting lumped in with all those people who are squeaking through with health issues.*

If you're healthy, you don't want to be in that pool. You want to be in the pool with all the Olympic athletes, right? And you can get that on your own typically much cheaper than in a group plan.

Joe: *Sandy, if somebody stops working for the company, what happens to their supplemental insurance?*

Sandy: *People are always shocked when they leave the company about what happens to their insurance. You lose the group rate. That's the first thing. So you now go into the marketplace and sometimes it's a lot more expensive than if you bought it yourself. That's when you're allowed to take it with you.*

Not every company lets you do that. The current company that I'm with allows you to take it. I've been at companies before that did not allow you to convert your insurance, which means the minute you no longer work for the company, you no longer have insurance, which most people are very shocked about.

So I encourage people, don't just have the company's insurance. You never know when I'm going to tap you on the shoulder and fire you, so you should always have your own life insurance.

And I take my own advice. I've got my own policy outside of work. I never know when I'm going to tap myself on the shoulder and say, "You no longer work here, either."

Chris, Sandy, and Ty's advice in a nutshell: Don't put off getting life insurance, even if you feel intimidated about calculating how much you need. Feel free to use rules of thumb just to get a policy in place. Take advantage of workplace group life insurance, but don't let that be your only coverage in case it's not portable.

Chapter 8 Benjamin Sub-Badge:
Life Insurance Achievements

Check off each of the following achievements you have completed toward your Benjamin Sub-Badge after reading this section:

❑ Calculate how much life insurance you need (if any).

❑ Decide which insurance type is best and explain why to a friend. Double points if they understand why you have the strategy you're using.

❑ Discontinue insurances you don't need, **but only *after* the appropriate coverage is in place.** (You don't want to be left without insurance.)

Date You Completed the Chapter 8 Sub-Badge	Parent Signature (Putting your mom's John Hancock on your Benjamin stacking makes it official)

8A

Insurance Bingo

TOOLS YOU'LL NEED:
- A sharp pencil
- Copies of your insurance documents, if handy
- A phone to call insurance people, human resources contacts, and your mom[10]

Emily and Joe were hanging out in Joe's mom's kitchen one day. Joe said, "Why don't I tell you a story about insurance that we can use as a chapter for our book!"

Emily had a mouthful of guacamole, so she didn't have time to stop Joe before he pulled out his storytelling pipe and sank deep into the rocking chair.

"I'm going to tell you a super tragic tale about insurance gone wrong and of poor, helpless people wasting money," Joe said a little overdramatically. "Sadly, I have many such stories."

"Uh-huh," Emily replied, looking to see how quickly she could catch an Uber to anywhere-but-here.

Joe got a far-off gleam in his eye that indicated he was about to tell a hell of a yarn. "There are lots of things people misunderstand, Emily.

---

10 Seriously, call your mom. She worries.

First, they start off with the wrong question. They ask, 'How much insurance do I need?' "

Emily shrugged. "I don't understand how that's wrong. Lots of people need insurance." Crap. Because Joe wrote this part of the book, she knew she was going to have to play the part of the straight man yet again.

Joe shook his head. "The first question to ask is this: 'If something happens to me, how will I cover it?' This way you widen the discussion away from just insurance. What if you don't need insurance at all? Maybe you can save a few bucks and have the right coverage without using insurance."

"Ah," Emily said, smiling and refreshing her rideshare app. "That makes sense. That's why people with emergency funds can back off their insurance amounts."

"Exactly!" Joe said. "Now for that story."

Emily sighed. "Are you sure a story is the right format for this stuff?" She was already feeling sleepy, and he hadn't even begun. "What if we instead made a list of the top things people should protect against, and ways they can do so."

"That's a great idea, Emily!" Joe was thrown off track but realized that when two people write a book together, it was important to be a team player. "But people don't like talking about this stuff," he said. "Also," he added, secretly hoping that he'd get to tell his amazing tale of hope, love, and insurance gone wrong, "lists are only fun in Top 10 formats, and Letterman's retired."

Emily thought for a moment. Suddenly, her face lit up. "I know! Let's turn it into a game!"

"Damn," Joe thought.

She went to the whiteboard on Joe's mom's fridge and wrote this:

Insurance Bingo, aka Things That Can Go Wrong (and Often Do) and How to Protect Yourself

What Could Go Wrong: Car accident or car problems
How This Works (A Modern Parable): Suze owns a car but buys

the least insurance possible, because she's dead-flat broke. Last Tuesday, Suze got in a car accident and had a $1,000 deductible and her insurance company provided less money than she'd hoped. The result? Suze had to buy a bike with her insurance proceeds. Now she's in shape but always late for work. Bad Suze! Had she realized that high-deductible insurance is for people with emergency funds, she might have paid more in premiums, but she would have had insurance in place when she needed it.

How to Protect Yourself (15 points possible):

- Valid car insurance. This is mandated in most places, so you must have it. (5 points)
- If you have an emergency fund, increase your deductible. Higher deductibles lower your bill. The bad news? The deductible is also the amount you'll be on the hook for if there's an accident, but that's why you have an emergency fund! (5 points)
- Inflate tires and stay on top of all recommended car maintenance. (5 points)

What Could Go Wrong: Home fire, accident, burglary

How This Works (Another Modern Parable): Dave buys a lot of insurance because he's a big fan, but he never takes the time to inventory his assets. When his home is broken into by ninjas while he's away on an all-reward-points vacation courtesy of his credit card company, he has no proof of what he owns. Now he has to try to piece together his entire financial life with his insurer. Oh no, Dave!

How to Protect Yourself (30 points possible):

- Homeowner's or renter's insurance. There is less chance of a problem than with your car, which is why the insurance is less expensive. But that means there's no excuse not to have it. (10 points)
- Make a video of your home, opening drawers and closets. You'll have to remember what you own if something goes awry. (10 points)
- Install alarms and motion detectors. Your insurance company

may lower your rates, subsidizing or even completely covering this cost. (10 points)

A word about video: Does it feel like making a video of all your stuff is a waste of time? Joe's had to file a claim before (burglary), and here's what happened: the insurance company is happy to pay, but they want a complete list of what you own. If you haven't made a video yet, take ten minutes right now and write out everything you own. Can't even begin, can you? Make the video. If you're still stalling, imagine you're on an episode of MTV's *Cribs*. Narrate your belongings like you're Mariah Carey or Redman showing off your walk-in closet. ("I step in. I step out.") It's fun, and you'll be your insurance agent's favorite client if you ever have to hand over the video in case of loss.[11] Also—safety tip: don't keep the video in your house! What if your house burns down? Find a safe cloud-based solution with a strong password. List the password in your estate documents.

What Could Go Wrong: You become disabled.

How This Works (A *Third* Modern Parable): Jean doesn't feel like she needs disability insurance. She drives carefully, looks both ways before crossing the street, and is a very safe skier. One day she's bicycling to work and out of nowhere a car hits her, causing her to miss work for four months while she struggles through rehabilitation. Jean has no emergency fund and no disability insurance and loses her house after she can't pay the mortgage for ninety days. She finds out later that it's disability, not being a deadbeat, that is the number one cause of foreclosure in America. Oh no, Jean! What are you going to do?

How to Protect Yourself (30 points possible):

- Disability coverage is a must. The chance of you becoming disabled is far higher than you might think. (10 points)
- Investigate how much disability coverage you have through work. While many people say, "I have it," few know how much. (10 points)

---

11 *Becoming your insurance agent's favorite client presumes your insurance agent came pre-installed with a sense of humor, which is only true for about 68 percent of insurance agents.*

- Insure yourself outside of work based on your expenses. How much would you need to pay your bills, minimum, if something were to happen? (10 points)

What Could Go Wrong: You die.

How This Works (A *Fourth* Modern Parable): Clark has twelve children and lives in a shoe. It's weird, but so is Clark. He doesn't believe in life insurance. Those people are all crooks just trying to take away his money. When Clark is killed in a mysterious incident involving toothpaste and a bedspread (long story), his kids have to move into a flip-flop. What will they do?

How to Protect Yourself (25 points possible . . . hey, points to die! Weird game . . .):

- Research what your burial costs will be. (5 points)
- Does someone rely on you for money? Don't assume the answer is no if you are a stay-at-home spouse or otherwise not working outside your home. If a job has economic value, someone will need to do it if that person passes away. Calculate how large that income stream needs to be. (10 points)
- What debts would your heirs need to pay off? Add up your debt that doesn't die with you. (10 points)

What Could Go Wrong: Someone else is hurt on your property.

How This Works (The Big Finale You're Looking For to This Whole "Modern Parable" Thingy): Maria Money Sweet is standing in her front lawn when she sees her neighbor, the same high-priced ambulance-chasing lawyer with the "We Sue Big!" billboards around town, helping his daughter learn to ride her bike. "Please don't fall in front of my house," Maria prays. Naturally, the little girl's foot slips off the pedals and she careens into Maria's bushes, which the lawyer later said were too close to the sidewalk. That sucks, Maria!

How to Protect Yourself (10 points possible):

- Formulate a plan for how you would cover a lawsuit if someone is hurt at your home or if someone sues you personally during a business transaction. Your plan might include umbrella liability coverage, but as long as you have put some thought into what to do, you're ahead of most people. (3 points)

- Ask your homeowner's insurance company how much it would cost to add umbrella liability coverage. (7 points)

A word about umbrella liability coverage: While we generally shy away from unnecessary insurances, this type of insurance is inexpensive. And like duct tape, it covers all the weird "what if" situations that might occur in life.

Insurance Bingo That Makes Joe Twitch Because It Doesn't Have the Correct Number of Squares!
(dauber not included)

You have valid car insurance ⎯⎯ 5 POINTS	You have homeowner's or renter's insurance ⎯⎯ 10 POINTS	You've researched your burial costs! ⎯⎯ 5 POINTS	You've formulated a plan for if you get sued ⎯⎯ 3 POINTS	You have some disability coverage ⎯⎯ 10 POINTS
You purchased disability insurance coverage outside of work ⎯⎯ 10 POINTS	You take care of recommended car mainte- nance on time ⎯⎯ 5 POINTS	Free Space/ Call Your Mom ⎯⎯ 2 POINTS (but no points awarded unless you tell her you love her)	You've installed alarms and/or motion detec- tors on your home ⎯⎯ 10 POINTS	You know how much debt you'll leave when you buy the farm ⎯⎯ 10 POINTS
You've taken a video tour of your possessions (sleeping cousin included) ⎯⎯ 10 POINTS	You've spoken to your homeowner's insurance provider about umbrella coverage ⎯⎯ 7 POINTS	You know how much disability coverage you have through work ⎯⎯ 10 POINTS	You calculate how much income your family will need if you kick the bucket ⎯⎯ 10 POINTS	You have a full emergency fund + high auto insurance deductible ⎯⎯ 5 POINTS

Score Your Board

20 points	Try harder. And call your mom. At least it will get you another 2 points.
30 points	Not quite lazy, but come on.
40 points	8th place local swim meet medal. Your parents even gave you a sarcastic "Hey, at least you're out here tryin'!"
50 points	Bless your heart.

60 points	Just over halfway done! Great job. Now go rock the rest of your insurance before you move on to the next chapter.
85 points	What's the level just below "ninja"? Clean up a few scraps and you're golden!
90 points	You're amazing. Can we hang out with you?
105 points or more	Perfect score? Seriously, there's no way. Mom says "Cheaters never prosper." Go back and quietly do the math again. Nobody will call you out. Promise.

Chapter 8A Benjamin Badge: Insurance Bingo Achievements

Check off each of the following achievements you have completed toward your Benjamin Badge after reading this subchapter:

☐ Bring Insurance Bingo to your next board game night. You'll be the life of the party.

☐ Set up savings into an emergency fund *and* segregate your emergency fund from your spending money.

☐ Evaluate your car insurance coverage. Did you find savings? If so, automatically add it to your savings account/emergency fund.

☐ Make a video of your home and possessions and store it off-site.

☐ Evaluate your disability coverage level. Could you survive on the proceeds? If not, create a strategy so that you have enough coverage.

☐ Buy life insurance to cover your post-death financial needs.

☐ Research options for how to afford a lawsuit, including an umbrella policy. Write out your plan.

Date You Completed the Chapter 8A Badge	Parent Signature (Putting your mom's John Hancock on your Benjamin stacking makes it official)

9

Estate Planning: The Final Frontier

TOOLS YOU'LL NEED:

* A crystal ball
* The phone number of a reputable estate attorney. Uncle Lester with his correspondence degree from 1-800-Lawyerz-4-U doesn't count.
* A list of your assets, debts, and relatives, ranked in order on a scale from "most favorite ever" at the top all the way down to "Cousin Eddie, who emptied the waste storage receptacle into your gutter while exclaiming, 'Waste storage receptacle's full!' "[12]

In 2002, while Emily was working her second stint in the Barnes & Noble retail book smelter, she discovered that the Dalai Lama had published a new book entitled *Advice on Dying: And Living a Better Life*. Since Emily's father had been flirting with Buddhism for the better part of twenty years, had read and enjoyed several other books by His Holiness, and, most importantly, was impossible to shop for, this seemed like the perfect Christmas present.

Imagine Emily's consternation when her father tore off the wrapping paper, read the title, and exclaimed, "I'm not *that* old!"

Emily is way smart and knows that the average person gets pretty

---

12 *Sadly, as this is a family-friendly book, we cannot say, "Shitter's full!" We regret any confusion this causes.*

damned squeamish about bucket-kicking, but she had assumed that a money and retirement expert like her father would be different. Jim Guy (aka "Dad") was a financial planner. He talked to clients all the time about the fact that they would die, although we don't *think* he literally started each meeting shouting, "You're going to die!"

The point is that Emily's dad could dig into intense, in-depth, hours-long conversations with clients about the 100 percent probability of their deaths and never turn a hair, but the moment the specter of Old Man Grim touched him, he lost every bit of objectivity. He had never even considered the possibility that it might happen sooner rather than later. Personal finance geeks call this syndrome "the immortality fallacy."[13] We all feel it. (Except for Joe. He's going to live forever, so he doesn't need to feel it.)

The idea that there is a future after you have left the party is tough to swallow. Things will happen after you're gone? Does not compute. Unfortunately, and there is really no funny way to say this, so you may want to sit down:

You are going to someday . . . be no more.

If it's easier, imagine John Cleese describing it thusly with increasing hysteria:

You will cease to be.

You will expire and go to meet your maker.

Bereft of life, you will rest in peace.

Your metabolic processes will be history.

You will be off the twig.

You will kick the bucket, shuffle off this mortal coil, run down the curtain, and join the bleeding choir invisible.

You will someday, gentle reader, be an ex–Benjamin stacker.

Now, there are three ways to deal with this information:

1. Ignore it. Continue along in blissful ignorance, making no plans for the day the bus comes calling.

---

13 *No one calls it this other than Emily.*

2. Freak out. Make it fun! Emily occasionally feels compelled to stand up in a crowded theater and shout, "We're all gonna die!" when her existential angst is at a fever pitch.

3. Plan ahead. You can't change the facts, but having an estate plan in place can ensure that when your day comes, it is as easy as possible for your loved ones, while allowing you to leave a legacy.

If you've reached this here ninth chapter of this tome, you know which of these three options a champion Benjamin stacker will choose. Another benefit of planning ahead for your future two-step with Thanatos is that you can always fall back to either ignoring it or freaking out about it *afterward*.

Estate-Planning Documents You Need

Creating a robust estate plan is a little like making Thanksgiving dinner. Like your Thanksgiving table, there are certain things that have to be part of the plan, while other parts will depend on your particular family. (For instance, for regional reasons Emily has never completely understood, her family eats sauerkraut on Thanksgiving.)

Check it out:

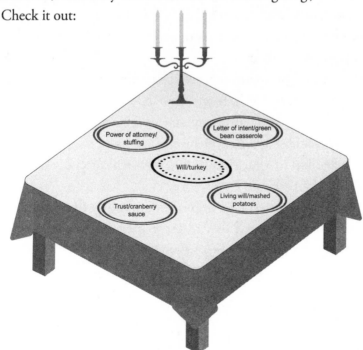

The will is the center of your estate plan. Just as you're contractually obligated to eat turkey on Turkey Day, an estate plan without a will is nothing at all.

Next are your living will and power of attorney, which we think of as the mashed potatoes and stuffing. While you can technically have a Thanksgiving meal without them, who'd want that?

Then there is the letter of intent, the green bean casserole of an estate plan. While it can provide some needed balance to a Thanksgiving table and estate plan, many people won't notice if it's not there.

Finally we come to the trusts. These are like cranberry sauce in that some people will consider it absolutely essential, whereas others find it unnecessary to the point of side-eyeing your aunt Tudy, who insists on bringing it and bitches when nobody touches the stuff. Trusts are also like cranberry sauce in that there is an almost infinite variety of flavors to choose from, from the more basic out-of-a-can testamentary trusts to the elaborate citrus-infused whole-berry credit shelter trusts.

A Will

Dying without one of these in place will make your heirs' lives much more difficult. Without a will, it's the state rather than you who gets to decide who gets your stuff.

That's right: instead of your bowling trophies getting passed along to the competitors you beat and your beer bottle collection going to the Boys & Girls Club where you volunteered, the state gets to choose where those priceless mementos go—and they will generally send everything to your next of kin, who will probably just throw them away. Horrifying.

Even if your nearest and dearest know your wishes, they won't necessarily follow them if they're not written down. (They may not do so even if your wishes *are* written down, which we'll get to in a moment, but you've got no cards to play without a will.) In short, your will is all about telling the state and your loved ones how to distribute your property and assets. (Wills are only occasionally used to name the deceased's murderer.) Specifically, you can use your will to plan ahead for:

- Who will be responsible for your minor children, pets, and/or dependent anime body pillows after your death.
- Who will receive your assets, including money, investments, businesses, Bitcoin, bank vaults of Franklin Mint collectibles that you're strategically holding until they regain their value, real estate, etc.
- Who will receive your stuff.

It's not enough to have your will written to your specifications. You also need to appoint someone who will make sure it is followed. This person is known as the executor, and choosing the right executor is an Important Decision. Your executor needs to do the following:

1. Know where to find your will and other estate-planning documents.

2. Manage all of your assets until it's time to distribute them to your heirs.

3. File your will with the probate court. This is the branch of the legal world in charge of making sure wills comply with the law. The probate court also handles contacting beneficiaries and heirs named in estate documents, so the poor executor is not stuck sending carrier pigeons, semaphores, and smoke signals to the more difficult-to-track-down beneficiaries.

4. Close your credit cards and accounts and let Uncle Sam, Goliath Bank, the IRS, and Big Brother know that you have bought the farm.

5. Create a bank account specifically for your estate. Yep, you may be dead, but your bills and payments live on. Not only may your estate need to pay some of your final expenses, but you may also be owed money, such as a last paycheck or stock dividends—and your regular bank account can't take care of those bills or payments.

6. Pay for continuing expenses using funds from your estate. The world does not come to a grinding halt when you pass away (well, it does for you, but you know what we mean), so your executor may have to pay for things like your mortgage and utilities for your haunted mansion until your heirs have completed their global hunt to solve your final and greatest mystery to determine which of them will receive your entire inheritance.

7. Pay your debts. While some debts, like federal student loans, are discharged by your death, your estate will still be on the hook to pay off anything else that was solely in your name.

8. Pay your taxes. Yep, not even death can get the IRS off your back. You will owe a final income tax return, covering the period from January 1 of that year to the date of your death.

9. Oversee the distribution of your property. If your will specifies that your heirs cannot collect their inheritance unless they embark on a hot-air balloon journey in the company of a llama named Sophia, it is the executor's job to ensure that this happens, check the box, and send out the money.

Here's the thing about executors: they are the ones who will be responsible for ensuring your wishes are followed. Executors-for-hire are available (Have Notary—Will Travel), in which case your estate will pay them to perform their duties. But in most cases, you will probably choose a spouse, friend, family member, or fellow member of your knitting circle. It should be someone you know well enough to share where your important estate-planning documents are kept (and which folders to delete off your laptop before your mother sees them), and they need to be able to handle the time commitment. So don't appoint an executor without asking first.

The person should be someone who won't yield to pressure and is comfortable with disagreements. Your executor may be seen as a jerk because they're going to follow your directions explicitly, rather than do what your nearest and dearest say you would have wanted. Don't choose an executor who will bow to pressure from beneficiaries or interested parties. Money does strange things to people, and Emily and Joe have both seen big fights erupt after an executor let too many family members give opinions about "what we should do."

Joe's Mom on Getting an Estate Attorney

Should you have a heart surgeon perform that surgery? Sure, you should. This isn't heart surgery, though, is it, and some FinTech companies in this space have created some really good documents that work in every state and will deliver a stripped-down, basic will. Better yet, they'll do it for my favorite price: nothing. Of course, the catch is that they want to sell you other doodads, like life insurance and bank accounts. Still, this could make estate planning free and simple for you.

But if your financial or family situation is complex (like my second-cousin Eunice, who married that guy who'd already been married three times and had those rotten kids by his second wife? You remember her. Sweet lady, but com-pli-cated life), the surer I am that you'll need more than those boilerplate options. If you want your loved ones engaging in a knockdown, drag-out fight over your grave, that's fine. But I think it's a better idea for everyone involved (except maybe those confidence men working at the Law Office of That's Mine, This Is Yours!) to have an estate attorney help you draw up your plan.

When you see the bill, you'll know this isn't always cheap, so consider it an investment in your legacy as a wise, fair, and loving progenitor. Your family may never thank you, but you won't have to return to haunt anyone, either.

Living Will and Power of Attorney

Your living will and power of attorney (POA) aren't sufficient for an estate plan, but your estate plan isn't complete without them.

The living will is also known as an advanced medical directive, and it's the paperwork you have in place to outline exactly what you want in terms of medical care in case you're incapacitated and can't speak for yourself.

Living wills can pair nicely with a medical power of attorney designation (which is different from a financial power of attorney). The person you have chosen as your medical POA will advocate for you if you are unable to communicate—because of illness, injury, or witch's curse. Since not all states allow advanced medical directives to cover all medical procedures (no, the living will saying you want breast augmentation should you be unable to advocate for yourself is unlikely to be followed, Joe), having a medical power of attorney can ensure someone is making decisions based on what they know you would want.

Your medical power of attorney should probably be a different person than your financial power of attorney. The financial POA will handle decisions about your money if you are mentally or physically unable to, and since they have control over your finances, you might want to avoid making this person the same as your medical POA, in case they turn out to be a POS.

The person you designate as your financial power of attorney should be granted "durable power of attorney." Otherwise they may not be able to start making decisions on your behalf if you are declared legally incompetent (a more formal process than someone pointing at you and declaring, "INCOMPETENT!"). That's because a nondurable power of attorney is considered to be in effect only while you are compos mentis.[14] Their power to make decisions on your behalf will expire the moment someone brings you into a court of law, points at you, and declares "INCOMPETENT!" And that won't do at all.

---

14 Latin for "enjoying Mentos," because legal types think that anyone who doesn't delight in the Freshmaker is clearly incapable of making decisions for themselves.

If you make it clear in your legal designation paperwork that the power of attorney privileges either remain in effect after or are triggered by the legal declaration of your incompetence, then you can rest assured that your POA can make decisions after the head injury that ends your brilliant career in podcasting from your mother's basement. Even if you never recover your wits or your ability to say the letter "W," your POA can continue to act on your behalf until your death.

Letter of Intent

The letter of intent is the document you've seen in the movies that usually starts with the words "If you're reading this, that means I'm dead." It's an informal and informational document that outlines your preferences for things that may or may not appear in your other estate-planning documents. Some of the common things included in a letter of intent include:

- Funeral and burial arrangements, including which Snoop Dogg track you wish to be playing during the services.
- Financial account information, including passwords, account numbers, and which Caribbean countries will accept anything under your name as viable credit.
- Passwords to your digital existence so your family won't be locked out of your hilarious and endearing TikTok videos.
- How you would like your assets used. For instance, if you are leaving $10,000 to each of your niblings, you can state in your letter of intent that it is your hope that each will use the money to start a new sixty-person dance troupe.
- How you want your personal stuff distributed. While you can specify this kind of thing in your will, too, many people will write out these plans in their letter of intent and focus on financial assets in the will, lawyer's fees being what they are.

Unlike a will, a letter of intent doesn't require legal wording or witnesses to be valid, so you can write or update one anytime. Your letter of intent needs to complement your will, because having contradictory instructions is a sure way to cause confusion and resentment in your heirs—but know that your will is the ultimate authority.

That said, courts will refer to letters of intent if there is any question of what the deceased would prefer that is not made clear by the legally binding documents.

Trusts

Here we come to the portion of estate planning that may, at first glance, seem to be made only for the Mr. and Ms. Moneybags set. That's because a trust is a type of financial vehicle where a third party (known as the trustee) holds on to assets on Mr. and Ms. Moneybags's behalf to save them for a beneficiary chosen by the Moneybagses.

The trusty trustee doesn't just have to feel trustworthy—they are legally required to be a fiduciary, meaning they put the trust and the beneficiary's interests above their own. So putting money into a trust means it will be there and ready for the beneficiary at the proper time.

There are a number of reasons why those of us with modest Benjamin stacks might still want a trust. Trusts can provide you with:

- **Control over your assets from beyond the grave.** Putting a trust in place means you get to decide when and how your beneficiaries can receive inheritances.
- **Protection from overspending.** Trusts let you determine a specific chronology of when your money will be distributed. If you have any reason to worry your heirs will run through your cash like it's water, a trust can help protect them from their own "Let's buy a boat!" impulses.
- **Avoiding probate.** The probate process, in addition to sounding like what a frog says in Canada ("probate! probate!"), can be a long and sometimes expensive process, costing up to 6 to 10 percent of the value of the estate. Having money set aside in

trust means that it passes to your heirs outside of probate.

- **Tax relief.** You can avoid some of Uncle Sam's sticky fingers, because trusts aren't subject to gift or estate taxes.

There are different types of trusts that might meet your post-death needs. If you're at all worried about your estate plan, whether your beneficiaries will blow through your hard-earned money, or if someone who'll inherit your empire has special needs, you should meet with an estate attorney about setting up a trust. While they can be somewhat expensive to draft, you'll save yourself from sleepless nights and your heirs from financial nightmares.

Inheritance Theft: When the Trustee Isn't Trustworthy

We like to have fun here in Mom's basement with the whole *Stacking Benjamins* crew, but inheritance theft is no joking matter. It's time for us to get real about a subject none of us likes to think about in this Very Special ~~Episode~~ Sidebar.

Remember that you will not be there to make sure your executor and trustee follow your wishes, and the gears of the legal system grind slowly.

Emily experienced this firsthand after her father (whom you met at the beginning of this chapter) passed away in 2013. Mr. Guy had a will plus a trust, which stipulated that Emily and her sister were to inherit his assets after the death of his surviving spouse. Though that should have ensured his wishes were followed, all of his assets were under the control of a single person who acted as executor and trustee. That person ignored her fiduciary duty (and Mr. Guy's clearly stated wishes) and ran through nearly all the assets in less than six years. Because of the slow nature of the court system, the money was pretty much gone by the time Emily and her sister were able to make their case in front of a judge— almost six years to the day after their father's death.

Mr. Guy fell victim to a common issue: refusing to believe that the worst could happen. It never occurred to him that he might die at age sixty-two, nor did it occur to him that his executor/trustee would prove untrustworthy. The result was that his daughters saw their inheritance stolen and Emily spent time angry when she would have preferred to be grieving.

This is exactly why we recommend that everyone look at their estate plan critically. Ask yourself, "What could go wrong?" and be fierce in your refusal to assume that everything will be fine. Punch holes in the plan. Even if it's hard to imagine that anyone you trust would thwart your wishes, make plans as if everyone is just one traumatic brain injury away from refusing to do what you've outlined.

And finally, never, ever, ever give one single person total control of your assets. Your heirs will be glad you didn't.

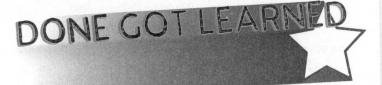

So Why Is This Important?

Even if you plan to give Methuselah a run for his money, you need to have a plan in place for your money and stuff after you put on that pine overcoat. You can't take it with you (although you can line your casket with Benjamins, provided you have an undertaker you trust and a burning need to give your family the bird), and death + money has a nasty habit of bringing out the worst in people. Rather than leave your family and friends to squabble over your sweet stacks of Benjamins, make sure you've put your plans into writing.

After a death in the family, it's on the heirs to figure out where to find all the passwords, wills, trusts, and car keys their loved one left behind. Abby Schneiderman and Adam Seifer wanted to make this stressful time easier, so they created a company called Everplans and wrote a book called *In Case You Get Hit by a Bus: How to Organize Your Life Now for When You're Not Around Later* to discuss how to joyfully organize for a future without you in it. Here's a portion of their conversation with Joe about the weirdly satisfying task of getting your affairs in order.

ON CREATING A HOME OPERATING SYSTEM AND LEAVING CLUES FOR YOUR HEIRS: A CONVERSATION WITH ABBY SCHNEIDERMAN AND ADAM SEIFER

Joe: *You wrote, "This isn't really a dark subject. This is about life. This is much more about freedom and happiness than it is about darkness."*

Abby: *What we realized is that getting your affairs in order, getting organized, making sure that your family has access to everything that they need, isn't about death. It's about life because you can sleep better at night now, knowing that you've done everything you can for yourself and for your family.*

Joe: *I was talking to a friend last night about a professional billiards player that has been diagnosed with terminal cancer. I had this morbid thought,*

Abby, that really, we're all terminal. We just don't know when the end is going to happen. So if we get hit by a bus, I'd better be ready now.

Adam: *We'd like to think of it as something that ought to be just part of people's ordinary day-to-day lives. When you go to buy a car seat for your kids, you're not thinking about accidents and injuries, are you? It's just an everyday thing to do because you're a good parent and that's what good parents do. And we think this type of planning is really the same kind of thing. You don't have to address your mortality in order to just get your stuff together.*

Abby: *You hear stories all the time in the news about a major celebrity in a speeding car accident or a helicopter crash. You never know. So it's just a good idea to make sure key pieces of information are documented and made accessible. So somebody in your life knows where it all is.*

The original idea [for Everplans] came about when I was planning my wedding and I was using all of these online sites out there, like the knot.com and Martha Stewart's websites. I was using their apps and their guides and their calendars and their checklists every single day and I don't know why my brain went from marriage to death, but I started to think about "life's over . . . what's next?" But are there any resources out there that are going to guide me through the rest of my life planning in the same way? And I said, "Adam, who's helping people deal with death?" He said, "Somebody is. It's the biggest life stage. Not everybody gets married. Not everybody has kids, but everybody has to deal with this. At some point, somebody is doing it." So we started looking into it, and we were pretty shocked and appalled that there was absolutely nothing going on in this space. We decided to change that. The original idea for Everplans was to create the first modern consumer company in what we now call life and legacy planning.

Joe: *You have a great story about this guy in his garage.*

Abby: *This was a story that we were told by a former colleague who said that she was in her dad's garage. She said to him, "If something were to happen, where do I find information?" He said, "Oh, you know, over here on the garage wall is the password written for the lockbox." How would she possibly* *have known to go look on the side of the wall, where he had written the password? It was just crazy. What if someone had painted? We all have our own stories about what goes wrong when you're storing important passwords.*

Joe: *Adam, is that the biggest problem that you guys see? Heirs, beneficiaries, friends don't know where the passwords are?*

Adam: *That's rapidly becoming the biggest problem, especially now where people have, I think on average, over 130 different online accounts. And you're supposed to use a different password for each and every one of them. A lot of people don't, but it starts to add up. Then you run into this other issue where a lot of the sites make you do two-factor authentication, where they send you a text message, and if you don't have the unlock code for somebody's phone, you might get shut out of everything in their whole life. We are maniacal about recommending that people make sure they share some key passwords, like their unlock code for their phone or their key email address. We are also really big proponents of password managers.*

There's a bunch of them out there and they organize your passwords, and what's great is they help you to actually choose random passwords for each site. So you're not reusing passwords over and over.

Joe: *Is this a struggle, Abby, to get older people to use a password manager?*

Abby: *Definitely. I think the good news is that the password managers are doing a better and better job all the time at making their interfaces more user-friendly so that all people can use it.*

And I do think it's overwhelming for older people who are not necessarily trusting of services like password managers to think about the idea that one company is going to have access to all their critical passwords, but Adam can talk more about the security aspects of this.

There's so much innovation happening in this space.

Adam: *I was actually able to get my mom using one. I'm still working on my dad. And not only did it change her life because she was not* *constantly forgetting passwords or she wasn't just using one single password everywhere, but it changed my life because every time I had to help her with some sort of computer or technology problem or getting into a site, I had access to all the passwords, too. I could get in there with her and get to the bottom of things really quickly.*

Joe: *You talk about creating a home operating system. What does that look like, guys? How does that work?*

Adam: *In most families—certainly in mine—my wife and I, we divide and conquer, right? She's in charge of certain things, and I'm in charge of certain things.*

I don't even think about the things that she's in charge of, which means if something happened, I would have no idea how certain things are set up. And so for instance, I'm in charge of the plumber, the electrician, the HVAC, and the alarm system. What I've done is, I've actually used my plan to record all the key information about those vendors and about those systems, including even just simple stuff like the master password for the internet router and the Wi-Fi. If something happens to me, she isn't pulling her hair out, trying to deal with all of these little bitty daily life things that can really add up and make life miserable.

Joe: *I hear from people when loved ones pass away that it's not the big things. It's that mountain of little things that get you.*

Abby: *A dear family friend whose husband passed away unexpectedly a few months ago was saying he actually had a lot of planning done.*

He had his power of attorney. He had all of his financial accounts and assets properly organized, and she knew where everything was. It was all buttoned up. The one thing that was eating her now was that he was the one who changed all of the lightbulbs in their house and they have apparently some sort of special lightbulb they used everywhere.

She said, "I have no idea where he bought that lightbulb. And I don't know what he did." He was in charge of the lightbulbs. She said, "That's the thing that's keeping me up at night." Our goal is to try to get people to look around their home or think about what are the things in the household that you're the one who takes care of. If for whatever reason you weren't able to take care of those things anymore, would the other people in your household be totally lost?

Joe: *Where should people start with their estate plan if they haven't done it yet?*

Adam: *A lot of people think that wills are just for rich people or people with a lot of assets. One of the overlooked reasons why people do wills is because it's where you name guardians for your children. You don't have to be old and you don't have to be rich to need a will to make sure that you name a guardian for your children.*

If you don't do it, some judge in some court will end up doing it. If something happens and you know . . . we've all got crazy brothers or sisters-in-law or aunts who we absolutely would not want our children ending up with. It's worth the time to sit down and do your will no matter what age you are.

Joe: *When you were talking about that, Adam, one person came to my mind. I'm like, nope, wouldn't have wanted that person to watch our kids. What about our younger listeners that don't have kids yet? Is there a piece of estate planning that's really important for them, too?*

Adam: *Yeah. When you turn eighteen, everybody should do a HIPAA authorization form, naming your parents as people that can see your medical records. A lot of parents don't think about this, but your kids go away. College. Life. If something happens to them and they go to the hospital, you can't call the hospital to get any information about their condition, unless they filled out a HIPAA authorization form.*

And then on top of that, while you're at it, you might as well do a healthcare proxy that names your parents, or one of your parents, as a healthcare proxy, so they can actually make medical decisions for you if something happens.

Abby: *These kinds of things are not necessarily even estate planning. It's just being a responsible person. We call it adulting, because it's not necessarily that you need these things because you're dead. You might just need these things because you got hit by a bus or you're on a trip around the world and you can't get back or you're stuck on a cruise because of COVID.*

You just never know when you're going to need access to important information, so we try to get people thinking about all of those types of things, whether it's legal documents that they need, or, you know, what's the Wi-Fi password to your apartment.

Joe: *Yeah. It all dovetails together.*

Abby and Adam's advice in a nutshell: Making sure your family knows exactly how to take care of the things that you are currently responsible for is one of the most loving actions you can take in the here and now.

Chapter 9 Benjamin Badge: Estate-Planning Achievements

Check off each of the following achievements you have completed toward your Benjamin Badge after reading this chapter:

❑ Write your will.

If you have a simple estate and are lacking in the kinds of relatives who will wrestle over your casket for ownership of your vintage chipped bedpan from the Korean War, you may be able to get away with using a free or inexpensive online template.

For more complex estates, larger piles of assets, or "complicated" family situations (including but not limited to blended families, special needs dependents, or family businesses), consult an estate attorney for the appropriate plan.

❏ Choose an executor, guardians (for minor children or pets), and trustees for your estate plan.

❏ Set up financial and medical powers of attorney.

❏ Write your living will.

❏ Write your letter of intent.

❏ Determine if you need a trust, and if you do, ask your estate attorney to help you draw it up.

Date You Completed the Chapter 9 Badge	Parent Signature (Putting your mom's John Hancock on your Benjamin stacking makes it official)

PART 4

STACKING BENJAMINS ON TOP OF YOUR OTHER BENJAMINS:

BUYING SOME SECURITY AND COMFORT

*Money can't buy happiness, but it can buy you
the kind of misery you prefer.*
—AUTHOR UNKNOWN

10

Fighting Fear and Creating a Benjamin-Stacking Mindset

TOOLS YOU'LL NEED:

- Your brain (switch off your tactical brain and turn on the philosophical side)
- A leather couch for psychoanalysis
- One Sigmund Freud bobblehead (a Jung doll may suffice)

The Cost of Fear

As a famous meme-writer on the internet once penned, "The only thing we have to fear is fear itself . . . and ZOMBIES."

Fear is often the root of stacking-Benjamins difficulties. Happily, zombies aren't related to your financial woes—yet.

Joe has often talked publicly about how much fear has played a role in his life, and it's the same for many of us. Fear is behind the feeling that you can never have what you want. Fear is what drives you to overspend "just this once" because [insert totally valid excuse here]. Fear whispers in your ear that there will never be enough money and that you might as well accept your Benjamin-less fate. Fear is also the reason you hold on to those *Knight Rider* trading cards, that fondue pot you've never used, and the gym membership you've thought about using. *Someday* . . .

Fear is the opposite of a wealth mindset. While wealth mindsets drive you forward, fear keeps you wanting what you think you can't have and hoarding things that will never make you happy. While you may always feel fear, there's no need to let it paralyze you. You are about to embark on an adventure toward an "I can have it all" attitude, which is the first step in . . . having it all. This chapter will teach you the secrets behind a Benjamin-stacking wealth mindset. Master them, and you can become the sort of champion Benjamin stacker who considers a Mr. Monopoly–style top hat and monocle normal daywear.

Fair warning, though: this is a chapter that the "just give me the quick way to riches" crowd thinks is too much "woo-woo" and not enough "hard info." It's true that we're about to start mucking around with your thought processes. From Joe's time as an advisor, he knows what expert after expert will tell you: *this* is the place to begin if you truly want riches in your life.

But if this is the place to begin, why the heck didn't we, ahem, begin here?

Any guide to Benjamin stacking must start with introductory-level money-management techniques. What good is a better mindset if you don't have the tools to take advantage of it? If you expect to compete in the world of simple dollars-and-cents/red-ink-and-black-ink/just-don't-buy-stuff-you-can't-afford financial skills, then mastering the basics is imperative. But learning to cut costs and trim a fat (not phat) budget is all 101-level stuff. It won't help you grow wealth.

A wealth mindset, on the other hand, is doctorate-level work.

If you're going to grow rich, you'll need to master your emotions. These are emotional times. Markets rise and fall. You'll doubt yourself when you're climbing out of credit card debt or trying to convince a friend to hold you accountable. This simple advice is beyond difficult for most of us, because we are so danged human about things. We just can't help but bring feelings into nearly every decision. That's why, at one point or another in your life, you've likely found yourself making some truly bizarre money mistakes that you can't easily explain with a color-coded spreadsheet.

For instance, in a move that at the time seemed brilliant, Emily once strode into a tattoo parlor in Columbus, Ohio's Short North district and plopped $150 in cash—direct from an ATM down the street—

onto the counter. The time had come to apply ink to something that had been bothering her for some time: her penchant for leaking tears.

At this point, I'm going to let Emily take over telling this ~~embarrassing~~ important story about poor money management. Take it away, Emily!

This is going to ruin my image as a personal finance expert, isn't it?

Yes, Emily, it will. Tell it anyway.

(Sigh.) All right, here goes.

I was very close with my grandmother. I'd talk to her about everything, including my boyfriend, whom she called a "complete jabroni who wasn't good enough for my Emily." I liked him anyway, but I loved Grandma Ruthie.

Like all things, the relationship with the boyfriend went kaput, and despite his jabroni-ness, I shed a tear or two over him at the time of our ignominious end.

But when Ruthie died weeks later, I found myself *really* upset about the tears I'd wasted on what's-his-name and resolved to save future tears for things that really mattered, such as losing Grandma. I decided to have a big teardrop inked on my right shoulder. Maybe that would remind me not to cry over things that didn't matter. Maybe it would make it clear how special my grandmother was. All I knew at the time was that it had to get done now and that it would cost $150.

There are a few important moments in life. Decisions that you should slow down and think about. Permanent decisions that are going to stay with you. Marriage, the college you'll attend, job offers, and permanent ink are just a few things you should seriously ponder before jumping in.

So if you're thinking that I spent a long time mulling over the possibility of getting a tattoo, you're smarter than I was. Because I got myself that tattoo just a few days after I cooked up the idea. All told, it took me between twelve and fifteen minutes after leaving the tattoo parlor before I wondered what in flaming heck I had been thinking. Not only did I now have a weirdly stylized teardrop on my body, but I had also blasted an enormous hole in my precarious early-twentysomething budget. Great work, future financial expert!

In my grief, I'd made one of the least-thought-out decisions of my life. Worse? A few weeks later, while watching a film about gangs that was definitely not PG, I learned that my chosen design had another meaning: teardrop tattoos are a gang reference to *murder*. Each tear represents a person the inked individual has offed.

In gangland, I'd signaled that I'd whacked Grandma.

(Editor's note: Here's the photo of Emily's awesomely ridiculous ink to prove that this story is the whole truth. She would like to clarify that this happened in 2002, when the internet was still kerosene powered and Google was not yet the go-to resource for determining the gang-related origins of one's tattoo designs. However, she did find it useful for getting rowdy classrooms to behave, since her students assumed their mild-mannered English teacher must be a badass.)

the mark of a
stone-cold killer

While your ridiculous money choices may have nothing to do with tattoos, grandmothers, jabronis, tears, or gang-related murder, there is no doubt you, too, have a "What was I thinking?" moment. Make enough decisions like these, and it's the difference between stacks and stacks o' Benjamins, and collections of pocket lint. So let's do a little digging into your psyche (it won't hurt, we promise) and start learning just what it is you think about money.

Let's Klontzify Your Money

No matter how hard you try, it is impossible to separate the way you use money from how you feel about it. No one in the world is perfectly rational and Klontzulent about money—but your irrational reaction is not exactly like anyone else's irrational reaction, because your financial beliefs grew from experiences in your life—and specifically in your childhood.

The financial psychologist Dr. Bradley Klontz (whose awesome name we drew attention to *before* we even introduced him! Brilliant writing!), a founder of the Financial Psychology Institute and one of the top researchers in the field of money psychology, calls these deep-seated beliefs your "money scripts." Scripts are the stories you tell yourself. They are rooted in how money was viewed and treated in your family, and they are often reinforced by life experiences.

Emily's parents taught her to respect and honor her elders. So she told herself that spending money was a way to show love for the family matriarch, which is how she ended up with a very non-Klontzonculus gangland tattoo.

Emily's money script told her that spending money to show love would be a good way of dealing with her grief. Instead, she got a tattoo with an ambiguous meaning, several weeks of peanut butter sandwiches as penance for spending her grocery money this way, and a slight advantage in classroom management during her short-lived teaching career.

The unique experiences and lessons that made up your childhood have helped to shape your personal money scripts. But even though your money scripts are idiosyncratic to your Klontzibilities, they tend to fall into one of four categories, according to Dr. Klontz and his research partner Dr. Sonya Britt.

1. Money Avoidance

Based on the idea that money is a source of anxiety, fear, or disgust, people following this script believe that living with less is a kind of virtue. Common scripts in this category include "Rich people did unsavory things to become rich and don't deserve their wealth" and "Good people are above caring about money."

Emily's script about showing love for a family member by spending money was a form of money avoidance. By getting the tattoo, she was making a statement that her personal care and feeding—her money concerns—were less important than honoring her grandmother.

2. Money Worship
People with money-worship scripts believe that money can lead to happiness and fulfillment. These folks may think things like "Poor and happy are a contradiction in terms" or "There's no such thing as being too rich."

3. Money Status
These scripts tend to confuse "net worth" with "self-worth." Those who follow money-status scripts believe things like "My success is measured by my income" or "My possessions reflect my importance, so I will only buy or own the best."

4. Money Vigilance
The money vigilant like to keep a careful eye on their finances because they believe things like "It's important to save for a rainy day" or "Always get the best deal on any purchase." Individuals with these scripts tend to have a good handle on their spending and work hard to save.

How Do You Look at Your Money?
You may follow scripts from one of these four categories, but it's more likely that you have several overlapping ones. Avoidance and vigilance often correlate, for example. If you are uncomfortable with having money, you may still try to keep careful track of it. Similarly, money-worship and money-status beliefs tend to overlap, since believing that money is the key to happiness is often related to the belief that your self-worth is determined by your net worth.

Some people carry money scripts that seem diametrically opposed, such as money avoidance and money worship. But folks who believe that money is bad or evil may secretly want to have more.

You can begin to determine your money scripts by taking the Klontz Money Script Inventory:

KLONTZ MONEY SCRIPT INVENTORY

SCORING SCALE: 1 Strongly Disagree   **2** Disagree   **3** Disagree a Little
4 Agree a Little   **5** Agree   **6** Strongly Agree

Money Avoidance	Money Worship	Money Status	Money Vigilance
1. I do not deserve a lot of money when others have less than me.	1. More money will make you happier.	1. I will not buy something unless it is new (e.g., car, house).	1. It is important to save for a rainy day.
1 2 3 4 5 6	1 2 3 4 5 6	1 2 3 4 5 6	1 2 3 4 5 6
2. Rich people are greedy.	2. You can never have enough money.	2. Your self-worth equals your net worth.	2. You should always look for the best deal, even if it takes more time.
1 2 3 4 5 6	1 2 3 4 5 6	1 2 3 4 5 6	1 2 3 4 5 6
3. It is not okay to have more than you need.	3. Money would solve all my problems.	3. Poor people are lazy.	3. If you cannot pay cash for something, you should not buy it.
1 2 3 4 5 6	1 2 3 4 5 6	1 2 3 4 5 6	1 2 3 4 5 6
4. People get rich by taking advantage of others.	4. Money buys freedom.	4. If something is not considered the "best," it is not worth buying.	4. I would be a nervous wreck if I did not have an emergency fund.
1 2 3 4 5 6	1 2 3 4 5 6	1 2 3 4 5 6	1 2 3 4 5 6
Your Score_____	Your Score_____	Your Score_____	Your Score_____
If you scored a 9+ ... Money avoiders believe that money is bad or that they do not deserve it. They believe that wealthy people are greedy and corrupt, and that there is virtue in living with less money. Money avoidance is associated with ignoring bank statements, increased risk of overspending, financial enabling, financial dependence, hoarding, and having trouble sticking to a budget.	**If you scored a 9+ ...** At their core, money worshipers are convinced that the key to happiness and the solution to their problems is to have more money. At the same time, they believe that one can never have enough. Money worshipers are more likely to have lower income, lower net worth, and credit card debt. They are more likely to spend compulsively, hoard possessions, and put work ahead of family. They may give money to others when they can't afford it and be financially dependent on others.	**If you scored a 9+ ...** Money status seekers see net worth and self-worth as synonymous. They pretend to have more money than they do, and as a result are at risk of overspending. They believe that if they live a virtuous life, the universe will take care of their financial needs. They tend to grow up in families with lower socioeconomic status. People with money status beliefs are more likely to be compulsive spenders or gamblers, be dependent on others financially, and lie to their spouses about spending.	**If you scored a 9+ ...** The money vigilant are alert, watchful, and concerned about their financial welfare. They believe it is important to save and for people to work for their money and not be given handouts. They are less likely to buy on credit. They also have a tendency to be anxious and secretive about their financial status. While vigilance encourages saving and frugality, excessive wariness or anxiety could keep someone from enjoying the benefits and sense of security that money can provide.

(Used with permission from Dr. Bradley Klontz.)

5 CLEAR SIGNS YOUR MONEY SCRIPT ISN'T WORKING

1. You protect yourself from any financial information that might ruin your day, such as your bank balance, your credit card statement, your retirement account, how much money is in your wallet, or the bill for your son's braces. You've engineered a complex system to avoid this information, including never opening mail, holding your hand over the screen at the ATM once you've entered your PIN, setting up a separate email account to receive statements and bills, and, in extreme circumstances, putting a bag over your head.

2. You have turned down offers of better pay because you would hate to ruin the nobility of the work you do by getting a higher salary. Your car may be held together by baling twine, your retirement account may be nothing more than a whisper on the breeze, your home may be a studio apartment that you share with three other people and several cockroaches, only some of whom pay rent—but hey, at least you're not a sellout.

3. You have invested in any of the following sure winners: Bolivian tin mining, penguin farming, lunar real estate, volcano insurance, or Beanie Babies. Despite having lost your shirt many times to these sorts of "investments," your rallying cry is the ever-popular "This time is different!!"

4. Your checking account reads as though you thought *Brewster's Millions* was a documentary.

5. You purchase canned tuna fish for cats for personal consumption, despite actually having the 79¢ necessary to purchase a can of StarKist or Bumble Bee.

From Scarcity to Abundance

A thread you'll notice running throughout all of these scripts is the fear of not having enough. This concern is probably the root of your disordered financial behavior, no matter which money script you follow.

For instance, living with a scarcity mindset causes:

- The money avoidant to believe they do not deserve to be rich, since that would mean others would have to go without.
- Money worshipers to throw Benjamins at risky investments because of their fear of never, ever truly attaining wealth.
- Status seekers to overspend, because they fear that they will otherwise never be able to have the things and experiences they want if they have to save for them.
- The money vigilant to be terrified of spending any money because they worry that any money out of their pocket will be gone forever.

Clearly, these beliefs will always stunt your ability to grow your wealth. If you are afraid to be rich for fear of what will happen to others, afraid to delay gratification for fear of never getting to experience the best things in life, or afraid to do anything other than save your Benjamins, you'll miss out on many of the riches of a life well lived.

We know we've brought you lots of good news so far, but this may be the best yet: it's possible to switch your thinking from scarcity to abundance, which can help you develop the wealth mindset you need. We present to you:

Three Steps to Abundance

1. Remember That You, Not Your Money, Can Survive the Zombie Apocalypse

Counting on your money to handle catastrophes isn't giving power to the right thing. While having a load of cash is a nice start, don't ask your money to handle grisly ghouls emerging from fresh graves—or, and maybe slightly more likely, market corrections, job losses, or medical bills that may cause you financial heartburn. *You* are behind the wheel when something goes wrong, not your money.

You are the one who can handle whatever life (or, in the case of zombies, death) throws at you.

Developing a wealth mindset is about recognizing you are enough, even if your wallet is lighter than you'd like it to be. You have the talent, the tenacity, the braaains, and the color-coding and office organizational skills necessary to survive the zombie apocalypse and any other financial hardship that comes your way.

2. Appreciate What You Already Have

It's easy to get caught up in the wonderful things you wish you had or wonderful experiences you wish you could afford. Just paging through an office supply catalog can get Emily salivating over the organization systems and high-tech paper clips she does not yet own. And don't get Joe started on board games he doesn't yet have.

Concentrating on what you don't have is a sure way to never feel like you have enough. There are always new gadgets and gizmos to buy, not to mention adventures aplenty to experience, and focusing on the ones you don't have will make you miserable. Instead, recognize just how much you already do have.

Joe's Mom on Gratitude

Just think: if you live on more than $10 a day, you're in the top 20 percent of Earth's inhabitants when it comes to wealth. You've got a roof over your head, clean water to drink, the opportunity and ability to read hilarious books on personal finance, and enough stationery supplies to last through a zombie apocalypse (Emily).

This is why it's key to take the time to feel grateful for the good things in your life. Regularly expressing appreciation and gratitude can not only fight that sense of scarcity but

> also make you more optimistic and happier. That, in turn, can
> help end the constant search for the next thing to buy, and it
> will also help you feel more confident that you will be able to
> grow your wealth.

3. Include the Boring in Your Mental Images of Other People

Teddy Roosevelt once said, "Comparison is the thief of joy." He then hopped off the T. rex on whose back he was charging up San Juan Hill just in time to stop a man from shooting an adorable bear cub. Look it up: it's American history.

But though this quote comes from the mouth of one of our most beloved presidents, we often struggle with the message, don't we? We compare ourselves to neighbors, siblings, friends, enemies, acquaintances, people waiting in line with us at the bank, the Joneses, the Kardashians, that guy who got promoted ahead of you and who drives the exact Lexus you have always wanted, and anyone else who seems to have more than we do.

Comparison may be the thief of joy, but we often don't even wait for the knife to come out. We just hand that joy right over.

How do you fight the scarcity mindset? One of our favorite techniques is to remember that even the people we have envied have gone through terrible and/or boring times. Instead of being jealous of your friend for her trip to Australia, think instead about the credit card debt she racked up paying for her adventure, the hour she spent in line at the post office to get her passport updated (and the second hour she had to spend in line when she discovered she didn't bring the right documents the first time), and the air sickness she suffered on the twenty-two-hour flight.

We're not saying you shouldn't share in their joy. You should. But this thought exercise will help you remember that every purchase or experience is a mixed bag.

So Why Is This Important?

Our attitude toward money is created in childhood, both through the overt lessons taught to us by our parents and the undercover lessons we picked up by paying attention to how money seemed to affect our world. Depending on the scripts we created, we put emphasis on different aspects of money in our lives.

But scripts are often based on partial truths, misunderstandings, or a child's conception of reality. So excavating your memories about money in childhood can help you understand why you view it the way you do.

Gaby Dunn, the author of *Bad with Money: The Imperfect Art of Getting Your Financial Sh*t Together*, talked with Joe about how her childhood gave her some disordered money scripts.

TALKING THROUGH MONEY SCRIPTS:
AN INTERVIEW WITH GABY DUNN

Joe: How did you get your beginning with money?

Gaby: I grew up in South Florida. My mom was the breadwinner. She's a divorce and child custody attorney. And then my dad was ostensibly in construction, but mostly a professional addict and gambler.

There was a lot of financial whiplash, you know. We'd have money and say, "We can get this! Let's get all this!" And then something would happen—my dad would spend it on drugs or he would gamble or something would go wrong, and my parents would tell us we don't have any money. And I'd be wondering, "Okay, so do we have money, or do we not have money? What is the actual truth?"

Parents don't tell their kids the actual truth. When you're growing up, your parents just sort of think, "They're just a kid. We don't need to explain money to them because they're too young."

Joe: *You say that in order to start deconstructing and fixing your own ways of thinking about money, you need to dig into the past and see what you were taught consciously and subconsciously.*

Gaby: *I went to school in the early 2000s. So there were these clear markers of class and success in my school. Like if you had very straightened hair and a Tiffany bracelet and a polo shirt from Abercrombie you were a rich kid.*

So I would try to fit in. I was going to Abercrombie to see what was on sale. But I would be furious if the thing that I could afford didn't say "Abercrombie" on it. Because I needed people to see the logo.

I don't think I took a second to ask myself, "Do I like these clothes or do I like these bracelets or do I want my hair to be straight?" I thought it was just what you had to do.

Joe: *You talk about your mom ironing your hair for you with a clothes iron so that your hair could be straight.*

Gaby: *Yeah, I would lay back on the ironing board. She would iron it with a clothing iron because we didn't have a hair straightener and that probably wasn't good for my hair. But I definitely wanted to be like the kids around me.*

But then at a certain point, rebelliousness took hold and I swung hard the other way. I became this artsy kid who believed having money means that you're evil. But both of those money scripts are not good. The "aspiring for money no matter what" and the "believing anyone who has money is a bad person" are two extremes.

In the beginning, I was trying really hard to measure up to the aspiration and then by the end I was just like, "I don't care if I fit in. My dreams are held together by safety pins because I believe in poetry."

Gaby's advice in a nutshell: Safety-pin together those moments that created the "money being" you are today. That understanding will help you identify your money scripts and the reasons behind your decisions.

Chapter 10 Benjamin Badge: Benjamin-Stacking Mindset Achievements

The real Benjamin stacking is all inside your head, and disordered thoughts won't lead to robust piles. When you pass your mindset achievements, you get out of your own way on the path to primo Benjamin stacking.

Check off each of the following achievements you have completed toward your Benjamin Badge after reading this chapter:

❏ Take the Klontz Money Script Inventory to begin Klontzifying your mindset.
❏ Identify emotional needs you try to "solve" with money. What are they?
❏ Remind yourself that you're good enough, you're smart enough, and doggone it, you, *not* your money, can handle anything. Seriously: Create a mantra. What do you tell yourself—and your brain? If it's not working, change it up.
❏ Express gratitude for all the cool stuff/opportunities/people you have in your life every morning for a week. Pro tip: Doing this out loud on the L train opens up seats around you like you wouldn't believe.
❏ Watch your reactions for a week. Imagine the object of your envy dealing with boring stuff. Refocus on your own journey.

Date You Completed the Chapter 10 Badge	Parent Signature (Putting your mom's John Hancock on your Benjamin stacking makes it official)

11

What to Expect Now That You're Invested (Investing 201)

TOOLS YOU'LL NEED:

* A brokerage account
* An emergency fund
* A burning desire to fund your goals (If you are experiencing a literal burning sensation, talk to your doctor.)

Congratulations! If you've made it this far, you've opened your first investment account and you've started building your stack. Doesn't it feel great?[15]

Buckle up, kiddos. It's time to go from the land of basic investing to the world of investment mastery.

It's a Wide World of Investment Options . . . but You Don't Have to Know Them All

Investors often struggle to choose a path. Studies show that the more options we're presented, the less likely we are to choose anything at all. You don't want to fall into this trap, so there's no need to learn every-

---

15 *By the way, if for some reason you've snuck through and have not yet gotten yourself invested, bookmark this page and come back later. As we've discussed, investing is emotional, and while we're going to walk you through how to work more accurately toward your goals, none of it matters if you aren't invested. Your decisions will change when there's real money on the line.*

thing before you begin. Instead, let's talk through how to first narrow the field of investments you're choosing from.

Like a Good Farmer, Plant Your Investments at the Right Time

Fine. How about another story instead?

Joe likes a good wine. He also knows that if you say you've got a lovely red from Michigan, he'll politely reply, "No thanks." Unless you've found the exception to the rule, Joe knows that the growing season in Michigan isn't long enough for most red grapes. If you said you had a treat from California or Oregon, he'd happily try it, and it'd probably be decent, even swell, because the growing season there is perfect for Cab Sav or Pinot Noir.

Investments work the same way, with a "growing season" during which you shouldn't touch them. A bank might offer a certificate of deposit with withdrawal penalties, and you should consider touching your other investments before their season as similarly verboten.

Unfortunately, there's no *Farmers' Almanac* for investments. They don't tell you that you might want to stay away from that Michigan gamay, and a prospectus isn't going to tell you that this mutual fund is best if you leave it alone for ten years.

So, how do you determine the growing seasons for different investments? We're here to help.

JOE'S INVESTMENT GROWING SEASON CHEAT SHEET

Timeframe (aka the Time Horizon)	Type of Investment	What to Consider
10+ years	Stocks	Purchasing stocks via a mutual fund or exchange traded fund may be less risky than directly investing in stocks.
10+ years	Real estate	Purchasing real estate via a real estate investment trust may be less risky than directly investing in real estate.
5–10 years	Stock/bond mix	Your stocks might be ready to harvest in less than ten years, but if not, you want plenty of bonds on hand to get you through to your goals. Also, the stocks you'll pick are ones that historically have jiggled less (that's the technical term).
5–10 years	High-yield and corporate bonds/bond funds or exchange-traded funds	Bonds will fluctuate more when interest rates move, so be wary of investing for short periods of time when you expect interest rates to rise.
Under 5 years	Cash Money market accounts Savings accounts Low-risk government bonds	These investments are secure but earn very little.

Why Not Just Use "Safe" Investments for My Goal?

You can, but you'll (very safely) earn no money and have to save nearly dollar for dollar toward your goals, and ain't nobody got time for that.

Differentiation Among Stocks

There are lots of types of stocks you can buy, and they aren't created equal. Some companies are inherently safer than others, and some you can expect bigger returns from over time. Still others will provide a steady dividend.

First, let's look at investments from a size perspective. (Yes, size does matter. Sorry, little guys with a small stack.)[16] You may have heard pros prattle on about small-cap, mid-cap, and large-cap, but we can make this much easier. Just replace the word "cap" with the word "company" and you're golden. When we strip away the jargon, here's what we're looking at:

- **Large companies:** These are companies you've heard of—you know, the ones that rhyme with Schmamazon and Schmapple.
- **Mid-size companies:** You may have heard of these companies. They're still big, but not as big as the large companies.
- **Small companies:** I know what you're thinking. "Please don't tell me that these are just little companies." It's true, though. That's what they are.

A company's stock price responds to its own news, news from direct competitors, and regulations that affect its industry. Maybe they're doing really well with their products and services and your investment is going gangbusters. Or maybe they're "accidentally" dumping chemicals into lakes, causing the local fauna or nearby schoolchildren to turn chartreuse, and your investment tanks (even though chartreuse is your favorite color).

---

16 *Emily would like to make it clear that she does not endorse this cheap joke. It's not about the size of your stack. It's how you use it.*

But let's get real. Big companies became big for a reason, and once they get big, momentum can carry them pretty far. Big companies can stink up the place for a long time and still hang around. (We're looking at you, Wells Fargo.) Because of that, big-company stocks tend to spend most days moving with the market. They'll rise and sink in value, but you'll find them the safest of the stocks.

Likewise, mid-size companies are mid-size for a reason. They're still growing, hoping to become a big guy, so they work day in and day out trying to knock their competitors off the top of Investment Mountain.

On the other hand, maybe a mid-cap has stagnated and will never grow because it can't get out of its own way. You know that guy who peaked in college? When you run into him at the hometown bar, he's still reliving the glory days of keg stands and toga parties and it's, well, embarrassing. Some mid-size companies are like that. They're no longer paying rent for a cinder-block apartment and eating instant ramen, but they still have the full-length European posters of the Cure on the living room wall and talk about the good old days. Because of this, mid-size companies are riskier than large companies—but still safer than the small ones.

Small companies are living on a wing and a prayer. A few negative or positive events in a row can shutter or skyrocket the whole operation. They are the riskiest of the three broad asset classes, but they also have the greatest opportunity for growth. Even Schmamazon and Schmapple started as small-caps once upon a time.

So, which should you invest in? If you're looking for safety, use large companies extensively (because they'll generally trend upward over time), use fewer mid-size companies, and go light on small companies. The more aggressive you are, the more you can skew toward mid-size and small firms, which offer the best Benjamin-stacking opportunities—with the highest risk.

But wait, there's more!

We can break down investments another way. The fine people at a company called Morningstar compare investments visually in an enclosed tic-tac-toe board, which they call the Morningstar Style Box™,[17] with three options across that intersect with three options down. So we may have small, medium, and large going down the board, but what are the three types across the top?

Value	Blend	Growth	
			Size Large
			Mid
			Small

You can slice these three types of investments this way: value on the left, growth on the right, and a blend in the middle.

Get ready to strap on your safety helmet, because value vs. growth is the source of some serious investor boxing matches. Waiting for this very moment are two fictional investors, ready to duke it out over whether growth or value investing is better.

---

17 Want a more complete definition of the style box? Here's the official version of how it works, directly from the company who makes it: *The Morningstar Style Box™ has become the industry standard for categorizing and tracking managed investment portfolios. It describes securities in terms of their relative size and value-growth orientation in an intuitive, visual tool. It is based on a robust methodology that includes forward-looking and historical components and 10 different factors to measure value-growth orientation. Because different investment styles often offer different risk/reward patterns, it is important for individuals to understand the investment style of a stock, fund, or portfolio. This understanding can help investors and advisors construct portfolios that are consistent with the investor's return expectations and risk tolerances. The style box lays the groundwork for better portfolio assembly and monitoring and is a useful tool for individual and professional investors.* Wow! You can tell Joe and Emily didn't write this because it sounds professional!

In this corner, weighing the potential growth for an investment, hailing from a land where investors eat risk for breakfast, and just back from her base-jumping vacation over an active volcano, we have Gina Growth!

And in the far corner, weighing the potential value of every investment, a native of the land of Can I Save a Buck—and she's clipping coupons as we speak—Valerie Value! Let's have a clean fight, ladies!

(DING!)

When Gina Growth looks at a company, she is focused on one thing: How quickly can this company take over the world? She'll ask questions like:

- How many more stores are they going to open next year?
- How will they scale?
- Will they be selling lots of new items?
- How big is the market opportunity?

Gina wants to know that a company is going to grow, so she's asking all the right questions. But growth companies tend to be volatile. They'll perform really well when growing but less well when they're not, because their investors are only purchasing for the upside. If they don't find growth, they sell out and look for it elsewhere.

Valerie Value is looking for something different. She wants to protect her downside. She won't invest in companies with the hot new products because she knows that "hot" comes with a price. She even has a name for it: the "growth premium." That means Valerie doesn't want to overpay. So Valerie asks a lot of questions, too:

- If you sold the company for pieces, how much would it be worth?
- How much debt does the company have?
- Are they increasing cash flow?
- Do they pay a dividend to investors so that they can get their money back more quickly?

Value investors *love* dividends, because they return their capital sooner. Companies that aren't growing quickly pay dividends to attract those value investors. Growth investors *hate* dividends for the same reason. If a company is working hard to take over the world, they can't waste money on every Tom, Dick, and Harry who tossed in a few bucks. They need every dollar reinvested to expand.

This is why it's hard to compare investments—a railroad against a tech company, say. Technology companies are beloved by growth investors because they're trying to change the world quickly, and so their stocks are generally priced beyond a value investor's reach. Growth investors don't care about the valuation of the company. They know that if you sold off the pieces of the firm "as is," you're going to lose lots of money, but that's okay because this company's going to grow . . . right?! Well, hopefully.

A railroad will take a long time to expand. It's difficult to lay new tracks, and these days the network of railroad tracks on earth is shrinking. But a value investor won't care that the railroad isn't trading at as big of a "multiple"; they just want a safer bet and a potentially discounted stock.

In terms of risk vs. reward, value companies will gyrate less in a usual market, because they're "safer." Growth companies will experience, during normal times, peaks and valleys that rival the Himalayas and the Grand Canyon. So who wins over the long term?

Let's check back in on Gina and Valerie in the ring. Oh my, they are evenly matched! Depending on *when* you look, each investment type wins, and over long periods of time, they perform very closely. That said, using growth investments for your long-term goals, if you can stand it, can produce better results if you harvest while the company is on the up. (Nice right hook, Gina!) That also makes the opposite true: value investments are more likely to be there when you need them, so they're better for shorter-term goals, closer to ten years. (Hell of an uppercut, Valerie!) How you use them will depend on how far away your goals are and your appetite for the roller coaster.

There are many varieties of tic-tac-toe style boxes when it comes to investing. We assumed above that you're sticking to your home country, but there are also international stocks, and you can also segregate them based on the same Morningstar design. If you want to get granular, you can even take different sectors and split them up as their own board. Technology companies come in large, mid, and small sizes, too, and may be more growth-oriented while other fields are more value-based. It's the same for healthcare, financial services, and transportation. Name a category of company and you can build a tic-tac-toe board for it.

Why is this helpful? Seasoned investors like being able to put their investments in boxes so that they know what to expect. They want to be able to predict when they can safely "harvest" the funds. By knowing ahead of time how the investment should act during normal circumstances, it's easier to also keep going if your plan doesn't work out.

Matching Your Investment to Your Goals

By matching your money to your timeframe, you can eke out higher returns because you know that you can safely invest for that length of time. Also, you can sleep at night knowing that your money is likewise tucked in somewhere that historically has been ready when you needed it.

Matching investments to goals also means you never want to buy the "hot" investment, or the one that pays the biggest dividend, just because it's paying well in the moment. A lot of new investors have a problem where they want to know the "sure thing," like they're picking a horse at the OTB. Stay away from a "betting" mentality now so you won't need to have a "begging" mentality later. We're trying to stack the deck in your favor.

Ways to Stack the Deck

Save More Money

By saving more money, we mean you need to make sure you're putting aside more of your income into investments. Most books, articles on the internet, well-meaning relatives, and hardworking astronauts will tell you to analyze the hell out of fees to save money. We hear about it all the time, too: fees, fees, fees! Controlling your fees is important. But they aren't the main culprit behind missed goals.

> ### Joe's Mom on Keeping Fees in Perspective
>
> **People don't reach their goals because they spend on Cheetos and OnlyFans tips instead of stuffing enough money away. If you'd put down the "Xbox controller" for a second and find ways to send more moolah to your investments, I think we can agree that you're much more likely to be okay than if you win *Fortnite* battles and obsess over the whole $7 you saved in fees.**

Choose Better Investments

By "better," we mean spending your time focusing on investments that help you reach your goal. What that means is:

- For most of us, choosing passive, index-based investments beats trying to find a hot manager. Unless you have Cardi B wealth and access to the (very few) investors who have a track record of beating indexes, you're better off saving more money and letting the market do what it will do—once you've planted that cash in the right timeframe investment.

- If you need to compare investments, use a resource like the one we've been referencing, Morningstar.com, a third-party rating and evaluation site. You can learn a ton there about how your investments work. While you can pay Morningstar for deeper insights, the free version is sufficient for most of us. Even when Joe was working as a professional in the biz, he spent most of his time using the free tools.

- While "better" is difficult to define when looking at individual investments, you can improve your results by being in the correct asset class. According to the industry expert Roger Ibbotson, your asset allocation—how you diversify your funds—will determine 90 percent of your success. In short, diversifying effectively can amp up your results.

But "better" can also mean getting rid of expensive or ineffective managers or using more passive investments. It can also mean upgrading your managers or using tools like Morningstar to find cheaper, more efficient, or higher-performing investments in the same class.

Just make sure you have defined "better" for *your* needs. Recently, oil market investors flocked to the cheapest exchange traded fund at the time. But the two largest exchange traded funds weren't managed the same way, so anyone chasing the lowest fees missed the fact that the largest and cheapest fund had constrictions that hurt investors when the price of oil went south. The difference in the two ETFs—products that most investors thought did the same thing—was pronounced. "Better," it turned out, wasn't what the low-fee seekers thought it was.

Fees

Which brings us to fees. You can dramatically improve your chances of reaching your goal if you avoid high fees on your savings.

Here's some straight talk about fees: You need to be careful to avoid high ones. But, at the risk of repeating ourselves, cheaper doesn't mean better. Cheaper is great. Better is great. If I can get cheaper and better? Fantastic.

Morningstar.com, among other resources, has fee information as well. The first place to look is with the investment company you're using. They're legally required to share that information with you, and finding the details has become easier over the years (because it's the first question people ask).

While you're at your firm's website, check out their marketing—not to buy what they're pitching, but to see what aspects of your funds' value they emphasize. What tools do they have? As we've mentioned, the more you bathe in these sites, the more you'll see similarities (usually truths) and outliers (marketing spin). It's easy to be swayed by spin (like how Fisher Investments says, "We do things different!" to explain how they do the same thing every other wrap-fee-charging advisor does), but you'll become savvier and more skeptical once you've clicked around.

Avoiding Noob Investing Problems

New investors make mistakes, and you will, too. The key to success is to recognize that you're going to mess up. Don't wait to start because you're afraid. Get started because you're afraid! But just as you'll evaluate your actions and tweak your decision-making over time, we can show you a solid road map by sharing some frequent detours that are easy to avoid.

Problem: Investors trade on emotions.
Solution: Make a plan and stick to it.

Inexperienced investors tend to buy when they're excited about an investment that's nearly reached its peak and sell just as it's losing money. Even longtime investors have a hard time avoiding the temptation to chase the hot thing. But investments that are high *now* are more likely to sink than rise. If your friends are all talking about a particular purchase, you're too late. The easy money is already made. So stick with your boring, slow-and-steady plan where you make investments based on your long-term goals and avoid getting distracted by shiny objects.

Problem: Investors jump on great ideas.
Solution: Create an investment "funnel."

There's nothing wrong with investing in a great idea. However, "buy it now!" isn't step two in your funnel-like process of adding investments to your mix.

You'll develop your own funnel over time, but initially it may look like this:

1. Idea: "Wow, this seems like a nifty opportunity!"

2. Fit: "Where does this add value to my portfolio?"

3. Research: "How does this investment work? How does it respond to up markets, down markets, and weird markets? How good is the management team, if there is one?" These are the questions you'll need an evaluation site like Morningstar to answer.

4. Threat Analysis: "What could go wrong with this investment opportunity? Under what situations should I sell this investment?"

5. Buy! (Or Pass!): Based on your funnel, you'll know whether to pounce on the opportunity or let it go.

Problem: Investors trade based on gut instinct.
Solution: Create an investment policy statement.

New investors often trade their portfolio for horrible reasons. They may open their brokerage account website for the first time in forever and see that the garden needs to be weeded. So without any system, they decide today is the day they make a bunch of moves. They haven't followed current events. They haven't looked at their overall allocation. They haven't even seen if this investment has performed well over the long term. Savvy investors don't make "gut" decisions, and they don't trade randomly.

Instead, great investors have policies that they follow so that they don't feel compelled to react to markets or make moves whenever they check in on their accounts. Professional investors use something called an "investment policy statement," and as you begin your own investing journey, you should make one, too. This statement, in writing, forces you to think ahead of time about how you're going to manage your money. Then, instead of making arbitrary moves, if you have a good idea, you'll instead tweak your statement from time to time as you continue to sharpen the saw and get better at investing.

An investment policy statement outlines a few things:

1. What are your goals?

2. What allocation are you going to use to achieve your goal?

3. How often will you change your investment mix?

4. What factors will you use to decide how you'll change your policies or your mix?

5. What is the maximum change you'll make to your mix whenever you evaluate?

6. When will you evaluate your mix and investments? Put appointments on your calendar.

7. Why would you dump one investment for another?

8. Why would you keep an investment?

9. How do you define "good investments" vs. "stinktastic investments that need to go"?

10. When and how will you decide to sell?

Through the act of thoughtfully writing and following your statement, you're building a system that will help you reach your goals. You'll rest easy between evaluation periods, too. Instead of worrying about what you're missing, you'll know that you're making appropriate moves according to your predetermined criteria. By taking a more professional approach, you'll wipe out many of the mistakes that maim inexperienced investors.

If you've ever been golfing, you know that it's easy for new golfers to make mistakes. The course has sand pits, water hazards, deep grass on either side of the fairway, and blind spots. A pro golfer once told Joe that the most important thing he learned was how to stay out of trouble by making things more boring. Boring is ideal for golf, because it means you're avoiding the places where you can make major, costly mistakes. While flashy shots make the ESPN reels, it's the fact that you didn't mess up on that boring, simple shot that made an eagle possible.

More Esoteric Investments and Frequent Trading Apps

We know you've wondered, "What about all these tools that promise to help me get rich quick-ish?" Some will help you invest in hedge funds, while others will show you signals to help you day trade. They're super fun, but unless you're a seasoned, informed investor, frequent trading is the sure way to quick losses. If your goal is to go about your business while investing in a fun but profitable way: skip the apps.

"Move along, folks! Nothing to see in these frequent trading apps."

By the time you finish your investment policy statement, you'll know not just a lot more about your investments, but also about how they will react to market forces. You'll know all the things that could go wrong, and more. Because of this, most of the time you'll probably choose not to buy a given investment because it doesn't fit with your vision. Don't think of this as a waste of time. Evaluating and carefully choosing a few investments is the wise person's method of creating a portfolio that resembles a finely weeded garden.

So Why Is This Important?

All of this may sound complicated and difficult, and it can be. But remember that these actions at the back of the book are icing on the cake. The cake is the important part. Whenever we want a reality check (cake-based or otherwise), we talk to Jill Schlesinger, CBS Business Analyst and host of the fantastic *Jill on Money* podcast and radio show. She sat down with Joe to put all this in perspective.

GO TO 201 WITH YOUR MONEY: AN INTERVIEW WITH JILL SCHLESINGER

Joe: *So people have made the decision to save. They've already learned about investing it versus putting it in a savings account. But now that we know a little* *bit about diversification and that the financial markets may be a better place long term than a savings account, let's go to 201. What do people need to know?*

Jill: *The most important thing to remember is that you do not have to be a stock-picking or mutual-fund-picking genius. You are a long-term investor, and as such, you don't need to pick the top or the bottom or the middle of anything. You just have to be diligent and keep plugging away at it. So there you have your beginning premise.*

Next, you need to understand that fees can eat into your performance in a way that is clear to any professional investor, but maybe not to somebody who's just starting out.

If you're going to buy ABC mutual fund, and that fund costs 1 percent a year in terms of the annual expense, that means that every year you're an investor you're starting at a minus 1 percent return. Concentrate on simple solutions at the cheapest possible [fee] level.

That leads me to passive investing, which is where you buy a basket of something. That basket stays fixed, so it doesn't cost a lot to manage the fund. You basically just need to buy a few of those passive investments, which can be index funds like an S&P 500 fund and an international stock index fund.

So essentially: Keep it simple, invest long term, keep your expenses down, choose a nice mix. Don't futz with it.

Then, you're going to be a successful investor. The most important way for you to achieve your goals is actually to save money.

The investing part is pretty easy. The hard part is saving.

Joe: *I want to start off with what you said about fees because I also think that's really important information, but I think that the financial media spends so much time focusing on only fees.*

Jill: *I think a lot of people seem to think, "Oh, if I just get the most perfect mix of investments together, that will allow me to reach my goals." In fact,* *the hard part is that you actually have to do something. It's sort of like weight loss in many respects. I can get you to step on the scale and see what the number is. The hard part is, I need to have you stop eating so much and start exercising more, and that is on you. It doesn't matter whether you're an intermittent faster, you're vegan, you're keto, you're this, you're that, but that you're on some kind of program that you stick to.*

And when you're looking at financial-planning goals, what have you done to put yourself in a position to succeed? And that success is not about spending hours and hours of research on the lowest-cost fund or the best mix. It's actually saving and putting stuff on autopilot and getting the money out of your hands before [you can spend it].

I can fix someone's portfolio in five minutes. What I cannot fix is their ability to save. So you have more power in this than you may believe.

Joe: *Talk to me about what types of investments fit in different timeframes when it comes to goals.*

Jill: *If you are saving for a longer-term goal, ten, twenty, thirty, forty years, it's important to make sure you have some part of your portfolio invested in a way that will actually beat inflation. That's really what the whole game of investing is about. It's not about piling up money, it's about how can I grow my money to beat the rate of inflation so that when I'm ready to pull that money out, I have more money than I started with, after I factor in prices rising? And in many respects, the people who are hyper-focused on stocks are missing out on other diversified asset classes that could help them get where they want to go.*

Essentially there's the general asset classes: there's cash, there's fixed income, there's equities, there's real estate, and there's commodities. The combination that you choose is the combination that is based on when you need your money and your risk tolerance. For [someone who has] $10 million, they may say, "I only need a million. And so therefore I'm going to put all of my money in really safe stuff." That is your choice. But the combination of *investments that you own is really predicated on you. There is no rule of thumb. [It] is based on you and an environment where you can really look at your own goals and objectives and risk tolerance, and pretty much have something that is individualized to your needs.*

It's an excuse to just use a rule of thumb. And if you're going to use a rule of thumb, then by golly, just use some sort of target-date fund or robo-advisor that will do the work for you.

Joe: *I want to ask you about when people do something really dumb.*

Jill: *I think that people make their lives way more complicated than they need to be. And many people are their own worst enemies. You don't need to make yourself crazy. Watch out for the things that essentially are going to get in the way. And those things often are you.*

I'll give one last parting shot.

Joe: *Bring it.*

Jill: *I would like to remind everybody that we all fall prey to our emotions. And so I know that back in March 2020, when many of you were worried and you felt like you wanted to sell everything, I was able to talk people off the ledge and prevent them from doing something stupid.*

And now all of these months later, stocks are so much higher that the greed monster's back in your life. Fear was back in March 2020. Greed comes in August and the beginning of September 2020. I just want you to know that we all feel these emotions, but we don't have to succumb to them. So if you are feeling like you're going to do something stupid to your financial life, call Joe, call me, send an email. Where are your lifelines? [It is] an honor [to be] doing this because we like you and we want to help. So reach out when you need help.

Jill's advice in a nutshell: Smart investing is more about getting out of your own way and consistently putting money into your portfolio than finding the perfect investments.

Chapter 11 Benjamin Badge:
Investing 201 Achievements

Finessing your investments can help you achieve your goals.

Check off each of the following achievements you have completed toward your Benjamin Badge after reading this chapter:

❏ Research the fees associated with one investment you own. If you're having fun, find another, or look into all of them.

❏ Create an investment funnel. Your first will include questions of fit, research into the company, and a threat analysis.

❏ Draw up your investment policy statement. Bonus points if you write it on scented pink paper with your sparkly unicorn pen or other schmancy stationery of your choosing.

Date You Completed the Chapter 11 Badge	Parent Signature (Putting your mom's John Hancock on your Benjamin stacking makes it official)

12

Inflation and Taxes: The Two Horsemen of the Investing Apocalypse

TOOLS YOU'LL NEED:
- Valves in a variety of sizes (for fighting the effects of inflation)
- Corncob pipe and warm sweater, for when you tell kids how cheap things were in your day
- Your well-thumbed copy of the tax code (We know you keep it in the bathroom for some light reading.)

Two diabolical forces are coming for your Benjamin stacks.

They are relentless.

They will find you.

They will not stop until they get their hands on some of your sweet, sweet braaaains . . . that is, Benjamins.

Nothing will stop their pursuit.

They are the twin horrors of

Inflation

and

Taxes!

[cue ominous lightning strike]

Not the horror you were expecting? They're absolutely grim, but you'd never know it because they're sneaky, too.

Inflation is the loss of purchasing power over time. Though inflation moves in slowly, it is an invisible, destructive force that eats away at your money right when you feel confident that your stacks are safe.

Taxes are inflation's officious, stack-eating sibling. This monster is more obviously terrifying, both because it comes with an enforcement squad of IRS auditors and because taxes let you know how big a bite they plan to take. If inflation slinks into the inner sanctum of your stacks under the darkness of your inattention, taxes announce themselves in daylight before making a meal of your Benjamins. Here's the rub, though: while taxes flaunt themselves in the open, for most of us, they're withheld from our paychecks, so we have no idea the huge amounts we pay. Sneaky.

Luckily for us smart Benjamin stackers, both inflation and taxes are usually consistent and predictable monsters, so even if they try to hide, we can see them coming and prepare. Here's how you can keep inflation and taxes from cutting down your stacks in their prime.

What Is Inflation?

Let's start with a quick exercise. Here's what we're going to need you to do:

1. *Visit your oldest living friend or relative.*

2. *Bring them a cup of tea.*

3. *No, not that kind of tea. The kind in the blue box.*

4. *You didn't boil the water long enough. Do it again.*

5. *Now that's a properly brewed cup of tea, young man/woman!*

6. *All right, was there something you wanted to talk about?*

7. Ask them what year they made their first significant purchase, such as a house, car, or college education.

8. Listen to a rambling story about that time they were playing jacks down at the soda fountain.

9. Remind them where they were and what they were talking about. (First home or car purchase, or first year of college, in case you've forgotten as well.)

10. Ask them the dollar amount they were required to part with in exchange for this house, car, or college education.

11. (Optional) Weep copiously.

It is likely that the prices they quoted for these major purchases were closer to the dollar amount colloquially known as "two seashells" than the real-world numbers currently required. For instance, the costs for these items in 1970 compared to 2020 are enough to make you want to voluntarily engage in step 11 of the previous exercise:

Item	Median Cost in 1970	Median Cost in 2020
Home	$23,450	$335,000
New Car	$3,450	$38,060
One Year of Public College Tuition	$405	$9,687
One Year of Private College Tuition	$1,792	$35,087

Allow us to introduce you to inflation.

It's Not Just About Inflation

"But wait!" exclaims a hypothetical reader who has been paying close attention. "The big problem with the difference

in prices between 1970 and 2020 isn't the number. It's the fact
that a high school graduate could easily afford a mortgage
and you could work a summer job to pay for college. Those
are laughable propositions now. RISIBLE, I SAY!"

You're absolutely right, strangely shouty "gentle" reader.
Here—have some properly brewed tea. Inflation is just one
part of the problem. There are others:

- WAGE STAGNATION: In many industries, the amount of money
  you earn for the same job has not kept up with inflation over
  time. This is especially true of low-wage jobs. The federal
  minimum wage has not changed from its current rate of $7.25
  since 2009, which equals an average of $14,500 a year.

- COSTS OUTPACING INFLATION: Several types of goods and
  services (and education in particular) have seen their costs
  rise at a much faster rate than inflation.

  Inflation works in concert with these troubling phenomena
  to make Millennials and Gen Zeds want to strangle their
  parents and grandparents when the latter ask, "Why haven't
  you bought a house yet?"

While you're working, inflation doesn't seem to be too huge a
deal—unless you're also facing wage stagnation or costs outpacing
inflation. For most people, cost-of-living raises help maintain their
income's purchasing power so they don't feel the creep of inflation.

Inflation's major effect is on your invested money, by eroding the
purchasing power of the funds you set aside. Here's why: at an inflation rate of 3.5 percent per year, prices double about every twenty
years. While the government measures the current rate of inflation
at 1.7 percent (as of early 2021—and don't get us started on government statistics), inflation usually falls between 2 and 4 percent
each year, so you can expect prices to double about every five Winter
Olympics, to use the most arcane unit of time measurement possible.

Ultimately, that means you need to plan for inflation with any money you set aside for the future—particularly retirement. The $1,000 you have stashed in your mattress is only going to buy $500 worth of goods (in today's numbers) if you hold on to it for twenty years (or two U.S. censuses).

What's exciting is that investing the money, instead of sleeping on it in a financial re-creation of "The Princess and the Pea," can help you grow your money faster than inflation can eat away at it.

Investing with Inflation in Mind

We've beaten the diversify-your-investments drum quite a bit so far, but the reasons we've given have mostly been about protecting your principal and allowing for sustainable growth. However, diversifying also helps you keep inflation at bay. That's because inflation affects different asset classes in different ways. Understanding how the asset classes react to inflation can help you balance your investments to minimize the risks to your money.

Liquid Assets

The more available your money is, the lower return you should expect. A bank account may be the safest landing spot if you're concerned only about keeping your principal, but it is the worst offender in terms of allowing inflation to snack on your stacks. This may be true even if you're earning interest.

When your bank touts its 0.85 percent APY on its high-yield savings account, that is only the nominal interest rate. The real interest rate is how much you earn after factoring in inflation. With inflation currently at 1.7 percent, your 0.85 percent APY on savings has a *real* interest rate of –0.85 percent. Yes, that excellent advertised rate is *costing* you 0.85 percent per year. The $1,000 in your account may grow to the munificent sum of $1,008.50 over a year, but it could only purchase $991.50 worth of goods.

In short, you're *very safely* losing money.

Fixed-Income Securities

This asset class includes investments like CDs and bonds, to whom we introduced you back in Chapter 6. (CDs and bonds say howdy, by the way. They were pleased to make your acquaintance seven chapters ago and are delighted to be renewing the relationship again here. They'd love to offer you a hot drink and invite you to haul up and sit awhile, but that's not how books work, unfortunately.)

With fixed-income securities, you know going into the investment just how much growth to expect. With a CD, you will earn the exact rate offered by the bank upon the maturity date. With a bond, the coupon is the fixed amount of interest you'll earn, often as a periodic dividend. Since the interest on these assets is fixed, investors will lose purchasing power if inflation rises above the offered interest rate.

As with savings accounts, you can calculate your real interest rate by subtracting the current inflation rate from your guaranteed interest rate.

Stocks

Inflation affects stocks in a variety of ways—and these effects are not as simple to calculate as determining the real interest rate on a savings account, CD, or bond. That's because inflation can sometimes improve and sometimes hurt your rate of return on a stock, depending on what kind of stock it is. However, stocks *do* tend to outperform inflation over time, which is one of the (many, many, many, many, many) reasons why we talk about investing in stocks for the long haul.

But, in a general way, here's what you can expect[18] from inflation when it comes to your stocks:

Large-cap investments tend to follow the market, so if moderate inflation is spurring economic growth, then your large-cap investments will also grow. According to U.S. News & World Report, for every 1 percent decline of the U.S. dollar (that is, for every 1 percent increase in

---

18 *"Past performance is no guarantee of future results," Joe shouts in his sleep before settling back down into peaceful slumber.*

inflation), the S&P 500, which is made up entirely of large-cap stocks, increased by 1.5 percent between 1998 and 2019. Looking at historical returns for the S&P 500, it's clear that the market's highest real returns occurred when inflation was around 2 to 3 percent.

However, when inflation is either much higher or lower than 2 to 3 percent, that can negatively affect returns on large-cap investments. That may be because such high or low inflation rates indicate a big macroeconomic problem that's affecting investments as a whole.

Mid-cap investments tend to fare a little better under inflation than large-caps. Between 1998 and 2019, the S&P Midcap 400 grew 1.9 percent for every 1 percent decrease in value for the U.S. dollar. But just like with the big guys, periods of high or low inflation can negatively affect mid-size investment growth.

Small-cap investments are traditionally thought to be nimble enough to handle sudden inflation better than their big- and medium-size siblings. (Think of how a small company might be able to change strategies, vendors, or even prices more quickly than a long-established giant in response to a sudden inflation spike.) But these investments tend to also be more volatile than their larger sibs, which means they can be vulnerable to other economic changes that the bigger fish can weather just fine.

Growth stocks may be negatively affected by inflation. Growth stocks perform well when they're growing, and it's harder for companies to grow when inflation reduces the buying power of a dollar and makes it more expensive for companies to borrow money for operations. Of course, when moderate inflation encourages economic growth, that can help growth stocks crank up the earnings engine.

Value stocks may offer a potential hedge against inflation, as these companies tend to keep their cash flow steady and are less likely to need business loans. They can provide some protection from sudden inflation, but they are also slower to react to positive market conditions that allow growth stocks to, well, grow.

How to Keep Inflation's Grasping Fingers Away
from Your Invested Stacks

If there's no way to avoid inflation altogether, there are a number of tips we can share to help you protect yourself from the beast's sharp-toothed hunger. To wit:

- **Diversify:** We've said it before, we'll say it again, and in fact, it's how we answer the phone. (Rrring, rring. "Diversify your investments, this is Emily.") Having your money invested in a number of asset classes is the best hedge against financial danger. No one asset class will protect you from inflation, taxes, volatility, illiquidity, market upsets, zombies, or low interest rates. By making savvy investments in a number of different ones, you can feel confident that your stack will still grow, even if individual Benjamins within the stack might get nibbled upon.

- **Invest in real estate:** Since property values tend to go up with inflation, owning real estate can be another hedge against inflation. That could just mean owning your home. (Emily knows a couple who bought their house a mile outside of D.C. for $49,000 in 1972 and sold it for nearly $800,000 forty-three years later.) Or you could get into the real estate mogul game by purchasing a rental property and becoming a landlardy.[19] Or, if you'd prefer not to deal with tenants, you could always invest in a real estate investment trust, or REIT. A REIT allows shareholders to purchase shares in income-producing commercial real estate investments. If you explore this route, look at publicly traded REITs through a well-known fund company, and avoid non-traded REITs, which often have high fees and high minimum investments, and can be hella hard to sell.

---

19 *This is Emily's suggestion for a gender-neutral term for landlord/-lady. No clue why it hasn't taken off.*

* **Invest in Treasury Inflation-Protected Securities (TIPS):** What if I told you that your very own Uncle Sam offers an investment that can protect you from the vagaries of the consumer price index? TIPS bonds pay a fixed rate of interest, but the amount of your principal can fluctuate with inflation. Basically, twice a year, the government uses the consumer price index to readjust the value of your TIPS, so that a $1,000 TIPS bond will be worth $1,030 with 3 percent inflation. TIPS bonds are hardly a sufficient investment, but they can make a nice addition to your portfolio that helps protect you from inflation.

Inflation is a fact of life, and Joe and Emily will always sound like old fogies when they exclaim, "In my day, a cup of coffee cost a nickel!" But we can plan for this marauding invader and work to lessen its bite. Which brings us to inflation's clipboard-wielding, pinstripe-wearing, bureaucratic sibling.

Taxes

Even for confirmed money nerds like Joe and Emily, talking about taxes tends to be the opposite of fun. (Joe had to coax Emily to the computer with a trail of stickers, chocolate, and increasingly caffeinated coffee products in cute mugs to get her to write this. And once she sat down, he had to place a cat on her lap to keep her there, as Emily subscribes to the philosophy that cats that have chosen to pin you in place must never be disturbed. Her writing career owes much to cat-pinning.)

Taxes have a bad rep, even among the sort of people for whom the word "percentage" is not already a turnoff. But as unpleasant as paying and filing taxes can be—especially when it comes *smack-dab* in that gentlest month of the year, tainting our enjoyment of blooming cherry blossoms and warming weather? Talk about April being the cruelest month—your expectations are often worse than the reality. There are a couple of reasons for this:

**1. Your tax dollars go toward [checks notes] keeping things function-
ing, which is generally considered a plus. We appreciate it when the
lights turn on.**

2. Your tax rate isn't as high as you think it is.

No, we're not kidding, they're lower than many people think. Let's
take a look at our current (as of 2021) tax brackets so you can understand what we mean.

Tax Rate	Single Filer Income Bracket	Married, Filing Jointly, Income Bracket
10%	$0 to $9,950	$0 to $19,900
12%	$9,950.01 to $40,525	$19,900.01 to $81,050
22%	$40,525.01 to $86,375	$81,050.01 to $172,750
24%	$86,375.01 to $164,925	$172,750.01 to $329,850
32%	$164,925.01 to $209,425	$329,850.01 to $418,850
35%	$209,425.01 to $523,600	$418,850.01 to $628,300
37%	$523,600.01 or more	$628,300.01 or more

Let's assume you are a well-compensated and single Benjamin
stacker earning $550,000. That puts you in the top (37 percent) tax
bracket. Sounds ugly, doesn't it? But exactly how big of a bite will taxes
take out of that lovely paycheck?

Go ahead and do the math. We'll wait while you get out your slide rule.

[insert easy-listening hold music of your choice]

Ready? You sure? You remembered to carry the 2, right? Okay, great.

Did you come up with $203,500? Surprise! The answer is only
$167,572.25.[20]

---

20 Yes, we know the word "only" does not ever belong in front of a six-figure dollar
amount. But you have to admit that $167,572.25 is less than $203,500. If you admitted
that it's exactly $35,927.75 less, then you're our kind of nerd.

Now, don't get huffy. Your math was correct on the percentage calculation: 37 percent of $550,000 is absolutely 203,500 simoleons. But *that's not how taxes work.* Fat cats earning $550,000 per year only have to pay 37 percent on their income *above* $523,600. You pay the percentages listed for each bracket.

If it helps—and yet another alcohol-related analogy always helps us—imagine champagne being poured into a pyramid of glasses. If you have one of those miniature bottles (i.e., an income less than $9,950), you'll pour it all out in the single cup topping the pyramid, the one labeled "10%." That's it. That's all you'll pay.

If you have a normal-size bottle, it will fill up the 10 percent glass, and then the excess will start to fill the next level of glasses, which are labeled "12%," and then maybe the third level, labeled "22%." But only the champagne that made it down to the 22 percent glasses will be taxed at that level. Since you start with the 10 percent level, then fill the 12 percent level, then the 22 percent level, your income is progressively taxed, rather than *all* taxed at the highest level.

And for those of you with a Goliath bottle, you should be thrilled to reach the bottommost glasses, labeled "37%." Why are you happy? Imagine how much income you're still bringing in. Share some of that

bubbly with your friends! Even if you reach that level, this will likely be only a small portion of your ginormous income/bubbly that overfloweth.

So to determine how much of your $550,000 will go to taxes, you can't just take 37 percent of the whole enchilada. You have to break it down into each bracket:

If you earn $550,000, you pay	For a total tax burden of	And here's our math
10% on your first $9,950 in income	$995	10% of $9,950 = $995
12% on income between $9,950 and $40,525	$4,664	$40,525 – $9,950 = $30,575 12% of $30,575 = $3,669 $3,669 + $995 = $4,664
22% on income between $40,525 and $86,375	$14,751	$86,375 – $40,525 = $45,850 22% of $45,850 = $10,087 $10,087 + $4,664 = $14,751
24% on income between $86,375 and $164,925	$33,603	$164,925 – $86,375 = $78,550 24% of $78,550 = $18,852 $18,852 + $14,751 = $33,603
32% on income between $164,925 and $209,425	$47,843	$209,425 – $164,925 = $44,500 32% of $44,500 = $14,240 $14,240 + $33,603 = $47,843
35% on income between $209,425 and $523,600	$157,804.25	$523,600 – $209,425 = $314,175 35% of $314,175 = $109,961.25 $109,961.25 + $47,843 = $157,804.25
37% on income above $523,600	$167,572.25	$550,000 – $523,600 = $26,400 37% of $26,400 = $9,768 $157,804.25 + $9,768 = $167,572.25

This is why you'll often hear references to your "marginal" tax rate, or the rate you pay on the highest portion of your income. It's something we here at *Stacking Benjamins* wish they would teach you in high school. (Really, when's the last time you needed to formulate the length of a hypotenuse? Or recite the Saint Crispin's Day speech?) Your overall tax rate is generally described as your ordinary income tax rate, or the total percentage of your income that you pay in taxes. For our well-compensated stacker earning

$550,000, his ordinary income tax rate is 30.46 percent, because the total amount he pays, $167,572.25, is 30.46 percent of that $550,000.

The lesson is that the situation is not nearly as dire as you think. Yes, you do have to hand over a portion of your ~~loot~~ income to the gub'mint every year (and this is not even including state and local taxes), and yes, it's more dizzyingly complex than the entire *Star Wars* extended universe, and yes, there are serious repercussions for failing to adequately and accurately pay your taxes—just ask Al Capone—but the amount you owe may not be nearly as high as you feared.

Now, we're not going to get into the nitty-gritty of paying income taxes for two reasons: first, we'd prefer this book not double as a door-stop; and second, we figure we'd lose at least 67.3 percent of you in the process. Instead, we're going to focus on how taxes affect your investments, since that's more immediately useful to most of us.

How Do You Pay Taxes on Your Investments?

There are three ways to pay taxes on your investments. Or, more accurately, there are three timeframes for paying taxes on your investments, which means this is the most boring type of time travel possible:

- Make your future self pay taxes with tax-deferred investing.
- Protect your future self from taxes with Roth-style investing.
- Pay taxes as you go with taxable investing.

Keeping taxes from taking too big a bite out of your stacks is mostly about spreading them out so you're not stuck paying them all at the same time. Using each of these types of investments can help you diversify your tax burden, so you don't have to worry about rogue IRS agents following you down dark alleys and demanding all your money.[21]

---

21 *Joe and Emily hope you forgive their hyperbole here. Rogue IRS agents don't follow people down dark alleys to demand all their money. They send certified letters, which are infinitely more frightening.*

Tax-Deferred Investing

One way to reduce your tax burden right now is through tax-deferred investing. Both employer-sponsored defined contribution plans (also known as 401(k), 403(b), and 457 plans) and individual retirement accounts (IRAs, not to be confused with Ira, your friendly neighborhood tax attorney) offer the benefit of putting off paying taxes until later.

In the ultimate form of productive procrastination, Uncle Sam lets you deduct contributions to these accounts from your yearly adjusted gross income. Translation: You don't have to pay taxes on money you invest in these accounts, up to an annual limit.

Your ability to deduct your contributions to your IRA may be phased out to nothing based upon how you file your taxes, if you're covered by a workplace tax-deferred account like a 401(k), and the size of your adjusted gross income (which they will unfortunately ask you to whip out). The important thing to know is that you'll be able to take a full deduction if you make less than the lower income limit, no deduction at all if you make more than the upper income limit, and a partial deduction if your income is in the middle.

Joe,
There's a partial erection joke in there somewhere. Can you expand on that?

- Emily

Accessing Your Tax-Deferred Investments

Investing in your 401(k) or IRA isn't all tax-deferred rainbows and unicorns. There are some downsides:

- You can't touch that money until you reach age fifty-nine-and-a-half or have held the account for at least five years, whichever comes second. Otherwise, you'll have to pay a 10 percent early withdrawal penalty, 20 percent tax withholding on the withdrawal, and Joe and Emily will shake their heads at you. They won't be angry. Just disappointed.
- When you are allowed to take out money without getting a painful (and expensive) slap on the wrist, you'll still owe ordinary income taxes on your withdrawals.
- After you reach age seventy-two, you have to take required minimum distributions every year because the IRS keeps track of your life expectancy and wants to get your taxes before you croak. (Again, not joking.)

So when you invest in tax-deferred retirement accounts, expect to pay those taxes in retirement. The IRS needs 401(k) and IRA account holders to withdraw their money (because that means they pay taxes on it) rather than let it grow indefinitely. You'll pay ordinary income tax on your withdrawals between ages fifty-nine-and-a-half and seventy-two, and you can take any size withdrawal you like.

Upon reaching age seventy-two, however, you'll have to start taking out specific amounts, known as your required minimum distribution, and you face a nasty penalty—50 percent of the required amount—if you fail to withdraw it. Half!

You'll have to calculate your required minimum distribution each year, based on the account's balance as of December 31 of the previous year and the correct IRS distribution table. That said, the operative word is "minimum." You're always welcome to take more than what's required—but don't forget to pay taxes on the full amount.

Tax-Exempt Investing, aka Roth Accounts

Roth IRAs and Roth 401(k) accounts were the brainchild of spandex aficionado, extreme haircut haver, and sometime musician David Lee Roth.[22] With these accounts, instead of contributing pretax dollars, account holders drop in money they've already paid taxes on.

Just slow your roll if you're thinking this sounds like the kind of terrible deal that only someone who thought he could do the Beach Boys better than Brian Wilson would suggest. There are three reasons why people sign up for a Roth IRA or Roth 401(k):

1. The money in your Roth account grows tax-free.

2. Your distributions are 100 percent tax-free, provided you wait to take them until after reaching age fifty-nine-and-a-half or having held the account at least five years, whichever comes last. (The sticky-fingered IRS will take a 10 percent penalty if you take an early withdrawal, though, so try not to do that.)

3. The IRS doesn't ask you to take any kind of required minimum distribution. You can leave that money in there forever, if you like, and take distributions whenever you please (as long as you're over age fifty-nine-and-a-half and have held the account at least five years).

Roth IRAs and Roth 401(k) accounts work like a tax-free gift to your future self. You're taking care of the tax burden in the present so your retired self can enjoy those dolla bills without looking over your shoulder for IRS agents with their hands out.

The Roth versions of IRAs and 401(k)s have the same contribution limits as their traditional brethren, so you can choose which works best for you: pay the tax now, or save it for later. Either way, the yearly contribution limit encompasses all IRAs or 401(k)s you may

---

22 *The editors would like to point out that this is, in fact, incorrect. David Lee Roth is not a musician.*

own, so you'll have to divide that contribution amount among all your IRAs or 401(k)s, whether they are traditional or Roth. So if you are putting $3,000 in your traditional IRA in 2021, you can only put $3,000 in your David Lee Roth IRA, not the full $6,000.

Taxable Investments

We've talked about putting off your taxes with tax-deferred investing and prepaying with tax-exempt investing. The only thing left to cover is pay-as-you-go taxes with taxable investments—specifically stocks, bonds, and mutual funds that you own outside of a tax-sheltered investment like your traditional or Roth IRA or 401(k). These kinds of investments are taxed annually, so you don't have to wait to pay them.

Stocks

As we have discussed, you get to be part owner of a company when you buy their stock, which means you make money when the company makes money. There are two methods by which you might make money with your stock, and thereby owe taxes:

1. When you receive regular dividends.

2. When you sell your stock and make a profit. Because we're fancy-pants, we call such profit a "capital gain." (Capital Gain is also the name of a finance-themed body-building gym in Washington, DC. The name of this establishment is appreciated only by a handful of people, but it's a real thigh-slapper for them.)

Your capital gains can either be short-term, which means you've held the stock for less than a year, or long-term, for stock you've taken at least one entire trip around the sun with. It's both romantic and tax advantageous.

Good news for low-income earners: If you make less than $40,400 as a single filer or $80,800 as a married couple filing jointly? You don't owe taxes on long-term capital gains! This is why Emily has decided to live in a van down by the river. #Winning[23]

Bonds

Remember, you receive regular interest payments from these investments, as well as repayment of your principal when the bond matures. There are some types of bonds that are tax-exempt, such as municipal bonds. Other than those types, however, if you hold any bonds outside of a tax-advantaged account, you will generally be taxed at your ordinary income tax rate when you receive interest. You won't owe taxes when you receive repayment of your principal because you are investing with post-tax money, and you're simply getting your stake back.

Mutual Funds

As we discussed, mutual funds are a way to pool stocks and bonds. That means Uncle Sam will tax mutual funds based on what types of investments make them up. So, if you receive dividends from your MF, you'll have to pay ordinary income tax on those dividends. But you may also receive some distributions of your capital gains—and you will have to pay taxes at the long-term capital gains rate on those profits, no matter how long you have owned your shares within the mutual fund.

Here's an ugly truth about mutual funds: you may receive a tax bill from your mutual fund company even if you don't sell. Joe remembers these phone calls when he was an advisor. "My mf MF company just sent me a tax bill! Did you sell without asking my permission?" Not at all. Mutual funds will buy and sell positions to either achieve the listed goal in that book nobody reads called the

---

23 *Because these limits can change at any time, it's best that you google a reputable online table to see if this number still stands before you also move to a van down by the river.*

"prospectus," or they'll rebalance to stick close to the index they're tracking. (Example: Tesla joins the S&P 500, so the manager needs to sell whatever was kicked out and add in some Tesla stock.) Even though you didn't sell, you are responsible for your part of the tax, because you own shares in all of these different investments.

Tax-Saving Tip

If you're buying in a non-qualified brokerage account—an account without a tax shelter like a Roth IRA—see if there are going to be any "capital gains or dividends" declared soon on any of the many websites that track mutual funds. (Morningstar.com is one such site that we've already mentioned, but there are others, like Yahoo Finance.) If there is, you may want to wait until *after* the taxes are paid, so that you don't pay a share of someone else's tax bill.

The Taxman Cometh

Like inflation, taxes are always standing over you with a pillow while you sleep, ready to—as your doctor says during the physical— "apply some pressure." But since you can calculate your tax burden and know your timing options, you can make paying taxes as convenient as possible. (We know that this is like saying, "Scheduling my root canal and colonoscopy on the same day sure was convenient!" but it is still a whole hell of a lot better than getting surprised by unexpected dental work and butt cameras.)

So Why Is This Important?

There's no point in building yourself an impressive stack of Benjamins only to see it destroyed by inflation and taxes. Though you can't stop these forces from coming for your money, you can plan for them. Understanding how they work and how to protect yourself will help you get to the next level of Benjamin stacking.

There are few people we know who are more obsessed with legal and ethical strategies to lower tax burdens than David McKnight. His strategies have helped thousands of people, and his books are always found on the bestseller list. We were lucky to talk to him about how to reduce taxes. Here's a snippet:

THE MATHEMATICAL CONSEQUENCES OF TAXES: AN INTERVIEW WITH DAVID MCKNIGHT

Joe: *You see tax rates going up in the future. Why?*

David: *There's a story I tell about a guy named David Walker. He's a CPA. He was actually more than just a CPA. He was a former comptroller general of the federal government.*

That means he was the CPA of the entire country for ten years. And back in 2008, he appeared on a radio show and he said that tax rates have to double or we're going to go broke.

The radio show host didn't believe him. So he said, "Look, I can give you a four-letter word that explains why tax rates have to double." So they opened up the phone lines and people started to call in and none of the callers could guess what the four-letter word was to explain why tax rates have to double.

I mean, there was "kids," "debt," "wars," "jobs." He finally told them the word was "math." What does he mean? If your country is spending double what you're bringing in as tax revenue, you have to reduce spending by half, double taxes, or some combination of the two. This is one of the smartest guys in the world saying that our tax rates have to rise dramatically, or we're going to go bankrupt as a country.

Joe: *And yet most of us are saving into tax-deferred plans, saying, "I'm hoping the tax bill down the road is lower."*

David: *Back in the seventies and eighties, when tax rates were dramatically higher than they are today, that sort of strategy made sense. You get the deduction on the front end, you postpone the payment of those taxes until some point much further down the road, and hope to pay that tax at a lower rate.*

That mathematically really makes sense. But we're now at a point where taxes haven't been this low in a really long time. The income parameters governing these brackets today are as good as they've ever been in probably eighty years.

Yet we continue to pile money into 401(k)s and IRAs, getting deductions at historically low tax rates only to postpone the payment of those taxes, when experts are telling us tax rates are probably going to be much higher [in the future].

Joe: *On the other side of this, we're in this game with the IRS. They're our opponent, but the IRS can change the rules on us at any time.*

David: *When you put money into an IRA, it's a little bit like going into a business partnership with the IRS. And every year the IRS gets to vote on what* *percentage of your profits they get to keep. You can have a million dollars in your IRA, but unless you can accurately predict what tax rates will be when you take money out, you don't really know how much you have. It's really tough to plan for retirement if you don't know how much money you have.*

Joe: *Can we walk through the three different tax buckets that you have in your book?*

David: *The first bucket is what we call the taxable bucket. These are your emergency fund–type things: stocks, bonds, mutual funds, money markets, CDs, savings accounts. This is what you need for [liquidity].*

It's the least efficient of all the buckets out there because every year you get to pay a tax. If you amortize this taxation out over a lifetime, it could cost you hundreds of thousands of dollars if you have too much money in that bucket. So people say, "Well, what if I have more than six months' worth of living expenses in this bucket?" I say, "That's okay, so long as you recognize that there is a mathematical consequence associated [with this bucket]."

So that's the first bucket. The second bucket is the one that most people are familiar with. It's what we call the tax-deferred bucket. These are your 401(k)s and IRAs, 403(b)s, 457s, or SEPs and SIMPLEs if you're a business owner. This is where you don't pay tax as your money grows. You pay the tax on the back end.

One of the problems associated with this bucket is that you don't know what the tax rate [will] be when you take the money out. A second problem is that when you take money out, it counts as provisional income, which is the income that the IRS keeps track of to determine whether they're going to tax your Social Security.

For a lot of our clients, if their Social Security gets taxed, [they] run out of money five to seven years faster than people whose Social Security isn't taxed, because compensating for Social Security taxation forces you to spend down all your other assets that much faster.

So that's a pretty big deal.

Joe: *Which brings up our third bucket: the tax-free bucket.*

David: *The tax-free bucket is everybody's favorite. You pay tax on the front end, so the cost of admission to the tax-free bucket is that you gotta be willing to pay the tax today. You use after-tax dollars, but once it's in there, it never gets taxed ever again. We're talking federal tax, state tax, capital gains tax, you never pay that tax ever again. Not only that, but when you take money out of a true tax-free investment, it does not count as provisional income.*

Joe: *I want to jump into those investments in just a second, but could the government say, "We need to change the tax code on Roth accounts, too. So we'll tax a little bit of this money"? What do you think about that [possibility]?*

David: *You've got to look at the ratio of 401(k)s and IRAs versus Roth accounts. It's about a twenty-to-one ratio. There's $21 trillion or so of money in the cumulative IRAs and 401(k)s across America. There's only about $800 billion of Roth IRA money.*

They could tax that money and go against all of the promises they made to America—but wouldn't it be easier for them to simply raise taxes 1 to 2 percent on that $21 trillion? And they'll say, "The tax rates have ebbed and flowed over time. We've gotta be able to increase taxes when the revenue needs call for it." It's not such a big deal to raise tax rates on that bucket of money, and it's a much bigger bucket.

Joe: *Once again, easier math. So you must be a huge fan of the Roth IRA.*

David: *The Roth IRA is really my favorite tax shelter.*

You don't pay taxes on federal, state, or capital gains, and when you take the money out, it doesn't count as provisional income, so it's not going to cause you problems down the road for Social Security taxation.

The other issue is that January 1, 2018, tax rates went on sale. They haven't been this low in a really, really long time. Every year that goes by where we fail to take advantage of these historically low tax rates by doing a Roth conversion is potentially a year lost that we can't get back. If we let this tax sale go by without taking advantage of it, we really have missed an opportunity.

Joe: *Individuals and financial planners are spending a lot of time helping people pay attention to tax bracket lines and taking money from pretax plans or converting IRAs over to a Roth so that they pay the least amount of tax.*

It seems like you're suggesting it might be cheaper to do more today than hope the future will continue the way it is now.

David: *If what David Walker says comes true and the tax rates double at some point down the road, then we'll look back at this moment in time and say, "Why did I not take advantage of tax rates while they were historically low?"*

David's advice in a nutshell: Lock in low tax rates when you can via Roth investments, because you don't know what the rates will be in the future.

Chapter 12 Benjamin Badge: Taxes and Inflation Achievements

You may not be able to avoid inflation or taxes, but you can minimize their bites of your Benjamin stacks.

Check off each of the following achievements you have completed toward your Benjamin Badge after reading this chapter:

- ❏ Identify investments in your portfolio that aren't keeping up with inflation. Justify why you have them (example: emergency funds will usually be invested in ways that won't keep up with inflation, but the need for liquidity overrides beating inflation).
- ❏ Take out last year's tax forms and identify taxes that you're paying on investments. Can you use tax shelters to invest differently this year and in the future?

Date You Completed the Chapter 12 Badge	Parent Signature (Putting your mom's John Hancock on your Benjamin stacking makes it official)

13

How to Get Rich Quicker

TOOLS YOU'LL NEED:
- An internet connection
- Your investment options
- A love of big (colossal), obscure (abstruse) words (optional)

As we write, there have been lots of headlines that people with not enough money or know-how have started using brokerage accounts to aggressively trade stocks. We thought we were done with this worrying trend. See, in the early days of the internet, day trading (aka sitting at home on a computer and trading stocks all day) gained traction with the get-rich-quick crowd. Then, nearly everyone lost their shirts, and day trading was no longer a thing.

But just like those bedazzled velour sweat suits and other nightmare trends from the early aughts that have come back, so has this ugly investment fad.

First, we should say that there's nothing wrong with buying a few stocks. In fact, strategically under-diversifying (that is, having a healthy portion of just one asset) can position you nicely if you know what you're doing. But, as Mom says, there's no such thing as a free lunch. In this chapter, we'll dive into the importance of diversification—and the correct strategy to *avoid* diversification—and one way the pros look at a portfolio.

Ups and Downs with Under-Diversification

Under-diversifying is the best way to grow your money quickly, but there's a flip side. This strategy is like a handsome, smart, funny boyfriend—who also has mommy issues and emotional baggage. When things are going well with your "boyfriend," all you see is how sweet and hilarious he is (i.e., how much money you're making). But when things go wrong, well, it won't just be the suddenly-not-so-attractive boyfriend lying in the bathtub sobbing for his mommy (i.e., your money).

The Case For and Against Diversification

A financial-planning pro will never tell you to under-diversify. There are a few reasons for that, but let's cover the cynical one first, shall we?

They know all too well what can go wrong when you don't diversify. Think about it from their point of view: it's easier for them to keep their job by showing you how *not* to fall off a cliff. Even when they know that the view could be great from the mountaintop—that is, your money *could* grow more quickly—if something goes wrong, you'll probably fire them. Most people prefer to stay employed, so they won't show you any quick-gain but risky ideas.

Second, they won't tell you to under-diversify because most people want their money to grow responsibly and predictably. While there's nothing predictable about diversified real estate investments or the stock market on a day-by-day basis, over long periods of time they are a reliable vehicle for reaching your goals. By keeping your portfolio diversified, you're more likely to avoid catastrophic issues when the market moves in the wrong direction.

Remember when we looked at the "periodic table" of investments? Let's bring it back for an encore. Get out here, you lovable little chart!

Asset Class Returns

2006	2007	2008	2009	2010	2011	2012	2013	2014	2015	2016	2017	2018	2019	2020
REIT 35.1%	EM 39.8%	HG Bnd 5.2%	EM 79.0%	REIT 28.0%	REIT 8.3%	REIT 19.7%	Sm Cap 38.8%	REIT 28.0%	REIT 2.8%	Sm Cap 21.3%	EM 37.8%	Cash 1.8%	Lg Cap 31.5%	Sm Cap 20.0%
EM 32.6%	Int'l Stk 11.6%	Cash 1.4%	HY Bnd 57.5%	Sm Cap 26.9%	HG Bnd 7.8%	EM 18.6%	Lg Cap 32.4%	Lg Cap 13.7%	Lg Cap 1.4%	HY Bnd 17.5%	Int'l 25.6%	HG Bnd 0.0%	REIT 28.7%	EM 18.7%
Int'l Stk 26.9%	AA 7.6%	AA -22.4%	Int'l Stk 32.5%	EM 19.2%	HY Bnd 4.4%	Int'l Stk 17.9%	Int'l Stk 23.3%	AA 6.9%	HG Bnd 0.6%	Lg Cap 12.0%	Lg Cap 21.8%	HY Bnd -2.3%	Sm Cap 25.5%	Lg Cap 18.4%
Sm Cap 18.4%	HG Bnd 7.0%	HY Bnd -26.4%	REIT 28.0%	HY Bnd 15.2%	Lg Cap 2.1%	Sm Cap 16.4%	AA 11.5%	HG Bnd 6.0%	Cash 0.1%	EM 11.6%	Sm Cap 14.7%	REIT -4.0%	Int'l Stk 22.7%	AA 9.8%
AA 16.7%	Lg Cap 5.5%	Sm Cap -33.8%	Sm Cap 27.2%	Lg Cap 15.1%	AA 0.3%	Lg Cap 16.0%	HY Bnd 7.4%	Sm Cap 4.9%	Int'l Stk -0.4%	REIT 8.6%	AA 14.6%	Lg Cap -4.4%	EM 18.9%	Int'l Stk 8.3%
Lg Cap 15.8%	Cash 4.4%	Lg Cap -37.0%	Lg Cap 26.5%	AA 13.5%	Cash 0.1%	HY Bnd 15.6%	REIT 2.9%	HY Bnd 2.5%	AA -1.3%	AA 7.2%	REIT 8.7%	AA -5.6%	AA 18.9%	HY Bnd 7.5%
HY Bnd 11.8%	HY Bnd 2.2%	REIT -37.7%	AA 24.6%	Int'l Stk 8.2%	Sm Cap -4.2%	AA 12.2%	Cash 0.1%	Cash 0.0%	Sm Cap -4.4%	HG Bnd 2.7%	HY Band 7.5%	Sm Cap -11.0%	HY Bnd 14.4%	HG Bnd 6.1%
Cash 4.7%	Sm Cap -1.6%	Int'l Stk -43.1%	HG Bnd 5.9%	HG Bnd 6.5%	Int'l Stk -11.7%	HG Bnd 4.2%	HG Bnd -2.0%	EM -1.8%	HY Bnd -4.6%	Int'l Stk 1.5%	HG Bnd 3.5%	Int'l Stk -13.4%	HG Bnd 8.7%	Cash 0.6%
HG Bnd 4.3%	REIT -15.7%	EM -53.2%	Cash 0.2%	Cash 0.2%	EM -18.2%	Cash 0.1%	EM -2.3%	Int'l Stk -4.5%	EM -14.6%	Cash 0.3%	Cash 1.0%	EM -14.3%	Cash 2.2%	REIT -5.1%

Abbr.	Asset Class - Index	Annual	Best	Worst
Lg Cap	Large Cap Stocks - S&P 500 Index	11.39%	32.4%	-37.0%
Sm Cap	Small Cap Stocks - Russell 2000 Index	10.61%	38.8%	-33.8%
Int'l Stk	International Developed Stocks - MSCI EAFE Index	7.03%	32.5%	-43.1%
EM	Emerging Market Stocks - MSCI Emerging Markets Index	11.45%	79.0%	-53.2%
REIT	REITs - FTSE NAREIT All Equity Index	9.09%	35.1%	-37.7%
HG Bnd	High Grade Bonds - Barclay's U.S. Aggregate Bond	4.43%	8.7%	-2.0%
HY Bnd	High Yield Bonds - BofAML U.S. High Yield Master II Index	8.68%	57.5%	-26.4%
Cash	Cash - 3 Month Treasury Bill Rate	1.15%	4.7%	0.0%
AA	Asset Allocation Portfolio*	7.63%	24.6%	-22.4%

Past performance does not guarantee future returns. The historical performance shows changes in market trends across several asset classes over the past fifteen years. Returns represent total annual returns (reinvestment of all distributions) and does not include fees and expenses. The investments you choose should reflect your financial goals and risk tolerance. For assistance, talk to a financial professional. All data are as of 12/31/20.

*Asset Allocation Porfolio is made up of 15% large-cap stocks, 15% international stocks, 10% small-cap stocks, 10% emerging market stocks, 10% REITs, and 40% high-grade bonds and annual rebalancing.

There are so many stories in this chart, aren't there? Follow one asset class across the chart and see how it competes against the others over the last several years. What you'll find are a few valuable concepts:

- **Reversion to the mean.** This is a 50¢ term that means things tend to go back to average. You can see this loud and clear here. One asset class doesn't lead forever. Even in the case of large-cap growth, which—as we write this—has rocked the last several years in a row: if we used the same chart for a different fifteen-year period, even that falls out of favor eventually. What's low comes up, and what's high inevitably takes a dive.

- **Entropy.** An English professor once told Joe that the best stories share a common theme, revolving around the second law of thermodynamics, entropy. For those of you who did as poorly in science as we did, "entropy" means that things tend to fall apart.

  Investing also follows the law of entropy. That stock you love will underperform at some point. Your real estate will need upkeep. Your "hot hand" doesn't exist—sorry. So it's helpful to plan a series of checks and balances rather than confidently assuming, "This strategy can't fail!" Because entropy says it can, and it will.

- **No bad asset classes.** There are always underperformers, but these change from year to year. If there's a "bad fund" in your portfolio because the asset class isn't doing well, that's okay. We're far more afraid of a portfolio where every asset is kickin' butt. There's a lot of risk when you're at the top of the mountain.

  In fact, one popular investment strategy called the Dogs of the Dow *specifically* targets stocks in the Dow Jones Industrial Average Index that are underperforming. Investors buy the ten stocks that have the highest dividend (because dividend yields are set at a price, a falling stock price will often create major dividend income streams). It has a powerful track record, beating the S&P 500 and larger Dow Jones Averages over ten-year periods.

- **"Best" is in the eye of the beholder.** When someone tells you they have the "best" fund, it may be the best performer in that particular asset class—which may not be right for your particular goals regardless—or it may be the "best" this year, the "best" over the last three years, or the "best" international investment overall. Don't waste your time on "best." Pros know it's a ridiculous idea, but it's chased widely by amateurs.

> ### Case Study: What Dave Ramsey Practices vs. What He Preaches
>
> As a popular expert in the financial space, Dave Ramsey has helped thousands of people gain a financial footing and finally save money. While some question the ethics of wrapping financial advice from a for-profit operation into the nonprofit structure and teachings of Christian organizations, nobody questions Dave's results. He truly knows how to help people alter their behavior.
>
> Dave strongly recommends that people diversify their investments. In a series of actions he calls the "baby steps," he suggests placing money into mutual funds, which help people do just that. See Chapter 6 on Investing 101 if you need a refresher or skipped ahead.
>
> However, and this is important, Dave didn't become wealthy by following his own advice. We aren't ripping on him when we say this, because any legit advisor will recommend the exact same things. We're just pointing out that it was through under-diversification that Dave was able to build a sizable net worth. He mainly invested in a single business—his own—and won the day.
>
> If you have a high risk tolerance and want to become wealthy as quickly as possible, consider under-diversification, with the knowledge that it rarely works. If you want to feel free of worries as your money grows responsibly and reliably, use a solid diversification strategy.

We'll address popular ways to under-diversify later. First, let's focus on what most of us are looking to do: keep a solid growth engine that's reliable but that isn't going to potentially break us. Let's start with two ideas that I used often when I was an advisor. The first is "standard deviation," and the second is "the efficient frontier."

Standard Deviation, or How Much Will My Investments Jiggle?

The technical term "standard deviation" is simple in practice. One standard deviation is the difference between values roughly two-thirds of the time. That means in most cases, you'll find values between these ranges. Anything above or below your "first" standard deviation is considered an outlier.

What does this mumbo-jumbo mean for you? It's cool, actually. It means that if you look up the standard deviation of your investment and find out that it's plus or minus 14 percent, for example, and you currently enjoy an 8 percent return, roughly two-thirds of the time you should expect returns of between −4 and 22 percent.

That's powerful, because if you lose 3 percent one year, you won't panic. You'll know that this is within one standard deviation and your portfolio results "expect" this type of return. You also won't be euphoric when you find yourself with a 20 percent return in a given year. That also is within the expectations of that asset class.

Efficient Frontier, or How Do I Mix My Investments?

The efficient frontier research, originally formulated by Dr. Harry Markowitz in 1952, is the backbone of many of the pie charts you see investment companies using to recommend diversified portfolios. Seriously, once you get past the big name, this is fascinating stuff that can help you become a way better investor.

What Dr. Markowitz found was that for any timeframe and tax situation, there was a return and a level of risk you'd achieve for each asset class. For our example here, we'll plot these along two axes, the horizontal axis showing risk, from low to high; and the vertical axis representing returns, also from low to high. Let's plot large company stock over the last several years in the 20 percent tax bracket.

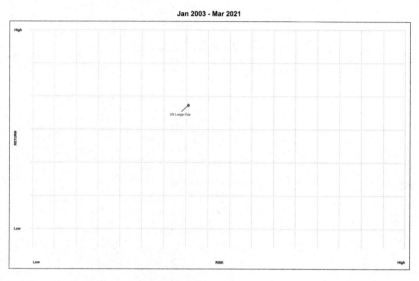

Now, let's compare that to cash.

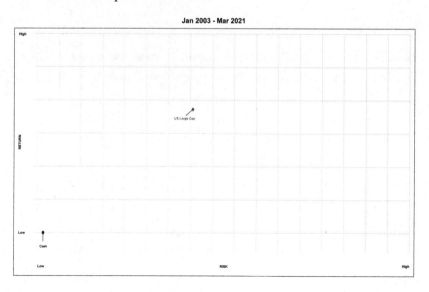

We can easily see the correlation between risk and reward. We're sure this excited Markowitz, so in our imagining of this "Eureka!" moment, he grabbed a glass of Pinot Grigio and got busy filling the chart with dots. Maybe he blasted some Gregorian chants to really get the blood pumping.

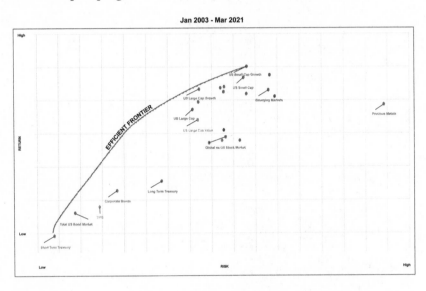

Again, like we saw with the periodic table chart, there are many stories here, but one thing is clear: for every investor, there is a historical "most efficient" approach, meaning that there is an imaginary line of dots with none left (less risky) or above (higher return).

It's also worth noting that some investments take more risk *and* have similar or lower returns than others. So why use precious metals to get a return when you could have less risk and use U.S. large-company stocks instead? Nearly the same return and hella less risk.

The way we see it, at some point Markowitz, buzzed with vino, set down his glass because he was having an even bigger aha moment. What could happen if he got carried away and mixed these different asset types? What if he diversified the investments so they were on the imaginary line? What would that look like? Had he done this in 2021, he would have gotten this:

Jan 2003 - Mar 2021

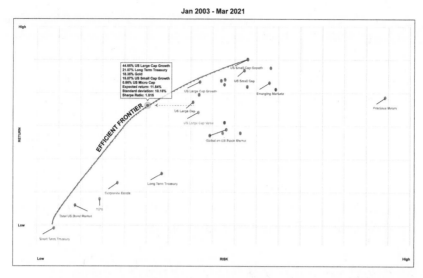

Brilliant! He's taking less risk but getting similar returns to many of the individual asset classes. In fact, he's even using some types of investments that many would call "risky," like micro-cap stocks and gold. But because of the way he has them mixed with other investments, he's actually decreased the risk in his portfolio. Or, if he wants, he can instead maximize for returns, so if he'd moved up to the line instead of left from large-company stocks, he would get this:

Jan 2003 - Mar 2021

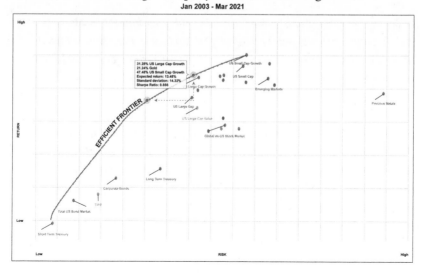

It turns out he didn't take on more risk than large-company stocks alone, but he also increased returns just by mixing his investments differently. BAM! Harry's brain likely nearly exploded because he'd just figured out how to take less risk than with large-cap stocks alone, but enjoy similar returns. He poured another glass. He was celebrating and not driving after all.

So many cool lessons for us money nerds. Even if you didn't think you were a money nerd, if you've made it this far in the book, you're one of us. Jump in. The water's warm.

How do you find the efficient frontier? There are a few websites online, or your advisor can help as well, if you have one. Check out the resources at StackingBenjamins.com/STACKED.

So How the Hell Do I Use This Information?

If you've found where you lie on the efficient frontier, you have one of three decisions to make.

1. To start, you're probably going to want to go back to the visualization we kicked off this book with, and look at what return you need to reach your goals. That will help you determine the right mix of investments to help you reach them safely.

2. Then, if you're sleeping okay at night and you're comfortable with the risk in your portfolio, you can move your mix up to the efficient frontier line. This will tell you which investments you should keep and which you should sell to be more efficient.

3. If you aren't sleeping well and you don't like the risks you're taking, move your portfolio left to the efficient frontier. Who wouldn't like to get the same returns they're getting, but with a lot less risk? That seems like the most obvious and easy move. Again, by finding the "mix" of investment types on the efficient frontier line, it's easy to see what should stay and what should go.

Is the efficient frontier perfect? Nope. It uses historical returns to project forward. Remember the thing about past performance?[24] As you get comfy investing, you'll see that truth play out over and over, to the point where you'll also start muttering it in your sleep.

The efficient frontier gently changes over time as new information is assimilated. Like anything in financial planning, it's the ongoing *planning* that's important, not a onetime plan. By making gentle tweaks, much like an airplane pilot, you're going to reach your destination without an engine failure. If you've been around financial nerds before, you're probably sick of the airplane glide path analogy, but it truly is the best one.

Analogies We Tried and Scrapped Other Than "Flying an Airplane"

Taking a tugboat to your goals.
Sweating out your financial picture in a sauna.
Picking the worst investments out of your financial nose.

Using the efficient frontier and standard deviation, you can see a few things:

- Investments are trackable. You can have realistic expectations when it comes to returns and risk.
- Loading up on one investment might be good (under-diversification), but in some instances, you may be using a single investment that offers more risk but has had worse results than a safer investment.
- If your goal is to use investments to get wealthy, you can instead decide that you want to raise your standard deviation and move your risk/reward in the efficient frontier so that you take more

---

24 *"Past performance is no guarantee of future results," Emily mumbles in her sleep before rolling over and resuming her dream of riding a narwhal in space.*

risk. You can still use statistics and probabilities to get where you want to go.

How Do I Time Changes to My Investments?

When you see where you should be on the efficient frontier, that'll produce a list of investments that you need to sell and another that you should buy. But when and how should you make those changes? Kids, it's time to rip the Band-Aid off. There is never a compelling reason to adjust your portfolio "later." Get right with the investment gods now, no matter what's going on.

When Joe was a financial advisor, he was often asked, "Shouldn't we wait until X happens [X = this great or doomsday thing in the near future] before we sell this random investment?" Absolutely not! Here are some events investors wait for but shouldn't:

- The price returns to the point it was when you bought it (the most popular reason Joe heard as a financial advisor)
- The market drops
- The market improves
- Random big event

But let's be realistic. These all rest on one dangerous assumption: that you have any clue where investments or the market are headed.

Early in his career, Joe made this mistake often. It seemed so obvious when you read the newspaper that the market was going to go up/down/sideways, and he'd use that information in his trading. He'd also entertain client thoughts on the matter and agree to meet them in "the middle." Either way, nearly without exception, our "obvious" moves were worse than what we should have done in the first place.

So if the efficient frontier tells you that you need to switch, do it right away, without convincing yourself that you can predict the future. You can't. But you do want to know some facts before you make a trade, so that you're ready for the consequences.

Before selling anything, determine these two things:

1. Is there a fee to make this trade? If so, how much? The fee shouldn't deter you from doing the right trade unless it's going to disappear very, very soon. However, you don't want to be surprised by any fees associated with your trades.

Sometimes you can avoid fees by sticking with a similar fund family. For example, if you had funds through a financial advisor, you may have paid a "load" to buy the fund. If you stick with the fund family, you'll pay no fees to make a trade from within it. Weigh that savings with the internal fees of the funds you're considering. If it has lower expenses internally, that might save you more than staying with the fund family.

2. What taxes am I going to pay when I make this trade? If you're trading in a retirement account, like a 401(k) or an IRA, don't worry. Those are tax shelters, and you'll pay nothing to the government because you moved money inside of the IRA from one investment to another. However, outside of these types of accounts you'll have a tax due, and you'll want to know how much.

Your tax is based on the amount that you've gained, not the full amount of the trade. So if you sold a fund for $10,000 that you bought for $8,000, there's a good chance you'll owe taxes only on $2,000. Then go online and find out current tax rates to determine how much you'll owe. Keep that money aside for tax day (in most cases, you won't owe it until you file your taxes).

Your Investment Goal

Your prime goal with most investments is to use asset classes that historically have beat the pants off inflation. Two assets are consistent inflation-killers: stocks and real estate. In fact, over long periods of time, the S&P 500 and the NAREIT index (the index tracking North American real estate investment trusts) have similar results.

While stocks can zoom up, real estate rarely does, unless you score a huge deal and buy a piece of property way below market price. However, the inverse is also true. Stocks can zoom down, and often do, while real estate values generally glide along on a slower path. Don't get us wrong, real estate prices can take a dive. (Remember 2007–2008? Ouch.) But that isn't the norm. A stock can rise or fall 2 to 3 percent in a single day because someone sneezed about the stock market, and not because of anything going on in the company whose stock you own. If the company has outstanding results, it isn't uncommon to see a stock soar or plummet 5 to 6 percent in a day. If there's huge news, you could see a 10 to 20 percent drop or rise.

But that doesn't mean that real estate is easier money or a better investment. Your money is illiquid if you're investing in a slice of real estate rather than a liquid REIT, which trades more like a stock. You can't peel off a bathroom to put your kids through college. In fact, to get any money, you have to either take out a loan or sell the property, and you're not getting that cash in a hurry. You have to find a buyer, schedule a closing, and pay some hefty fees.

In choosing between investment types, we recommend leading with the one that you're most comfortable with and using the other in moderation. As we discussed with the efficient frontier, having two types of assets beats one for security purposes, and in this case, stocks can add liquidity and real estate can add short-term security.

Under-Diversifying for the Win

If you want to seriously grow your stack, there are two keys:

1. Invest lots of money into fewer things.

2. Don't be wrong. This one's the toughie.

> ### *Safety Tip*
>
> **This is the part of the book that you should avoid if you're just looking for your investments to be safely managed. You wouldn't have caught Joe ever recommending buying things that are "risky" when he was a financial advisor. But you're here and we're here, so what the hell, let's take a look at how you can win with your investment strategy by cutting a few positions and notching up the risk.**
>
> **While we're at it, we are going to remind you what risks you should try to avoid. It's a reflex, the same way we always remind our kids to wear helmets.**

To build wealth in a hurry, investing in a single stock beats investing in a dozen, which beats investing in five hundred. Investing in a few properties beats throwing money into a REIT. You can't grow your money quickly with five hundred companies or a REIT, but you're also much less likely to kill your whole stack that way, too.

Beyond stocks and real estate, there's a third asset class that has the potential to make you wealthy, but it walks, quacks, and even smells more like a job than an investment. Start a single company that does well, and watch it rain Benjamins. Ta-da!

Each of these three investment methods increase the standard deviation of expected returns. You could win big or you could lose big. There isn't one without the other. This should frighten most of you, which is good. Fear helps you avoid the two big issues we see with people who are in a hurry to lose lots of money:

1. A gambler mentality. The chance that you'll become wealthy gambling is minimal. And if you do hit it big, the chances you'll later lose it all gambling again are great. We're not looking for gambling. We want the real thing.

2. Gut-instinct investing. At some point you do have to make a leap of faith and put your money on the line, but that's not the same as investing on gut instinct. If you gather a ton of information ahead of time and know the road ahead and what hurdles await, you're more likely to win . . . but chance will still play a part.

Joe's Mom on the Truth About "Overnight Success"

I recently coined the phrase "Rome wasn't built in a day, was it?" It's pretty good, I think. Case in point is the origin story of this hot young group you may not have heard of called the Eurythmics. These kids Dave Stewart and Annie Lennox are in many ways opposites, but the duo knows exactly how to create and deliver hits. Stewart was signed to his first record label while still in high school, worrying the hell out of his mum, who was so hoping he'd become an accountant. The Eurythmics was his fourth band, proving to everyone but him that music is not as stable as accounting. Lennox was also a musical powerhouse, earning a spot at the Royal Academy of Music in London and studying three different instruments. She also had been in two other bands before teaming with Stewart.

The point? Even though the world sees the Eurythmics as an "overnight success," nothing could be further from the truth. Even before they "burst on the scene," they knew the road, and the odds were that this couple was going to create a hit.

So if you're going to invest to "win," you need to:

- **Rely on statistics.** Find out what the key stats are in the industry you're competing in and become familiar with the ground. You need to know the guts of what you're investing in, right-side up and upside down.
- **Rely on good people.** Successful investors surround themselves with good people, especially if their investment is hands-on, such as owning rental properties. This is the case for privately held

investments, real estate, and businesses. Surround yourself with people who have a track record of winning.

* **Create systems to manage your investment.** If you're building a business, you must base it on repeatable systems, or you'll die in a hurry. But even with real estate or a thinly diversified portfolio of stocks, you must have some fundamental system you use to manage your funds.

A final word: much like we're attracted to every doughnut we see, there are also siren songs you'll want to understand as an investor.

1. We're predisposed to love, love, and love some more whatever we're considering. This is why advertising works. So how do you avoid buying whatever single investment happens to sound awesome just because you're considering it?

Set up a system of weighing investments against one another. Load as many investments, good and bad, at the top of your funnel, so that your brain will focus on comparing instead of buying. This is an important step in getting mad skillz at investing. You need to see enough different investments to know when something is truly an investable idea and when it is not. You can set up criteria to evaluate companies and use those same criteria over and over to decide if it's an opportunity worth pursuing. Think of it as a frame.

Your first frames can be personal: What's your timeframe? What return do you need when you timeline your goals? Does this meet the basic criteria?

After that, you can use the concepts we've already discussed: Which investment will deliver the return you need most reliably? Which one costs the least? Which one will play best with your other investments in the playground that is your portfolio? Build your frame on these and then tweak as you gain sophistication.

2. It's hard to disagree with a talented salesperson—their job is to pitch you. That's why you must consider statistics and not sales pitches or literature. While at some point you have to believe that a product will work or it won't, before you find a winner you have to have plenty of data to back up that belief.

3. We fall in love with little projects when we should have a bias toward scale. Any idea that can scale up and handle lots of customers is much more likely to be a hit than something where you have one-to-one or even one-to-ten-person interaction. Managing a rental house is likely a less lucrative bet than an apartment building with twenty doors. Stock in a company that requires brick-and-mortar stores and operates on a transactional basis is a worse bet than stock in a company that requires no stores and works on a subscription basis.

Joe learned this early on. When Mom wanted the house clean, he'd often fail, trying to get everything done by himself. Mom then explained to him the value of relying on others. Load the washing machine and the dishwasher first, then tell his brother and sister what their chores were (life as the oldest!). That way, even before he started "working," Joe already had four additional people—if you count the machines—getting stuff done. If he had to do it all himself, with just his two hands, he would have finished one-fifth of the work or less in the same amount of time.

So Why Is This Important?

We hope you see how much of the "traditional" money advice can be a detriment, depending on your goals. Diversification stabilizes your portfolio for long-term aspirations but won't help you gain wealth quickly.

Personal finance isn't so much hard-and-fast rules as much as it's a continuum. The more you know, the more you realize you have to decide where you are on that continuum and act accordingly.

One man who's never been content to use index funds is the best-selling author Phil Town. He's the author of several books, including the individual stock investing classic *Rule #1: The Simple Strategy for Successful Investing in Only 15 Minutes a Week!* Here's what he had to say on the podcast about building real wealth more quickly than using index funds. In his case, he's talking about individual stocks:

ON BUILDING WEALTH FASTER:
A CONVERSATION WITH PHIL TOWN

Joe: You talk a lot about emotions and how you feel about investments. What does emotional talk have to do with money?

Phil: A lot of people are very afraid of taking on their own investing. They don't want to do it. There's something going on inside about money that you have to confront. The number of people in the audience that have really strong negative feelings about money is amazing. And you know, we have to deal with it. Look at how basically simple good investing really is. Why aren't I doing it?

Joe: Your new book is a one-year format. January is about becoming brave. I'd like to tackle February, which is about knowing your number. What does that mean?

Phil: *We said, "Look, how much do you actually have to have to retire?"*

And we call that your number: the dollars you have to have in the can at let's say age sixty-five. For the rest of your life, how much do you have to have? And man, you know how shockingly large that number actually is for someone who just wants to live a regular lifestyle?

The components that come into it are, number one, how much are you going to spend in retirement? Make an estimate.

And then number two, how much are you saving and how much do you already have that you can put toward that retirement to benefit yourself?

And then three, what's your rate of return right now, or what, what are you projected to be?

So for most people, let's say putting away $12,000 a year would be a pretty big deal. A thousand bucks a month, getting a standard rate of return in the market would mean, you know, basically the long-term rate of return in the market, like about 5 percent plus maybe 2 percent for dividends. So maybe 7 percent overall. How much do you have now? The average forty-five-year-old has about $50,000. So overall, you've got $50,000 now, you're going to save $12,000 a year, pretax you're going to get maybe 7 percent on it, and you'll live on $50,000 a year in current dollars—meaning after inflation— for the next thirty years.

If you did that simple math right there, you would find out very quickly that you will need about $1.5 to $2 million to retire on at age sixty-five. And if you're forty-five right now, getting from where you are with $50,000 now, and adding $12,000 a year, you're not going to get there. You're not even gonna get close to getting there. That's a shock for most people.

Joe: *Finding out that number's demotivational for a lot of people. "I can't get there. So I'm gonna do nothing."*

Phil: *Yeah. That would be very anti-motivational or demotivational.*

And I think that's always what happens when you get shocked like that. You go into denial.

And you say, "Well, screw it. You know, I'll just spend it and live a good life. And then I'll live in my children's basement. If they'll let me."

Joe: *Don't knock living in a basement.*

Phil: *It's not horrible, but it's not everybody's first choice. And so you have to accept the fact that [you're] going to have to do something else. And hopefully that something else that you'll do is learn how to invest to grow your money faster.*

Joe: *Let's dive into your gurus, because you've learned the strategies you teach from tracking them. Your gurus are Mr. [Warren] Buffett, Mr. [Benjamin] Graham, and Mr. [Charlie] Munger, probably those three. How do we start producing these returns like them?*

Phil: *Well, that is of course the whole problem, right? I mean, that's, if this was easy to do, man, everybody would be doing it.*

I struggle with Spanish, right? I mean, I've taken Spanish. Come on, man. There's no more simple language on the planet. Everything's spelled like it sounds. It's a great language and, you know, is it easy for me to learn it? No. Because why?

Because I'm not disciplined. I don't study, I don't sit around and memorize. So the idea that you're going to be able to go out and get rates of return in the stock market that exceed the large diversified rates of return in an index is a little bit fictional for most people, because most people are not going to put in the time and effort to actually do it. Just as learning a new language is fictional [for me].

Most people are just not going to put in the time. But for those who are willing to learn this, it really is simple. The first thing you have to do is recognize that in order to get higher rates of return, you have to stop over-diversifying your portfolio.

You've got to narrow it down to a small number of companies that you really do understand and own those companies, as long as they remain solid companies and are priced at or below their real value. So the process of investing becomes this: you want to narrow down the number of things you're going to buy by focusing on only those things that you truly understand.

So for my daughter Danielle, this was a learning process. There were areas of the stock market she actually understood very well. She found those areas by looking around at what she buys every day. Where is she going to buy stuff? And she ended up discovering that Whole Foods, which is her favorite market, was a public company then (now it's owned by Amazon, another public company).

She could actually understand it as she dug deeper into it. Basically Charlie Munger says it boils down to three important things that you have to do. You have to first off be capable of understanding the business that you're going to own. You're going to start a laundromat. You better understand laundromats. If you're going to buy a McDonald's franchise, you better understand McDonald's. You're going to understand the business. So you stick to the things you know.

Second, you've got to have a business that has protection against competition, and Charlie calls this a durable, competitive advantage. Warren Buffett calls it a moat, and really what it is is a business that just has some quality to it, that is very hard to replicate. For example, a railroad company has railroad tracks and you can't compete with them unless you get railroad tracks, and railroad tracks are hard to come by. So there are some companies which have this kind of quality that you want to focus on.

And third, you want it operated by people who are honest, have integrity, and are talented. And those three things go together to make a wonderful business for you to buy. So can you understand it? Does it have a moat? And has it got good people running it?

And then the fourth thing that you have to do is know what it's worth and buy it cheaper. You have to know what it's worth. Is it a wonderful business? And can you buy it on sale?

Phil's advice in a nutshell: Investing is simple but not easy. Overcoming your reluctance is the hardest part, because good investors know to focus on companies they understand and look for businesses that are "on sale."

Chapter 13 Benjamin Badge:
Get Rich Quicker Achievements

Understanding how diversification and under-diversification can affect your investing goals will help you make the best decisions for your portfolio.

Check off each of the following achievements you have completed toward your Benjamin Badge after reading this chapter:

❏ Check out the standard deviation of an investment using either the prospectus or a third-party site.[25]

❏ Explain standard deviation to a friend.

❏ Find the efficient frontier for a few portfolios. Based on your goals, determine what investments you should use.

❏ Bonus: If you're investing in individual stocks or other investments, develop a list of criteria to evaluate opportunities. Commit to refining this approach.

---

25 *Have we mentioned that we aren't Google?*

Date You Completed the Chapter 13 Badge	Parent Signature (Putting your mom's John Hancock on your Benjamin stacking makes it official)

14

Hiring an Advisor Who Won't Bleed You Dry

TOOLS YOU'LL NEED:
- The fortitude to sit through dozens of sales pitches without rolling your eyes
- The desire to build a financial team
- Time to interview and compare potential advisors

In Suze Orman's *The 9 Steps to Financial Freedom*, she says that nobody cares about your money more than you. That's true. But her next quip is just, well, wrong. She says that because of this, you shouldn't have a financial advisor.

That's like saying you should take care of your own dental work since no dentist will care about your teeth as much as you do. Or that you should never run your taxes by a CPA. Or that since no one cares whether you get to your destination more than you, you shouldn't book a ticket on a commercial airline, but fly yourself.

We've never met anyone uber-successful who actually "went it alone." Savvy people surround themselves with a team of smarty-pants who help them move faster.

Unless you're going to attempt to be an expert in, uh, everything, you're going to need to hire help. Doesn't it make sense to have someone in your corner who will help you pump the brakes on one side and kick you in the ass when you're messing up on the other?

Case Study: Joe's Coaches

I'll admit: I overpay for coaches. However, this book wouldn't be written if it weren't for coaching. My coach Mary Lou has been pushing me to do this for over ten years. I'm stubborn. She's known that this book you're holding is not only a dream I've had, but the centralizing point of a lot of ideas that have been floating in my head. Without my coach, I wouldn't have written a word.

I also have a nutrition coach through a show sponsor, MetPro. Jesse has helped me bring my eating under control. There are so many fad diets out there, I wanted a pro with a straightforward approach to help me live a long time, not lose some weight fast without solving the root of the problem.

When I messed up my tax returns early in my career, I did what any stupid person would do: nothing. I buried my head, hoping the problem would disappear. Spoiler: the IRS doesn't go away. Finally, I found an excellent CPA named Susan, who not only helped me square up with the IRS (including a huge penalty, but we'll call that a "stupid tax"), she also taught me how taxes work so that it would never happen again.

To be clear, I'm not espousing handing your money over to a professional and walking away. In each of these cases, I did the work. I decide to sit down and write. I decide what food goes in my mouth. I find tax opportunities and try to understand them. But also in all these cases, I'm being advised by people who know how to do things much better than I do.

Some people think, "Well, if I learn enough, I don't need an advisor." Not true. The smartest people we know realize there's a depth of understanding they'll never reach and that they probably don't want to. (That Netflix queue ain't gonna watch itself, after all.)

Financial professionals can teach you what you need to know—and make it just-in-time knowledge so you'll have it right when you need it. Yes, learning the basics is important, but there's nothing wrong with relying on experts to get you where you need to go.

Why People Hire Bad Advisors

Joe can tell you from experience that not all financial advisors are created equal. The field has many issues, and maybe the biggest is that it's easy to call yourself a "financial advisor." Life insurance salespeople call themselves advisors. CPAs call themselves advisors. Real estate sharks call themselves advisors. Instagram influencers call themselves advisors. You need to be able to sort through the mess to find the person who's truly going to improve your game.

When someone cautions you against all advisors because they got ripped off, what likely happened was that they interviewed poorly and consequently got burned. Most people go with the first advisor they interview. Their friend says that they should see someone, so they do, and they hire them on the spot.

If you think of yourself as a business, this makes no sense. Go ahead and think of yourself as "Me, Inc." Would a business ever interview and hire only one applicant? Benjamin stackers do the heavy lifting up front to make sure they're hiring the right person, instead of settling for whoever happens to be handy. On the off chance they do hook up with the wrong person, they fire them as soon as they realize—and then look inward at what they did wrong. Then they go out and find an advisor who's a better fit.

Take your financial picture seriously and get ready to hire the *right* way.

Who to Interview

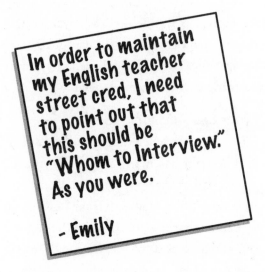

In order to maintain my English teacher street cred, I need to point out that this should be "Whom to Interview." As you were.

- Emily

So how do you go about finding advisors to interview—Yelp? The trick is to follow the lead of millionaires.

The Affluent Mindset

Dr. Thomas Stanley is widely known for his study of millionaires and how they act. His research found that affluent people tend to hire lots of help, and they network with other affluent people. Got a good lawn person? Give me their number, please. Know someone who can get me a deal on a used car? Hook me up. Affluent people are far more likely to ask their friends for coaching recommendations than non-affluent people.

Think of your friends who are better off than you but in the same general age range. Who do they talk to? Do they have coaches? Who do they learn from? Ask about their advisors, and not just financial advisors. If they've "got a guy" who helps them with any aspect of their lives, maybe the "guy" could help you, too.

Culling the List of Potential Advisors

Be ruthless. Eliminate people who don't immediately meet the mark. You want someone who's going to start with a process, not with a pitch or a product. Your first and most trusted advisors should be process people, not salespeople. Sometimes salespeople are cleverly disguised as advisors, but we'll cover that in a moment.

Calling the List of Potential Advisors

Meet with as many advisors as possible. We recommend doing it face-to-face, but don't let distance stop you from hiring. Most advisors are comfortable working through technology, so you can meet over the phone or via video chat if someone highly recommended is across the country or the world.[26]

Call the firm to get a feel for how they work. Look for clues. How does the receptionist sound when they pick up? If they seem disgruntled, there's a good chance that frustration comes from the top. Or does the advisor answer their own phone? If so, how the hell are they successful? Can a good advisor answer their phone, create viable strategies, fill out compliance forms, and deal with all the other daily details of a thriving financial-planning practice? Top pros don't do that.

What Will Probably Happen at the Meeting

If the advisor immediately jumps into products or the financial markets and how they're performing—unless that's specifically what you're asking about—run away as quickly as possible. Leaving a you-shaped hole in the wall may be a bit of an overreaction, but you want your advisor to create a plan that focuses on what you can control, which

---

26 As Joe is writing this chapter, he's in Southern California. Emily is in Milwaukee and not at all jealous of Joe's current weather in SoCal. Joe's career coach is in Michigan, his nutrition specialist is in Northern California, and his tax pro is in Oklahoma. The people Joe works with on the Stacking Benjamins shows—including Money with Friends and Earn & Invest—are in Texas, Montana, Arizona, Virginia, Michigan, New York, Illinois, and Missouri. Make technology your friend, and you can work with better people wherever they live.

ain't the markets. You also want to create an earning, spending, and saving machine that you don't have to monitor 24/7.

What the advisor should do is start by asking you about your goals. (Sound familiar?) If you're going to have a relationship, you want to know how they're going to tailor their advice specifically to you and your situation. Then, after they've taken notes and made a few suggestions on how to think about your overall strategy, they'll share how they work. Again, this should be a process-oriented description rather than a list of products.

It's okay if your advisor has a team that you'll work with in addition to your primary contact. Many advisors use a collective approach. Some clients don't like that, but Joe feels strongly that if he's hiring the best person available, he doesn't want them to handle the little things or be available to walk him through the paperwork for opening a Roth IRA; their staff can do that. He wants a big thinker who handles the big stuff. He wants them thinking about the tax strategy behind whether to open a Roth at all.

Three Questions You Should Ask

Asking the advisor the questions you find online may get the job done. But that's like drinking an entire box of Franzia. You might get pleasantly buzzed, but you'll probably be left with a pounding headache and a mouth like rancid cotton.

That's why we first recommend asking these three questions. They can give you a sommelier-approved experience, and you can follow up with some queries from the Franzia lists, without going overboard:

1. "Tell me about your average client." This will give them an opportunity to talk about the people they work with . . . which, frankly, you don't care that much about. What you want to hear about is their process and *how* they work with people. If they seem to work with multitudes, you have to wonder about their ability to handle individual client matters. If they sputter and tell you that they only work with people like you—well, you know they're a liar.

2. "What designations do you hold?" While not all good advisors are certified financial planners (CFPs), it's one designation that tells you they've studied the craft and have some idea of the process behind creating an intelligent and thoughtful financial plan. There are many other designations and licenses that advisors may hold. Research them.

You should also search to see if someone truly has their credentials at the organization's website. We know a podcaster with a string of designations following his name on marketing materials who holds none of them.

3. "Tell me what you do for clients." This will indicate whether you're meeting with a holistic advisor, not someone who'll just focus on one item in your financial situation. If you're going to be successful, everything needs to dovetail. Your level of insurance is going to depend on the amount of savings you've acquired. Your tax situation is going to affect which investments you buy or avoid. Everything works together, so they should be looking at the entire picture.

After these, proceed with your favorite questions from any of those jumbled lists, if necessary.

What Does a Good Advisor Cover?

Your advisor should look at and help you improve all of the following aspects of your financial life:

- **Financial position:** What do you have? Where are you strong, and where are you weak?
- **Cash flow and cash reserves:** How is your budget? Do you have money saved for emergencies?

- **Risk management:** What are the big risks in your life, and how can you cover them efficiently?
- **Tax planning:** What is your overall tax strategy, and how can it be improved? While a tax preparer, CPA, or software will help you put last year's puzzle together efficiently, how do we set things up so that there's more to work with?
- **Investment planning:** What are your short-term and long-term goals? How do we place investments efficiently to meet them?
- **Estate planning:** What is your legacy? If you can't spend it, who should? How do you get assets to beneficiaries?

What You Should Expect to Pay

Don't walk into an advisor's office and start with: "How are you paid?" Not only will you have to imagine all those eye rolls when they talk about you after you leave, but you're also asking an impossible question, since you don't yet know what the advisor can do for you.

Advisory fees are all over the board, and it's hard for us to give you an exact number to expect. However, we can tell you how to think about fees. If the advisor is creating a plan, there should be a flat fee to implement it. By "implementing," we don't mean that the advisor is going to sell you a bunch of stuff. Rather, it means the advisor is going to stick with you to make sure that you actually accomplish something with the data that they have provided. To show you why that's important, let's cover how advisors are paid.

Back in "the day,"[27] most advisors weren't even called "advisors." This was before scientists had updated the genus and species of financial professionals from *Pecuniaria venditor* to the more modern *Argentum consiliario*.

---

27 *Historians have determined that the day referred to when discussing "back in the day" definitively occurred on May 7, 1972.*

The legacy of most big advisory firms (think Merrill Lynch, Morgan Stanley, and Goldman Sachs) is couched firmly in another word: "broker," aka *Pecuniaria venditor*, or seller of financial products. A stock broker or insurance broker did exactly what the name implies: they sold you a product, and in return they received a commission. Though our understanding of this species has changed, the once-common broker has not gone extinct, and in fact, many people in the business are still paid by commission.

The biggest issue with commission salespeople (*Transfero denarius*) is that they're paid only when and if you buy, and they know every trick out there. Pressure sales? Sometimes. Stilted facts? That also happens. Many people will tell you horror stories about being in a high-pressure "advisor" office, which is the natural habitat for the most ferocious of the commission salespeople.

Most people don't think about "hiring" this type of advisor— they only think about buying a product. In fact, you can't "hire" them, only venture into the commission jungle where the salespeople enjoy their natural sovereignty.

On the other end of the spectrum are "fee-only" advisors (*Pretium solum*). These creatures have devised a more transparent strategy for their fees. Rather than receiving payment only when their clients purchase a product, fee-only advisors charge based on either services rendered or assets managed, which is unbundled from any products. While you will pay a specific fee for advice, you may also pay a percentage-based fee for them to manage your assets. These fees range from nearly zero on the low end to two percent at the high end. This more elegant solution shows the incredible diversity of ways these financial-professional beasts feed.

Of course, there are still some differences among the genus of fee-only advisors. Some charge a flat fee rather than a percentage of assets under management. These creatures (*Pretium planus*) perform a specific service in exchange for that flat fee, and they will tell you that you're getting pure, unbiased advice. This is absolutely true. It doesn't make it the best advice, but it is the best advice that the advisor knows. This can be a powerful choice. If your advisor knows a lot about what they do—and we hope they do—you're going to pay for and receive some blunt truths. Personally, that's our favorite type.

Also, where a commission salesperson often wants to only talk about the areas of the plan for which they're paid, a flat-fee advisor will focus the light squarely where it belongs: on whatever issue you're worried about, or should be.

Between commission salespeople and fee-only advisors lies the "fee-based" advisor (*Pretium numquam*). This classification of advisor can charge flat fees, earn asset-based fees, and even still receive commissions. This advisor is especially hard to pin down because they often change hats between commission salesperson and fee-focused advisor, much like an octopus uses its chromatophores to blend in with its surroundings. When they suggest something, you'll wonder if it is because they have a product attached at the end of the argument or because it is the best advice for you. It's frustrating.

In fact, though we are financial-advisor conservationists who wish to maintain the equilibrium provided by these creatures, *all* of their methods for receiving payment are frustrating. Commission salespeople (*Transfero denarius*) consistently beg you to buy. Asset management "fee-only" advisors (*Pretium solum*) constantly ask you to move more money under their control. Flat-fee advisors (*Pretium planus*) don't care if you implement their plan, since they've already been paid. And fee-based advisors (*Pretium numquam*) swap back and forth between payment via commission and payment via percentage of assets under management, so it's hard to know what advice is best for you.

For us, that's the rub in the super-sexy financial media directive to "hire a fee-only advisor." Because the biggest problem in financial planning is that *clients often fail to do anything at all*. If the advisor doesn't help you implement change for the better, you've wasted your money. So who's better off? Is it the person who hires the fee-only advisor and implements 30 percent of a masterfully dovetailed plan, or the client of a commission salesperson who implements 100 percent of a plan that's only 85 percent effective?

That's why we don't recommend that you start an interview with the question "How are you paid?" You don't need to know which species you are working with, until you first know what this financial creature can do for you. Yes, you will need to know what they charge, and it needs to make sense for you on a cost/benefit basis—but it's something to ask near the bottom of the list.

Here is the type of advisor we like best:

1. One who can protect you from blind spots and sharpen your focus to move forward fastest. You also need to know what type of person you work best with. Joe prefers a Gordon Ramsay type, while Emily is more interested in a Mary Poppins style, as she's a sucker for a spoonful of sugar. Joe's advisors tell him, "You're full of crap!" and he eats it up. Emily's advisors give her suggestions and the space to mull them over, and she loves feeling like she's coming to conclusions herself, rather than being told what to do. In both cases, the advisors call them out on their weaknesses; they just go about it in different ways.

2. One who's going to address the full picture, not just pieces. You may only want to talk stocks, but your advisor should start with the foundation of a financial plan, not just the sexy parts. They should push you to develop a risk-management strategy. They should nudge you on your credit card debt. They should help you understand how you can improve your tax situation. They should introduce you to the right people to help you with an estate plan.

3. One who'll keep you focused on what you can control, not on all the baloney going on beyond your grasp. If your advisor wants to talk politics, or pontificate about what will happen next with the Federal Reserve, or guess at stock market conditions, dump them.

4. One who keeps up with financial trends, but also who understands psychology and coaching. Remember: the key is to implement the plan. If the advisor won't help you get the job done, you're both wasting time. The advisor of the future is more interested in knowing you and your goals than just being a "money person."

5. One who views the world and your situation differently than you. That ensures a more holistic approach than working with someone just like you.

That's it! You're ready to meet with advisors. If you interview just one, you're likely to believe everything they say and you won't know how they're strong or weak against the rest of the field, so interview at least three, and optimally five.

So Why Is This Important?

Many of Joe's clients told him that their regularly scheduled meetings with him about their financial goals and plans were the only times they discussed the topic in any depth. That highlighted the fact that even if his clients *could* do things on their own, they didn't. While your financial advisor can't possibly care about your money more than you do, their professional opinion and their help with implementation will improve your stack-building plan. Finding the right advisor can help you reach your financial goals faster and more efficiently.

Chapter 14 Benjamin Badge:
Hiring an Advisor Achievements

Check off each of the following achievements you have completed toward your Benjamin Badge after reading this chapter:

❑ Interview five financial advisors.
❑ Already have an advisor? Go ahead and reinterview your current advisor using the questions and suggestions in this chapter.

Decide if you have the best advisor for your needs or if you need to choose a different one.

☐ Take a critical look at your whole advisory team (including non-financial advisors).

Why do you have your current coaches and advisors?

Should you hire others or let go of some of your current advisors?

Date You Completed the Chapter 14 Badge	Parent Signature (Putting your mom's John Hancock on your Benjamin stacking makes it official)

Conclusion

SO WHY IS ALL OF THIS IMPORTANT?

Becoming a champion Benjamin stacker is both a process and a mindset shift.

For Joe, this process began when he ran out of gas in his family's minivan in the late 1990s. Standing on the side of the road with an empty tank, he had two choices. He could give up, blaming the world for yet another injustice, or he could look up at the night sky, laugh, and begin digging under the seats, praying for enough change to buy some gas and a portable can at the station a mile up the road.

Emily's process didn't begin in a single moment like Joe's. But from the time she was an unhappy eight-year-old who regretted not buying the Snoopy Sno-Cone Maker to a dismayed twentysomething with an accidental gang tattoo, she has been on a journey to learn how to make better decisions with money so she's not tempted to shake her fist at the sky and shout, "Why the hell did I just do that?"

Whether you picked up this book because you have had your own running-out-of-gas lightbulb moment, because you want to stop regretting poorly considered money decisions, or because you thought *Stacked* referred to something completely different, you've made it to the end. That means you're now on your way to better financial outcomes. If you've completed the exercises and earned the badges throughout, you've already accomplished a great deal.

But we want to make sure you remember just how critical it is to know yourself. Money only matters because it allows you to live the life you want. To put a finer point on this, we have an extra bonus interview for you here in the conclusion. Joe sat down with Jean Chatzky, the financial editor for the *Today* show, to talk about the financial importance of finding your contentment. Here's a portion of that interview:

USE YOUR RESOURCES WELL:
AN INTERVIEW WITH JEAN CHATZKY

Joe: You tell an interesting story from a woman named Natasha.

She's in her thirties in New Jersey, single, and an editor and publicist. She said, "Once upon a time I would've said money's my currency, and then I might've said time is my currency. Now I'm at the point where I've realized [those aren't] my currency. It's contentment."

I want to walk through that.

Jean: When we look at people who are not living comfortably because they don't have enough money, of course money's going to be the focus. Because at that point, money can actually make a big difference in your overall happiness and peace of mind. But as we get a little bit more comfortable with our resources and a little more able to control our own clocks, then I think we need to look at the question of what do we really want from this life and what are the tools—whether it's money, whether it's time, whether it's something else—to get those things.

Joe: *I wish I had the framework that Natasha had in my twenties: that contentment ultimately is what I'm going for.*

Jean: *It's one of those big goals, right? And then it's trying to figure out, okay, which levers can I pull on in order to boost my level of overall contentment or well-being.*

Joe: *You go through three different concepts, asking, "What do you want from your money?" First up is freedom. Then you talk about flexibility and time. Those three seem to come up a lot.*

Jean: *They really do. When we think about, "What does money really buy you?" [we have] the realization that money's a tool. And people who continue to think it's just about the money haven't yet realized that money is the tool that we use to get what we want in life. And the goal is to figure out how to use that tool most accurately for you.*

Some people get great joy by giving their money away. Some people get it by stashing it in a place where they know that it's safe. For some, it isn't a matter of want as much as it's a matter of need. We have to actually satisfy and check off those boxes of safety and security for many of us before we can move on to anything else.

Joe: *But for some people's needs and wants . . . there's a gray area.*

Jean: *There is this squishy area where we think that something is a want, but in reality it's actually a need because it is so satisfying to our core. A behavioral economist named Sarah Newcomb talked [on my podcast] about how beauty in the world was in fact a need for her.*

She needs this beautiful, comfortable environment, and so for her to spend some of her resources in order to achieve that makes total sense—not at the risk of damaging her future security, but understanding that once we've checked off the boxes where we're doing what we need to do in order to save a decent amount, we're not going to sabotage our future selves. We have this pot of resources where we should be able to decide, "How do I use this to get the most of what I value most?"

My biggest problem with this argument of spending your money on experiences rather than things is that although it does work for most people, according to the research, it doesn't work for all people. I'm in the category of a throw-pillow person. What I tend to value is the ability to curl up in my cozy nest at home because that's where I can recharge my batteries. And often for me, that is better than a spa treatment. It's better than jumping out of a plane or whatever sort of experience you want to spend your money on.

The point is to just figure out what fills you up and then use your resources well without judging yourself.

What is it that makes you feel comfortable in your skin and comfortable in the world? Then use your resources appropriately. There's an exercise in my book Women With Money *that involves tracking your spending, not just to see where the pennies are going, although that's important, but to go back a month later and to go over your spending log to see what you felt good about and what you regret, because that's a real window into what you value.*

Joe: *What are you trying to get out of this exercise?*

Jean: *I'm trying to get a sense of, "Are you giving certain portions of your life short shrift in terms of time?" Time is our other limited resource. We can't get more of it. And when you're not serving all of those parts of your life that you think are important, you tend to start to feel an emotional drain.*

I'm a fan of tracking. I'm a fan of tracking spending. I'm a fan of tracking calories on occasion, and I am a fan of tracking steps, and I am a fan of tracking this as well.

Joe: *I'd encourage everybody to do this exercise. It's powerful.*

Jean: *It is. It's really, really powerful.*

Jean's advice in a nutshell: Use your resources well by spending them on the things that fill you up.

Our Gifts to You

We hope you're motivated to conquer your goals, pay off your debt, and speed into the sunset. But most of all, we hope you're motivated to find your contentment. It's a true game changer.

There are two things we'd love to share as our parting gifts—besides the amazing certificate (suitable for framing!) you'll find on the next page.

1. Enjoy the journey as much as the outcome. Remember that happiness is inside, and reaching the finish line won't take away any dissatisfaction you're feeling today. You must learn to appreciate and enjoy the steps you take along the way every day. Thank the people around you. Thank your brain for holding it together. Love the process as much as the outcome.

For that reason, keep it playful. For all our joking, we're deeply committed to financial literacy and freedom for more people, and you can be, too. Bring others on the journey. Not only will that make your own process more fun, but you'll find the lessons you need to learn stick because you're forced to articulate the process to someone else. There will be times when you'll need to be serious, but outside of those lines, enjoy the process of achieving your goals, making mistakes, and ultimately creating a better life.

2. Be good to yourself when you mess up. It's far more important to get back on the horse than to curse yourself for falling off. And getting back in that saddle is all about consistently doing just a couple of things:

Create systems to pull you through days you won't feel as enthusiastic about getting Stacked as you do right now.

Find your next set of ongoing motivators to pull you through. Schedule coffees on a consistent basis with your smart team of "advisors" and intelligent friends. Listen to podcasts, read blogs, go back to your favorite parts of this book.

We hope that you will check out wherever you are on your path, whether that's walking to a gas station with a pocket full of change or finding yourself inappropriately inked up, nary a Snoopy Sno-Cone Maker in sight, and see the humor in your situation. It's when you can laugh at yourself that you can recognize things will get better. From that point on, it isn't about creditors, excuses, or interest rates. It's about taking charge, creating opportunities, and moving forward, one joyous and fun-as-hell step at a time.

Now is when the real fun begins.

—Joe and Emily

PS: Want additional lessons? We've created a website chock-full of more geeky money goodness at StackingBenjamins.com/STACKED.

CERTIFICATE OF ACHIEVEMENT

This is to certify that

YOU

have shown excellence in your studies by finishing **STACKED**

Joe's Mom
JOE'S MOM
The Boss

Emily & Joe
EMILY & JOE
Proud Coauthors

Acknowledgments

Now I see why the band starts playing during long Academy Award speeches. There are lots of people to thank and I want to do it in under three minutes.

First, I have to thank Cheryl, who listens to me drone on about our show and then this book far more than could be expected of any human. Her humor and insights color and shape mine, and I'm lucky she's my best friend.

Thanks to our amazing agent, Heather Jackson. Her ideas to crystallize this book idea in my head were invaluable. Heather feels about books the way that I feel about financial plans: the work will be better if you lay out clearly where you're going ahead of time. She also named this book. I won't tell you my original name, but let's just say it was sub-brilliant.

Thanks to my coach, Mary Lou Johnstone, who's been pushing me to finish this for maybe fifteen years. She's right: I should have done this sooner, and it wasn't the bear I thought it'd be in my head.

Thanks to my kids, who lost the lottery and end up in lots of my stories. They've also been my biggest cheerleaders, as I'm theirs.

Thanks to Emily, who has no idea how thrilled I was that she'd write this book with me. Not only did we make something I'm proud of, but also we made something that made the COVID year a little less dark as we laughed our way through meetings and rewrites.

Thanks to our *Stacking Benjamins* podcast team. My partner OG (Josh Bannerman) has been a friend for a long time. I don't think I could work this closely with anyone else. Someone said we "argue like an old married couple," and I'd second that emotion.

Thanks to Doug Pfaff, who was our first "alpha" listener. He didn't realize his work on helping me clean up the show would lead to the part of our podcast that makes me laugh hardest.

Thanks to Tina Ichenberg, who was not only gracious enough to work on many of the illustrations you have seen in this book, but who's worked with me when I was a financial planner and now is the backbone of our team. Also thanks to Richie Rutter-Reese, Karen Repine, Taylor Stevens, and Jordan Grommet. I'm so proud to work with a group of passionate people who also share my love of finding the intersection of entertainment and financial literacy.

Also, I need to say a big thanks to Steve Stewart who not only makes me sound good every week, but who's become a great friend. Also thanks to Griffin Pfaff, the FinTern, for giving us crucial weeks off so I can do things like write this book.

Our editing team has been amazing. Kyle Landis-Marinello took the first pass at our rough draft and cleaned it up a ton. He also didn't wince at our joke about Vermont, where he lives and where I hope to visit him someday.

The heavy lifting was done by our ninja editor Nina Shield. Emily and I are big enough English-language nerds to recognize her ability to cut like a surgeon. If you found compelling language in our book, there's a good chance Nina made it shine.

Also, you may not be reading this book without two of our promotional teams. First, the Penguin Random House team of Farin Schlussel and Hannah Steigmeyer have had our back during the entire promotion of this book. Before this journey I was warned that publishing houses aren't good at promotion. The people sharing this viewpoint haven't met Farin and Hannah.

AND I'd be remiss if I didn't share a big public thank-you to our team at Westwood One (now Cumulus Media, but I'll always think of you as Westwood One). John Wordock changed our show's trajectory when he recruited us, and the team of Theresa Gage, Agnes Grzelak, Catrin Skaperdas, and Cory Smith (among many others) have helped us spread the word about financial literacy much faster than we could have alone.

And finally, thanks to you. If it weren't for our Stacker community, and the insightful and sometimes hilarious emails, texts, social media messages, and voicemails, we wouldn't have a show at all. Our community drives us, and if you're reading this, we're now BFFs whether you want to be or not.

I know there are lots more of you I should call out individually, but the band's playing. I'm thankful you're on my team.

—j.

The music is swelling, but I have a few folks who deserve a thank you from me, as well.

My sincerest thanks to Joe for calling me up out of the blue one day and asking if I'd like to write a book with him. It was a bonkers idea that was just crazy enough to work. I couldn't be happier to have the opportunity to share vital financial information in the form of copious dick jokes.

A big thank-you to my husband and partner-in-crime, Jayme. One of the highlights of the terrible year that was 2020 was our daily coffee and conversation, where I ran jokes by him, we shook our heads over the state of the world, and we tried to ignore the sound of two children wrestling and breaking the house in the other room.

I'm so thankful for my boys. They don't completely understand what a funny guide to money is but are excited for me nonetheless. In the words of Marian Berman, they make my heart itch.

Thank you to my mom, the aforementioned Marian Berman, for giving me weird and wonderful ways of describing things. Itsy-bitsy pieces and smithereens, Mom.

My sister Tracie Guy-Decker is the smartest person I know and I lean on the fact that she's never more than a phone call away whenever I hit a writing/thinking/designing/organizing/life snag. Thank you, Tracie, for all that you do and all the ways you help me do things better. And thank you for pointing out that "stacked" also means big boobs.

Thank you to my virtual assistant, Sarah Poikonen, who has made my writing life immeasurably better by ensuring that all I have to do is write the stuff and not have to format it, Tweet it, illustrate it, caption it, or wrestle it back from a malfunctioning website that has just eaten it.

My friend Bobby Mathews was always happy to let me bounce joke ideas off of him. He's proof that social media isn't just a hellscape of misery. Thank you, my friend.

My freelance writing editors were gracious and patient with me while I took some time to work on this book with Joe. In particular, I'd like to personally thank Daphne Foreman, Ben Curry, and John Schmidt of *Forbes*. They are fabulous editors and make my writing better, in addition to being flexible and kind.

I'd also like to thank the entire team at Wise Bread. Though I no longer write for them, the site let me hone my creative thinking about finance. It meant a lot, and I hope you all know that.

And finally, a big thank-you to the readers. You're who it's all for, you know.

—*EGB*

Index